MIDDLE EASTERN SECURITY

MIDDLE EASTERN SECURITY

Prospects for an Arms Control Regime

Edited by

EFRAIM INBAR
AND
SHMUEL SANDLER

FRANK CASS • LONDON

First published in Great Britain by
FRANK CASS & CO LTD
Newbury House, 900 Eastern Avenue
London IG2 7HH, England

and in theUnited States by
FRANK CASS
c/o ISBS
5804 N.E. Hassalo Street, Portland, Oregon 97213-3644

Library of Congress Cataloging-in-Publication Data

Applied for.

British Library Cataloguing in Publication Data

Middle Eastern Security: Prospects for an Arms Control Regime
I. Inbar, Efraim II. Sandler, Shmuel
327.1720956

ISBN 0-7146-4644-X (hb)

ISBN 0-7146-4168-5

Printed in Great Britain by
Antony Rowe Ltd, Chippenham, Wiltshire

This group of studies first appeared in a Special Issue on 'Middle Eastern Security:
Prospects for an Arms Control Regime' in *Contemporary Security Policy,* Vol.16,
No.1, published by Frank Cass & Co. Ltd.

CONTENTS

DOCUMENTS

List of Abbreviations

ABACC	Argentine–Brazilian Agency for Accounting and Control of Nuclear Materials
ACRS	[Working Group on] Arms Control and Regional Security
CBW	Chemical and biological warfare
CDE	Conference on Disarmament in Europe
CFE	Conventional forces in Europe
CFSP	Common foreign and security policy
CoCom	Co-ordinating Committee for Multilateral Export Controls
CSBM	Confidence- and Security-Building Measures
CSCE	Conference on Security and Co-operation in Europe
CTBT	Comprehensive Test Ban Treaty
CW	Chemical warfare
CWC	Chemical Weapons Convention
CWW	Chemical warfare weapons
DOP	Israeli–PLO Declaration of Principles
EEC	European Economic Community
EP	European Parliament
EPC	European political co-operation
EU	European Union
G-7	Group of seven members of the International Monetary Fund with the largest economies
IAEA	International Atomic Energy Agency
IAEC	Israel Atomic Energy Commission
IEPG	Independent European Programme Group
INF	Intermediate-range nuclear forces
MENWFZ	Middle Eastern nuclear-weapon-free zone
MFO	Multinational Force and Observers
MTCR	Missile Technology Control Regime
NPT	Non-Proliferation Treaty
NSG	Nuclear Suppliers Group
NWFZ	Nuclear-weapon-free zone
OECD	Organization for Economic Co-operation and Development
P-5	[five] Permanent members of the UN Security Council
PLO	Palestine Liberation Organisation
SSM	Surface-to-surface missile
START	Strategic Arms Reduction Talks
UNDC	United Nations Disarmament Commission
UNSCOM	UN Special Commission [on Iraq]
UNTSO	United Nations Truce Supervision Organization

Preface

The need to introduce some form of arms control to the Middle East has long been apparent, but until recently neither the regional parties nor international powers had placed the issue at the top of their agendas. Recent developments, however, have taken Middle Eastern arms control out of dormancy; the (second) Gulf War of 1991 and the diplomatic process begun in Madrid demonstrated, respectively, both the urgency of and the possibilities for arms control. Since Madrid, Israel and its neighbours have been meeting regularly on the topic, through the Multilateral Working Group on Arms Control and Regional Security.

In November 1993, the Begin–Sadat (BESA) Center for Strategic Studies at Bar-Ilan University organized an international conference to study 'Arms Control in the Middle East' in depth. The conference, held on Bar-Ilan's main campus in Ramat Gan, Israel, was well attended by academics, practitioners and the public at large. BESA Center Senior Research Associate Dr Gerald M. Steinberg played an important role in preparing an interesting and attractive programme.

This volume presents a selection of papers delivered at the international conference. We have found them to be particularly valuable because the contributors, as a whole, related to the topic specifically within the realities and constraints of the Middle East. Consequently, the ideas and findings presented herein should prove useful to policy-makers involved in regional arms control negotiations, as well as to the academic community. The authors, who laboured to revise and up-date their papers to a deadline, deserve our gratitude.

The 1993 arms control conference was co-sponsored by the Konrad Adenauer Foundation. In the meantime the BESA Center and the Foundation have developed a fruitful working relationship, and we are deeply indebted to the Foundation for its continuing support for the Center's activities.

Efraim Inbar
Shmuel Sandler

The BESA Center for Strategic Studies

The BESA Center for Strategic Studies at Bar-Ilan University was founded by Thomas O. Hecht, a Canadian Jewish community leader. The Center is dedicated to the memory of Menachem Begin and Anwar Sadat, who concluded the first Arab–Israeli peace agreement. The Center, a non-partisan and independent institute, seeks to contribute to the advancement of Middle East peace and security by conducting policy-relevant research on strategic subjects, particularly as they relate to the national security and foreign policy of Israel.

The Global Environment

American Hegemony, Regional Security and Proliferation in the Post-Cold War International System

ROBERT J. LIEBER

The most useful starting point for an assessment of the American role in proliferation and regional security exists not at the local or regional level, but through an assessment of the end of the East–West conflict and its implications both for the international system and the United States.[1] In essence, the end of the Cold War has had an impact far beyond the Central European setting in which it began and ultimately ended, and its implications affect many more actors than were members of NATO or the Warsaw Pact. Initial hopes for greater international stability after the Cold War have given way to the realization that the decline of the Soviet Union and the emergence of the United States as the only superpower are having mixed effects. Indeed, in some areas, particularly outside Western and Central Europe, there is more rather than less instability. This instability, coupled with the increased likelihood of nuclear proliferation, creates cause for concern. Indeed, it has even been suggested that in the coming years the world may see the use of an atomic bomb as a weapon of war for the first time since Nagasaki.[2] Under these circumstances, the question of whether the United States can successfully establish international or regional regimes capable of limiting proliferation of nuclear weapons and of other weapons of mass destruction takes on an enormous importance.

In assessing the possibilities and limitations of the American role, this paper proceeds first by assessing three momentous changes which in recent years have affected the Middle East and the role of the United States in the region. These include the end of the Cold War, the experience of Operation 'Desert Storm', and the Israeli/PLO agreement of 13 September, 1993. All these events have created great opportunities as well as risks, and they particularly enhance the importance of the United States. However, the result is a paradox: the very factors which have led to the emergence of a one-superpower world make it more difficult for America to play the kind of global and regional leadership role which is widely expected of it and for which no alternative country, regional organization or international body is available. As a consequence, the ability of the United States to act as an effective hegemon is uncertain, and the risks of regional instability and of proliferation are correspondingly greater.

Three Changes and Their Impact

First, the end of the Cold War brought major consequences at a regional level and for the structure of the international system itself. In the Middle East, one immediate result was the weakening of the rejectionist position within the Arab world. Even before the December 1991 dissolution of the Soviet Union, it was evident that external support for countries such as Syria and Libya had eroded substantially. Mikhail Gorbachev had previously signalled that the USSR would not provide resources for Syria to match Israel, and subsequent events left Moscow less capable of doing this even if it had so wished. For the Arab states, the end of the Cold War and collapse of the USSR meant a dwindling of weapons, money, diplomatic support and deterrence of Israel and the United States.

Syrian President Hafez Asad proceeded to draw the necessary conclusions from this change, and its implications influenced his participation in the coalition against Iraq and in the opening of the Madrid peace process in October 1991. For Libya, which was not inclined to proceed similarly, the result was a still greater degree of marginalization.

The emergence of the United States as a lone global superpower had an impact in moderating Arab state behaviour and in fostering a greater degree of Arab pragmatism toward Israel. However, there were also systemic consequences with more ambiguous long-term effects. The Cold War, for all its intensity and the dangers of superpower nuclear confrontation produced a bipolar system with a considerable degree of stability and predictability. The stability of the bipolar world and of superpower strategic nuclear deterrence has been widely discussed and does not require extensive elaboration here,[3] although it is worth recalling the observation of Kenneth Waltz that, 'The longest peace yet known rested on two pillars: bipolarity and nuclear weapons.'[4]

In the aftermath of the Cold War, there has been speculation about the likely consequences for international stability. Although Western Europe can be expected to maintain a relatively robust degree of order, conditions elsewhere are likely to vary a great deal, and some regions may well face greater instability. Pierre Hassner, for example, has noted the political decomposition and anarchy that have emerged as a dominating feature in important parts of the post-Cold War world:

The bipolar era severely limited the sovereignty and the freedom of states (particularly within the Soviet sphere)...Thus it was natural that communism's decline would encourage the rebirth of nations and increase their openness to external influences. What was unclear was whether the future would feature a new bipolar cleavage (this time based on a North South confrontation), a new multipolar equilibrium or global cooperation...The surprise is that, although indications in the direction of each model have emerged, their course has been troubled, distorted and, in some respects, dominated by another more powerful development – political decomposition and anarchy.[5]

Moreover, as Robert Jervis has observed, areas without a recent history of stable co-operation are likely, in the aftermath of the end of bipolarity, to witness increased conflict.[6] In essence, the Cold War and nuclear deterrence not only prevented war between East and West, but the bipolar system and extended nuclear deterrence also fostered a degree of regional stability. In this regard, Erich Weede has observed that general nuclear deterrence prevented war between East and West, but that stability is likely to be more precarious elsewhere:

> The end of the Soviet Union and her bloc implies the abolition of extended deterrence without its replacement by another pacifying condition. Moreover, some nuclear proliferation to developing countries is to be expected. Unfortunately, the combination of precarious balances of terror with domestic instability among poor countries seems unlikely to make nuclear deterrence work as well in future as it did in the Cold War past.[7]

Apart from the end of the Cold War, a second major change resulted from Saddam Hussein's August 1990 invasion of Kuwait and the American-led response in Operations 'Desert Storm' and 'Desert Shield'. The ousting of Iraq from Kuwait and the rout of Saddam's armed forces made abundantly clear America's preponderance of conventional forces and its unique capacity to project power. Along with the end of the Cold War and the retreat of the Soviets, this indisputable fact contributed importantly to Asad's entry into the peace process. In taking Syria into negotiations with Israel, Asad sought to build a working relationship with the United States, whose might he had clearly appreciated and understood.

The American-led UN coalition effort against Saddam thus intensified the consequences resulting from the end of the Cold War. The outcome of the crisis further undercut the rejectionist position in the region and severely weakened the PLO. The outcome of the Gulf crisis also made it possible for the United States to play a leading role in UN efforts to destroy the Iraqi nuclear weapons programme. Moreover, it had become increasingly clear that only the United States could maintain the balance of power needed in the Persian Gulf in order to preserve the autonomy and security of the Persian Gulf states and Saudi Arabia. The Clinton administration's concept of 'dual containment' of Iraq and Iran was a reflection of this reality.[8]

The overwhelming American military strength demonstrated against Iraq has had, however, an unintended consequence. As Eliot Cohen observes, the Gulf War made it clear that no country can hope to match the United States in a conventional conflict and it thus creates an incentive for nuclear proliferation:

> To a hostile general staff, nuclear weapons look increasingly attractive as a means either of deterring either the Yankees or (more likely) their local clients, who provide the necessary bases from which American military power operates.[9]

A third major change has resulted from the September 1993 Israeli–PLO Declaration of Principles (DOP), which was made possible by the outcomes of the Cold War and the Gulf War. Despite protracted delays in its implementation and the murderous actions of those on both sides determined to destroy it, the DOP marks a watershed in the region. Prior to the agreement, studies of regional arms control prospects had concluded that without substantial movement in the peace process there would remain serious limitations on what could be achieved.[10] However, the signing of the DOP, the subsequent May 1994 Cairo Agreement, and the implementation of Israeli withdrawal from Gaza and Jericho create new opportunities. To be sure, practical steps toward significant arms control measures remain elusive. Measures to deal with chemical and biological weapons and missiles, as well as with nuclear weapons, are unlikely to proceed unless or until the security concerns of Israel have been dealt with effectively. None the less, the contingency is at least imaginable.[11]

Related to the above, however, is the broader relationship between peace and security. And it is here that the role of the United States remains particularly important in providing reassurance and deterrence for Israel, as well as for the Gulf states and potentially for others who may face challenges from rejectionist actors such as Saddam Hussein's Iraq and the Islamic Republic of Iran. This reassurance is essential for the peace process, yet the very same circumstances which have brought momentous changes in recent years also have the effect of creating a measure of uncertainty about the American role in regional stability.

Opportunities and Risks

The three profound changes which have taken place provide impressive opportunities. These stem from the great reduction in the role previously played by Moscow, the preponderance of power and influence available to the United States, and the defeat of the military challenge presented by Saddam. As a consequence, there is at least the potential for improvement of regional security, settlement of the Arab–Israeli–Palestinian conflict, development of regional economic co-operation, and agreement on measures to control weapons of mass destruction.

Optimism, however, must be tempered with great caution in addressing Middle East problems, and the risks which accompany recent change are at least as conspicuous as the opportunities. First among these remains the still unresolved transformation of Arab and Islamic societies from tradition to modernity. A tumultuous process which occurred over the course of some three centuries in the West has been truncated into a few generations in the region. Moreover, it is occurring in the presence of modern weaponry, mass communication, and nothing yet approaching a consensus on the social and political values around which societies are to be organized internally and in their relationship to one another.

Fouad Ajami has written eloquently about the competing and deeply flawed visions which have contended with secularism in the struggle for domination of the modern Arab world.[12] Among others, these alternatives have included Arab nationalism and Nasserism, Ba'thism, anti-Zionism and, most recently, Islamic fundamentalism. This latest challenge not only represents a peril to secular and moderate governments within states such as Egypt, Tunisia and Jordan, but also is reflected in rogue or pariah states such as Saddam Hussein's Iraq, Gaddafi's Libya, and the fundamentalist regimes of Sudan and the Islamic (though non-Arab) Republic of Iran.

These regimes, as well as Saddam Hussein's Iraq, represent a major source of instability through their rejection of the existing international and regional agreements, threats against neighbouring states, active support of terrorism, opposition to the peace process, often brutal repression of their own populations and active pursuit of weapons of mass destruction. Moreover, although active backing from the Soviet Union and Eastern Europe is no longer readily available to these states, the end of the Cold War also means a lesser degree of outside restraint on their behaviour. Thus it is at least arguable that Saddam would not have moved to invade Kuwait in 1990 had the Cold War still been in existence.

A second set of problems results from the disintegration of the USSR. While the Soviet regime regarded proliferation as against its own interest and was willing to co-operate with other major nuclear supplier states in co-ordinated non-proliferation efforts, the successor states not only have less interest in the issue, but reduced capability as well. Moreover, their desperate economic predicament makes them seek out export opportunities of any kind, even where these involve the supply of modern weapon systems and sensitive technologies or materials which may accelerate the development of weapons of mass destruction in recipient countries. In addition, chaotic conditions within the former Soviet Union increase the risk that sensitive materials may be exported against the wishes of Moscow, or that a brain drain may occur in which skilled scientists sell their services to would-be proliferators.

A third major problem concerns the increasing number of Middle East states with advanced capabilities or programmes for the development of surface-to-surface missiles, chemical and biological weapons, or nuclear weapons. As noted above, this tendency is compounded by evidence from the Gulf War that high technology and advanced weapon systems are fundamental to modern military power. Saddam's rudimentary missile capability in the Gulf War momentarily sent shock waves through the region. This was evident even though Iraqi Scuds had no significant military impact and embodied a 1940s technology (based on the old German V-2 rocket) which was countered by a 1950s technology (Patriot missiles as an outgrowth of what was originally an anti-aircraft system).[13]

Fourth, the availability of Third World suppliers of modern weapons and technology also becomes more evident in the post-Cold War regional environment. Countries such as China (submarines and nuclear reactors), North Korea (missiles) and Pakistan (nuclear technology), as well as India, Brazil, Argentina and others represent actual or potential sources, and are less easily incorporated into existing anti-proliferation efforts.

The American Role: International Opportunities and Constraints

The United States stands as the lone superpower. Moreover, its primacy has become self-evident not only in the Gulf War but also in its sponsorship of the peace process. The symbolism is further evident in the fact that although the Oslo agreement between the Rabin government and the PLO was achieved without active American involvement, the parties none the less came to Washington for the public act of signing the document on the White House lawn.

The United States also functions as security guarantor for small states in the Middle East.[14] This is particularly evident in the Gulf, where not only the sheikhdoms but also Saudi Arabia depend on America to counterbalance the power of Iraq and Iran. In this sense there exists some comparison with the role played by England in Europe of the eighteenth and nineteenth centuries. As an outside actor, England was able to throw its weight into the scales against whatever power threatened to dominate the Continent. In the Gulf case, it is in the interest of the United States to ensure that neither Iran nor Iraq achieves effective domination of the region and of the two thirds of the world's proved supplies of crude oil which exist there.[15]

This does not require the United States to play the kind of role it did in Europe where containment of the Soviets meant creation of a formal military alliance in NATO, maintenance of a vast network of military bases and facilities, and the long-term stationing of 325,000 American troops. In the case of the Gulf, and indeed of the wider Middle East, this degree of activity is not only undesirable but unnecessary. The nature of Arab and Middle East politics, as well as the multiple cleavages and conflicts among regional actors, makes a formal alliance impractical. Moreover, a large network of bases or the stationing of American troops in significant number would become a focal point for local opposition and a target for terrorism.

Instead, the elements of the American role allow for a more restrained presence but a none the less evident commitment. As the Saudis concluded after the Gulf War, if the Americans were willing and able to send 500,000 troops half-way around the world to save a Kuwaiti regime with whom they had no formal agreements, then they could certainly be expected to do so if the far more important kingdom of Saudi Arabia faced a comparable threat.

In essence, the American regional role involves an ascending order of interests and commitments. These begin with reassurance that the United States is committed to the security of Israel, the Gulf states, and moderate Arab regimes. It next implies deterrence of a range of military threats; and ultimately, as shown in the case of Kuwait, it implies that the United States will be available to intervene militarily under extreme circumstances. Beyond this security guarantee, however, the United States also plays a unique role in creating and energizing arrangements or regimes for non-proliferation, as well as in seeking to foster the Arab–Israeli peace process and in contributing to regional order.

The events of recent years have left the United States in a unique position; however the same events have created conditions which constrain its freedom of manoeuvre and make regional co-operation more difficult to achieve. One set of problems stems directly from the end of the Cold War and of the Soviet threat. In the past, this threat and the existence of an American-led bloc to contain it placed limits on the degree of friction which could develop among the Western partners and Japan. The need to co-operate against the Soviets meant that disagreements in economic and other realms were prevented from escalating beyond a certain point because of the perception that too bitter an intra-allied confrontation could only benefit their adversary and thus weaken common security.[16]

In the aftermath of the Cold War, Europe, Germany and Japan are better off in security terms, but the disappearance of the common threat, as well as domestic economic problems, makes it increasingly difficult for them to agree with the United States or each other on matters of shared interest. As a result, co-operation, has become more difficult. This is manifested by disagreements over Yugoslavia, responses to terrorism, trade policy toward Iran, and effective measures to combat proliferation.

The problem facing American policy-makers of gaining co-operation among former allies is far more acute than that of dealing with former adversaries. During the Cold War, though the clash over basic values and interests was severe, there was little doubt that any agreement reached between Moscow and Washington would effectively bind not only the two parties but also their blocs. In the post-Cold War era, however, not only do the weakness and chaos of the truncated Russian state make it harder to reach or implement agreements between Washington and Moscow, but the intentions of the erstwhile members of the two blocs can never be taken for granted. Moreover, the specific problems of Russia, Ukraine and other former republics of the USSR and ex-members of the Warsaw Pact make it far more difficult for the United States to ensure that even agreed non-proliferation efforts will be pursued or that weapons and technology will not find their way to would-be proliferators.

Finally, and within the region, the United States faces a new potential obstacle. It is that the presence of chemical and biological weapons, and of missiles, may raise the cost of military intervention in the event of a crisis which would otherwise call for the dispatch of troops.[17] Nuclear weapons in the hands of regional actors would increase this peril by orders of magnitude. Indeed, it has repeatedly been observed that had Saddam delayed invading Kuwait until his nuclear weapons programme had come to fruition, the United States would have found it far more difficult to organize the UN coalition against him or defeat the Iraqi forces with miraculously light casualties.

The Role of the United States: Domestic Constraints

The ability of the United States to lead effectively in a regional security regime is shaped not only by international considerations but also increasingly by domestic constraints as well. The most evident of these, particularly in the post-Cold War environment of reduced threat, is an exceptional sensitivity to casualties. The interaction of this sensitivity with the proliferation of advanced weapon systems in the Middle East poses a potentially serious problem, the evidence of which can be found in the horrified domestic reaction to the body of an American soldier being dragged through the streets of Mogadishu in October 1993.

The rubric for American intervention since Vietnam has been bluntly expressed in the words of William Schneider as 'Win quickly or get out'.[18]

Interventions in Panama and Grenada during the 1980s succeeded at a domestic level because the Reagan administration could indeed win quickly and at little cost. The one more costly Reagan era intervention, in Lebanon in 1983–4, did not prove to be a domestic political liability because the administration opted to withdraw the Marines rather than remain in a potential quagmire. From this standpoint, the Bush-led intervention against Iraq's take-over of Kuwait also succeeded because of a clear goal, light casualties and the rapid withdrawal of forces after the 100-hours' war. Had the conflict proved to be of longer duration, however, and the casualties significantly higher, the ability of the administration to maintain public and congressional support might well have been called into question. Indeed, it is worth remembering that congressional resolutions authorizing President Bush to use force against Iraq in support of the UN Security Council mandate, passed the Senate by the narrow margin of 52–47.

Domestic constraints on the ability of the United States to act effectively abroad have increased significantly in the aftermath of the Cold War and the change of administrations in Washington. Just as the end of the traditional Soviet threat has made it significantly harder to gain agreement among allies, so it has also made it more difficult to gather sufficient public and congressional support for ambitious foreign policy measures, whether these involve the possible commitment of troops abroad, funds for the defence budget (now declining toward 4 per cent of (GNP), foreign assistance, or even an active and assertive foreign policy posture.

The end of the Cold War has permitted the strong reassertion of domestic priorities and a concentration on efforts to address problems neglected at home during the twelve-year Reagan and Bush era. The reduced salience of foreign policy is thus evident. Only 9 per cent of voters in the 1992 presidential election listed foreign policy as among the top two issues influencing their vote,[19] and opinion polls in February 1994 indicated that as few as 1 per cent of Americans identified foreign policy as the most important issue facing the country.

The Clinton presidency in foreign policy has become emblematic of these changed domestic circumstances. Clinton himself campaigned for office by emphasizing domestic issues, particularly the economy, and his priorities since taking office have reflected that fact. In addition, commitment of additional time and political capital to foreign policy does not offer evident political advantages. Not only have some of the most pressing problems been without clear solutions (as in Bosnia, Somalia and Haiti), but those Americans for whom foreign policy has been a priority tend to favour Republicans in any case. As evidence of this, 87 per cent of those for whom foreign policy was a priority in the 1992 elections favoured George Bush.

There is thus little domestic incentive for the Clinton administration to give higher priority to foreign policy, and this position is supported by the experience of the President and those around him. Whereas George Bush's generation saw America's world role as marked by the failure of isolationism in the 1930s, and the successes in defeating Nazi Germany and Japan in World War Two and subsequently containing the Soviet Union, the Clinton generation's formative experiences included the Vietnam debacle, the fall of the Lyndon Johnson presidency which became embroiled in it, and an aversion to the use of force. However, domestic public opinion polls also indicate that perceived weaknesses in Clinton foreign policy contribute to disapproval not only of presidential performance in that area, but of the administration itself.[20] This public perception thus has the effect of motivating the administration to devote more attention to foreign policy than might otherwise be the case.

Regardless of domestic constraints, however, there remains a compelling need for the United States to provide leadership in Middle East regional matters. In the post-Cold War environment, co-operation on the part of major powers in seeking to limit proliferation is unlikely to be sustained without an active, continuing role by the hegemonic power – in this case the United States. Though non-hegemonic regime maintenance may be possible elsewhere (as in the case of the European Union), the various *ad hoc* efforts, understandings and weak organizational bodies which deal with the proliferation problem are unlikely to be effective in the absence of American leadership. Whether the United States will be able and willing to sustain this role remains at issue.

Conclusion: The US Regional Security and Proliferation

The picture which emerges abounds in reasons for instability and motivations for the proliferation of weapons of mass destruction. The sources of instability include ethnic conflict, a traumatic modernization process, the absence of democratization, and the fact that the United states and Russia no longer have the same degree of interest in preventing the escalation of regional struggles which previously might have dragged them into open confrontation.[21] Moreover, the interrelationship of instability and proliferation is perilous. As Weede and others have noted, some degree of nuclear proliferation can be anticipated and local balances of terror are likely to be precarious. Coupled with domestic political instability, these factors mean that nuclear deterrence is unlikely to be as stable in the developing world as it was between the United States and the USSR during the Cold War.[22]

In this setting the ability of the United States to address the proliferation peril involves both international and domestic dimensions. At regional and global levels, the United States has long been the principal actor, and its continuing role has been evident both in support of United Nations measures to eliminate the covert Iraqi nuclear programme, and in efforts to deal with North Korea's dangerous nuclear proliferation programme and its blatant violations of the International Atomic Energy Agency (IAEA) inspection regime.

Proliferation strategy remains, however, the subject of considerable debate. Some have argued that it is better not to focus on specific *ad hoc* measures or the type of anti-proliferation measure characteristic of the Cold War, but instead seek major new diplomatic initiatives and treaties.[23] Others, to the contrary, find that grand schemes will not work and that it is more productive to focus on a limited agenda.[24] In addition, it is argued that American strategy can do no more than delay the pace of proliferation, either because of the end of bipolarity and its replacement by a more unstable multipolar international structure,[25] or because proliferation is inevitable and radical measures to address it will be impossible until after a weapon is actually used.[26]

The evidence of recent decades is that, in the absence of the United States, neither other individual countries nor international institutions such as the United Nations or the IAEA will by themselves take sufficiently vigorous action against proliferation. The record of the Europeans in the export of sensitive nuclear materials to Iraq is evidence of this, as is the feebleness and credulity of the IAEA towards Iraq's programme prior to the Gulf War and the subsequent discovery by inspection teams of a covert programme whose scale was vastly greater than had been imagined. Similarly, the evidence from East Asia case is that without American leadership, pressure on the North Korean regime would have been far less significant.

Despite these American-led efforts, both Iraq and North Korea remain potential nuclear weapon states. If and when sanctions against Iraq are ended and its exports of oil resume, the behaviour of Saddam's regime makes it likely that there will be a renewal of measures to resume the covert nuclear programme. In the case of North Korea, subtle changes in the wording of Clinton administration statements (which draw a distinction between possession of a nuclear device and achievement of a real nuclear capability) suggest that the nuclear threshold may have been crossed.

The difficulty of the proliferation problem internationally is compounded by the American domestic environment. For the reasons discussed above, the ability and willingness of American governments to give high priority to a vigorous non-proliferation effort are uncertain. This is so even though the 1992 Clinton presidential campaign suggested that non-proliferation would be given enhanced emphasis in a new Democratic administration.

The conclusions are thus sobering. They are that there is no effective alternative to American leadership; that even with this leadership it is likely that some degree of nuclear proliferation will be delayed but ultimately not prevented; and that in the post-Cold War international system, the ability of the United States to commit itself to a maximum effort in this realm remains to be demonstrated.

NOTES

1. For their thoughtful comments on an earlier draft of this paper I wish to thank Efraim Inbar and Aharon Klieman.
2. This observation is by Eliot Cohen in *The National Interest,* No. 34 (Winter 1993/94), p. 38.
3. Among others, see Kenneth N. Waltz, 'The Stability of a Bipolar World', *Daedalus,* Vol. 93, No. 3 (Summer 1964), and 'The Emerging Structure of International Politics', *International Security,* Vol. 18, No. 2 (Fall 1993), pp.44–79; John Gaddis, 'The Long Peace', *International Security,* Vol. 10, No. 4 (Spring 1986); Robert J. Lieber, The United States and Western Europe in the Post-Cold War World,' in Kenneth Oye, R. Lieber and D. Rothchild (eds.), *Eagle in a New World: American Grand Strategy in the Post-Cold War Era* (New York: Harper Collins, 1992), pp. 315–34.
4. Waltz, 'The Emerging Structure of International Politics', p. 44.
5. Pierre Hassner, 'Beyond Nationalism and Internationalism: Ethnicity and World Order', *Survival,* Vol. 35, No. 2 (Summer 1993), pp.49–65, at p.50.
6. Robert Jervis, 'The Future of World Politics: Will it Resemble the Past?', *International Security,* Vol. 16, No. 3 (Winter 1991/92), pp. 39–73.
7. Erich Weede, 'Conflict Patterns During the Cold War Period and Thereafter', paper presented at Conference on The Impact of Global Political Change on the Middle East Haifa University, 4–6 May 1993), p.1. Moreover, Benjamin Frankel argues that while bipolarity inhibits nuclear proliferation, multipolarity will encourage it. 'The Brooding Shadow: Systemic Incentives and Nuclear Weapons Proliferation', *Security Studies,* Vol. 2, No. 3/4 (Spring/Summer 1992).
8. The concept of 'dual containment' has been elaborated by Anthony Lake, Assistant to the President for National security Affairs, in 'Confronting Backlash States', *Foreign Affairs,* Vol. 73, No. 2 (March/April 1994), pp.45–55, especially 48ff. The administration's original statement of the policy was made by Martin Indyk, special assistant to the President for Near East and South Asian affairs, in a speech to the Washington Institute for Near East Policy, 18 May 1993. Also see Washington Institute, 'Special Report: Clinton Administration Policy Toward the Middle East', *Policy Watch,* 21 May 1993.
9. Cohen, *The National Interest,* p. 37.
10. Alan Platt (ed.), *Arms Control and Confidence Building in the Middle East* (Washington, DC: United States Institute of Peace Press, 1992), p.3.
11. Geoffrey Kemp, 'The Middle East Arms Race: Can it be Controlled', Middle East Journal, Vol. 45, No. 3 (Summer 1991), pp.441–456 at p.454.
12. See, for example, Fouad Ajami, The Arab Predicament: *Arab Political Thought and Practice Since 1967* (New York: Cambridge University Press, updated edition, 1992).
13. See Theodore A. Postol, 'Lessons of the Gulf War Experience with Patriot', *International Security,* Vol. 16, No. 3 (Winter 1991/92), pp.119–71. Note, however, that Postol finds the Patriot system to have been essentially ineffective in countering Scud missile attacks against Saudi Arabia and Israel.
14. Kemp, for example, notes that after the Gulf War the performance of the American weapons

and armed forces 'resurrected the belief that the United States has the power to assure the security of the region.' See 'The Middle East Arms Race', p.441.

15. See Lieber, 'Oil and Power after the Gulf War', *International Security*, Vol.17, No.1 (Summer 1992), pp.155–76.

16. Kenneth Oye elaborates on this point in 'Beyond Postwar Order and the New World Order', in Oye, Lieber and Rothchild, *Eagle in a New World*, pp.3–33. Note too the argument of Stephen Walt that states balance against threats rather than versus power *per se*. See *The Origins of Alliances* (Ithaca: Cornell University Press, 1987), p.5. By implication, the disintegration of the threat represented by the Soviet Union removes the basic impetus for NATO's existence. On the other hand, Russia does remain the most powerful state on the European continent and concerns about its future policies provides sufficient motivation for the Western countries to retain their alliance rather than abandon it altogether. Also see Gunther Hellman and Reinhard Wolf, 'Neorealism, Neoliberal Institutionalism, and the Future of NATO', *Security Studies*, Vol. 3, No. 1 (Autumn 1993), pp.2–43.

17. Lewis A. Dunn, 'Rethinking the Nuclear Equation: The United States and the New Nuclear Powers', *The Washington Quarterly*, Vol. 17, No. 1 (Winter 1994), pp.5–25, at p.5; and Brad Roberts, 'From Proliferation to Antiproliferation', *The Washington Quarterly*, Vol. 16, No. 3 (Summer 1993), pp.139–73, at 155.

18. Schneider finds that 'If a vital national interest is at stake, Americans want to take action that is swift, decisive, and relatively cost-free.' '"Rambo" and Reality: Having it Both Ways', in Kenneth A. Oye, R. Lieber and D. Rothchild (eds.), *Eagle Resurgent? The Reagan Era in American Foreign Policy* (Boston: Little, Brown, 1987), p.59.

19. Source: Voter Research & Surveys. Election day poll conducted by a consortium of CBS, NBC, ABC and CNN.

20. A decline in public confidence in President Clinton's handling of foreign policy has been reported as undermining the public's belief in the president's ability to take sound decisions. A May 1994 poll indicated that a majority of Americans disapproved of Clinton's handling of foreign policy. Specifically, 53 per cent of those interviewed disapproved and only 40 per cent approved. See Dan Balz and Richard Morin, 'Public Losing Confidence in Clinton Foreign Policy', *Washington Post*, 17 May 1994, p. A1.

21. See, for example, Jervis, 'The Future of World Politics', *International Security*, loc. cit.

22. Erich Weede, 'Conflict Patterns During the Cold War Period', p.1.

23. Roberts, 'From Proliferation to Antiproliferation', p.173.

24. Kemp, 'The Middle East Arms Race', p.443.

25. For example, Weede, 'Conflict Patterns', and Frankel, 'The Brooding Shadow'.

26. Cohen, *The National Interest*, pp.37–8.

Prospects for a Common Arms Transfer Policy from the European Union to the Middle East[1]

MICHAEL BRZOSKA

Introduction

A substantial share of modern arms in the Middle East comes from Western Europe. Arms export policies in Western Europe therefore have some influence on possible arms control in the Middle East. Western European governments have repeatedly proclaimed their support for any such regime but they have done little in practice to bring it about. Considering the benefits EU (European Union) member states have recently reaped from arms control and disarmament in their own region, and the possible benefits of a stable peace in the Middle East, more activity might be expected.

But arms export policies of the member states of the EU differ widely, despite long-standing attempts to co-ordinate foreign policies. Harmonization of arms transfers policies in the EU is at an early stage. Discussions among governments in the EU have not proceeded to difficult political issues such as arms transfer control to the Middle East.

A low degree of harmonization of arms export policies in Western Europe is a complicating element in efforts to control arms transfers to the Middle East. More harmonization, under political control, would reduce the number of actors, and thus co-ordination costs, in any arms transfer control regime. A united Western Europe would almost automatically become a 'leader' in regime creation politics simply because of the size of its arms industries.

At the same time that political harmonization is lacking, integration is growing at the industrial level. Economics partly substitute for an explicit arms transfer policy. Differences among Western European arms exporters are narrowed albeit on a low level of control. Also, industry-led integration makes the exercise of political restraint more difficult. Improvements in political control over arms production are necessary for any common arms transfer control initiatives by EU member states or at the EU level.

Three elements shaping the prospects for harmonization of arms transfer policies in the EU are described in the following sections. First, national arms transfer policies of the major arms exporting states in Western Europe are discussed. Then efforts to provide a framework for the arms industrial integration at the Western European level are described. The next section summarizes recent negotiations about better harmonization of arms exports and exports of dual-use goods from the EU. The paper ends with a look at the prospects for arms transfers from Western Europe to the Middle East.

Western European Arms Exports to the Near East

International data sets for arms transfers demonstrate the importance of the Near East[2] for Western European arms producers (see Table 1). According

TABLE 1

ARMS SALES FROM WESTERN EUROPE TO THE NEAR EAST

	France	UK	FRG	Italy	'Big 4'
Percentage share of supplies to Near East countries in total deliveries, US government data					
1985–88, total Near East	73	84	29	52	72
1989–92, total Near East	84	97	50	25	87
1985–92, Saudi Arabia					57
Iraq					8
UAE					3
Egypt					2
Israel					0
Syria					0
Percentage share of supplies to Near East in total deliveries (1988–92), SIPRI data					
1988–92, total	64	61	29	38	56
Saudi Arabia	24	52	2	16	31
UAE	22	0	14	5	12
Iraq	6	0	2	3	3
Egypt	3	0	2	9	2
Israel	0	0	1	0	0
Syria					
Percentage share of supplier in total sales to Near East countries, US government data					
1985–88, total Near East	11	11	1	1	24
1989–92, total Near East	11	21	2	0	33
Saudi Arabia					53
Iraq					15
UAE					58
Egypt					14
Sales in total sales to Near East countries (1988–92), SIPRI data					
1988–92, total Near East	14	12	2	1	29
Saudi Arabia	18	36	1	2	56
UAE	72	1	14	2	89
Iraq	8	0	1	1	9
Egypt	7	0	1	3	11
Israel	0	0	1	0	1
Syria	0	0	0	0	0

Sources: SIPRI Yearbook 1993 (London: Oxford University Press), pp.444–5, 480–2; R.F. Grimmett, *Conventional Arms Transfers to the Third World 1985–1992,* Congressional Research Service Report 93–656F, 19 July 1993, Washington, DC, pp.60, 68.

to data accumulated by the US government, more than three-quarters of all arms deliveries from Western European countries went to countries in the Near East. The importance of these countries for Western European arms producers increased in the early 1990s according to the US data. SIPRI data also reflect the dominance of Near Eastern markets for West European arms exports. In the SIPRI data, the share of Near Eastern importers in Western European exports is on a somewhat lower level than in the US data. The major reason for the difference seem to stem from the pricing procedures used and from the extent of military goods covered. For instance, deliveries to Saudi Arabia, by far the most important recipient of Western European arms during the late 1980s and early 1990s, are valued much higher in the US statistics than by SIPRI. The US government records a much wider spectrum of weapons than SIPRI which only reports data on transfers of major weapons, such as ships, aircraft, armoured vehicles and artillery, missiles and major electronic equipment.

In addition to Saudi Arabia, the United Arab Republic, Egypt and, until 1989, Iraq provided Western European producers with large business opportunities (Table 1). The two statistics record hardly any deliveries to Israel, Libya or Syria.

Some states in the Middle East are important to Western European arms producers and Western Europe is an important source of supply for a number of states in the Middle East, most notably Saudi Arabia and the United Arab Republic, but also Bahrain, Kuwait, Oman, Qatar and Tunisia, where a third or more of all weapons imported from 1982 to 1992 came from Western Europe. A somewhat reduced future importance of Western European countries can be expected judging from the distribution of recent orders from states in the Gulf.[3]

There used to be large differences in the patterns of arms transfers from Western Europe to the Middle East. The differences were the result of political preferences, arms production economics and explicit arms export policies. In the late 1980s and early 1990s, differences have narrowed. There is no room here to recount the extensive and convoluted history of West European arms export marketing and diplomacy with respect to the Middle East, but only a few points are relevant for the later discussion. Because of their quantitative importance, focus is on the 'big 4' in Western Europe: France, the United Kingdom, Germany and Italy.

Political Preferences

Historical factors still count, though their importance has declined. For instance, in British foreign policy, the Gulf states have a special status, not only because of their economic importance. Another case in point is

Germany, where relations with Israel are an important, though not always dominating, aspect of foreign policy. In the judgement of Italy's foreign policy establishment, geostrategic considerations, for instance with respect to Libya, have a major role.

Since the late 1960s, the member states of the EEC (European Economic Community) have been trying to harmonize their political views on foreign policy interests, including the Middle East. The framework chosen was that of informal meeting outside of EEC institutions, later called European Political Co-operation (EPC). With the ratification of the Single Act in 1986, the EPC became attached to the EC though outside of its institutional apparatus. In the Treaty on European Union, concluded at Maastricht in late 1991 (and therefore often called the Maastricht Treaty), the EPC is transformed into the Common Foreign and Security Policy (CFSP), as the 'second pillar' of the European Union. The stated aim of a common foreign and security policy is to be achieved step by step through the agreement and implementation of joint actions in specific policy areas (article J and following section of the Maastricht Treaty). Defence policy is to be coordinated in the Western European Union (WEU), instead of the CFSP.

The EPC process has resulted in greater harmonization of foreign policies towards the Middle East. One field where co-operation was notable is that of arms transfer limitations. For instance, in 1986 arms embargoes against Libya and Syria were on the agenda of the EPC and in August 1990, Iraq was embargoed by the EC. EC countries also co-ordinated their restrictions on the transfer of some chemicals deemed to be of particular use in the production of chemical weapons in the EPC framework from 1984. It was transformed into an EC Council Regulation in 1989 (No. 428/89).

Arms Production Economics

West European arms producers, especially France and Britain are often classified as 'commercial suppliers', driven more by economic than politico-strategic motivations. The search for financial gains fuelled the expansion of arms transfers to Middle Eastern countries in the 1970s and 1980s and is the major driving force behind current marketing efforts. But no Western European supplier state ever gave industry a totally free hand; commercial interests were fed and tamed by political interests, albeit to different degrees over time and with respect to different categories of military goods.

One factor shaping the degree of political intervention has been the pattern of industrial competitiveness. In general, 'newcomers' tend to be less inhibited by political reservations than established producers.[4] Established producers are often preferred by recipients because of their past records and presumed future reliability, for instance with respect to spare

parts supply. Producers entering the arms market have better chances at the
fringes of the market, where more respectable suppliers are reluctant to
deliver. One market niche comparatively open to newcomers has been
licence production. Established suppliers prefer to keep control over
technology and production; newcomers have tended to be more responsive
to recipient requests for the transfer of arms production technology. Among
the producers in Western Europe, none is a newcomer any more, but,
excepting Britain, all were in the not so recent past: France in the late 1950s
and early 1960s, Germany in the 1960s and Italy in the 1970s. Some of the
particularities in the patterns of arms transfers from Western Europe to the
Middle East, for instance the French connection to Israel in the 1950s and
1960s, or Italy's role in supplying Libya and Syria in the 1970s and early
1980s, or Germany's role as dominant supplier of small arms factories since
the 1960s,[5] partly resulted from limits in competitiveness. With the
increased maturation of arms industries in Western Europe, the pressure to
supply questionable recipients decreased in the late 1980s. Unfortunately,
the recent downturn in procurement and export orders has increased export
pressures again.

Another economic factor that shaped past differences among West
European arms exporters was the degree of integration between arms
production and civilian production. France and Britain provided opposite
cases: the Gaullist project of modernization of the French arms industry
assigned arms production the role of one of the locomotives to pull the
civilian economy.[6] In Germany, integration of military and civilian
production in the same enterprises, with the civilian part dominating, was
the preferred strategy from the 1950s to this day.[7] Both strategies ran into
problems with respect to arms exports: in the French case, arms exports are
so important for industrial development, that foreign policy, for instance
towards Iraq in the 1970s and early 1980s, was partly driven by a
dependence on arms transfers. In the German case, the predominance of
seemingly civilian products made the government reluctant to interfere with
exports beyond the range of obvious weapons. So German companies were
uncomplicated suppliers for a wide range of 'dual-use' goods in the 1970s
and 1980s, in the field of chemical weapons as well as conventional
weapons.[8] The differences in the arms production 'philosophies' remain. A
major change with respect to dual use goods was brought about, though, by
the Rabta affair and the Second Gulf War. Notably Germany has tightened
its regime over the export of goods useful for military purposes.[9]

Explicit Arms Export Policies

In Germany especially, arms export policies are a sensitive domestic policy
issue. Governments have therefore been careful to avoid exposure on this

issue, not always successfully. One result of this overriding consideration has been rather strict official guidelines on arms exports from the late 1960s. Another result has been a peculiar special treatment of warships: the guidelines were never applied to warships, which could be freely exported anywhere. German law does not allow the export of weapons to areas at war or close to war. In the political guidelines of 1971, this criterion was extended to 'areas of tension'. The whole of the Middle East was judged to be such an area. But the export of warships was almost always[10] authorized, for instance to Iran in 1977, Kuwait in 1980 and Israel in 1991. All other West European states also have specific legal and political guidelines on arms exports. As in the case of Germany, their interpretation has been dependent on specific interests, such as the ones mentioned above, and specific circumstances.

Efforts to harmonize these diverse export policies, with respect to content, institutions involved and interests to be considered will be reviewed after first looking at production as the phyiscal basis of exports.

Internationalization of Arms Production in Western Europe

Arms production is one of the best guarded fields of national sovereignty. Even among the states in Western Europe, by and large members of the same military alliance and with economies integrated in a free trade area, political regulation of arms production has remained a national prerogative. But economic integration in the EC and military integration in NATO had a profound effect at the industrial level. With respect to internationalization of arms production in Western Europe, politics has clearly lagged behind economics, despite a number of efforts at policy harmonization. These efforts and their failures are instructive as they demonstrate the difficulties of harmonization typical also for arms export policies.

Between Co-production and Concentration

Calls for better co-operation in arms production in NATO,[11] or at least Western Europe, date from the 1950s. An ever increasing number of organizations, working groups and committees were created but had limited success.[12] Co-production projects were initiated, but usually only among two or a few member states. Some co-production projects paved the way for more long-term co-operation among arms producing companies. The British, German and Italian producers of the MRCA (Multi Role Combat Aircraft) Tornado fighter, for instance, went on to propose and develop a follow-on project, the Eurofighter. But in general, arms producing companies in Western Europe benefited from the high level of national protection and favoured the continuation of procurement policies oriented towards domestic manufacturers.[13]

The situation changed in the 1980s. A major event was the British procurement reform of the early 1980s initiated by Sir Peter Levene.[14] Procurement became more comptetitive and the level of protection was lowered substantially. As a result, concentration in British arms industry increased substantially. The same happened in Germany without procurement reform when the government got rid of its extensive holdings in arms production. Daimler-Benz took over and consolidated much of the West German arms industry. Italy lagged behind until the early 1990s, when restructuring under government sponsorships became a fiscal necessity.[15] Even in France, with its strong state-industry network around the Direction Générale d'Armement, some changes were introduced, for instance the commercialisation of GIAT, the ordnance producer.

Institutionalizing International Competition

The British government tried to carry the spirit of the 'Levene reforms' into the West European arena via the Independent European Programme Group (IEPG).[16] There, Peter Levene and his minister (at that time Michael Heseltine) found open ears for a review of the nationally oriented procurement practices. A 'wise men' committee under the chairmanship of former Dutch defence minister and EC commissioner Henk Vredeling[17] was established to analyse proposals for a more open Western European arms market.

The 'Vredeling' report, presented and discussed in the IEPG in 1986 and 1987, contained a mixture of British ideas about the benefits of open markets, French insistence on the strategic role of national arms production and Spanish, and Greek and Italian hopes to build up their arms industries under the umbrella of the IEPG. Tenders should be open to producers from all member states. But no procurement agency should be forced to accept foreign offers. 'Less Developed Arms Industrial Countries' should get special treatment.

The IEPG adopted the Vredeling Report in its 'Action Plan' of 1988. Procedures for open tenders were established. But in practice not much happened. In December 1992, the IEPG was quietly dissolved.[18] And the Lisbon office closed. Although theoretically still in operation, the Action Plan was effectively dead.

The Role of the EC

The British government might have fared better if it had tried to involve the EC instead of the IEPG. But initial obstacles in the EC were very high. Article 223 of the founding Treaty of Rome establishes that arms production and exports are national prerogatives. Until the late 1970s, this article was interpreted as forbidding EC institutions any consideration of matters related to security policy and armaments. This interpretation was rejected by the European Parliament (EP). In 1978, after a stormy session, a slight majority of conservatives (but without Gaullists) and Liberals voted in favour of commissioning the 'Klepsch' Report on armaments issues. This was the first in a now long string of EP reports on armaments and arms export policy.[19]

The EC Commission avoided openly touching the issue[20] until well after the passing of the Single Act of 1986. Still, it was obvious to all political and economic actors that the creation of the Single Market from 1993 would have effects on arms production, at least with respect to those many companies producing civilian goods alongside military goods.

The negotiations leading up to the Maastricht agreement on a Union treaty provided a good opportunity to change the political framework in accord with the changing economics of arms production in Western Europe. Early on in the negotiations, the EC Commision made its preference clear: the abolition of Art. 223. With that simple measure, the commission would have dramatically increased its own power over arms production and arms exports.

The EC Commission received some support for its proposition. The EP repeatedly voted in favour of dropping Art. 223.[21] Germany and the Netherlands were in favour of amending Art. 223 or dropping it provided some national control over exports would be encoded in the new treaty. France and Britain opposed these proposals. A common reason was the objection to handing over another part of national sovereignty to bureaucrats in Brussels. The French government was more flexible on this point provided that an intergovernmental body of EC members was created to oversee an arms industrial policy. That was totally unacceptable to the British government. These discussions on armaments policy were soon overwhadowed by the contentious issue of a possible future European security policy and did not come to a conclusion. Discussions were effectively postponed until 1996 when the Union Treaty will be reviewed.

Without unanimous consent, Art. 223 survived the Maastricht exercise intact, and no West European framework for arms production was established.

Industrial Transnational Activity

The announcement of the 'Action Plan' and of the 'Single Market' had signalled to many of the decision-makers in the arms industry that the economic environment of the 1990s would be dramatically different. In preparation, arms producing companies in Western Europe greatly increased the number of links between them in the late-1980s. Some of these were called 'strategic alliances', such as the one between British Aerospace and Dassault on the next generation figher aircraft; others were more concrete co-operations in sectors of arms production, such as between GEC and Thomson on aircraft radar; and some involved the acquisition of capital. The decrease in procurement orders connected to the end of the Cold War hastened the restructuring process.

After this initial surge, internationalization activities lessened in the early 1990s. The Action Plan was not implemented, and the EU would not provide a policy framework. Company managers realized that the West European arms market would remain a national affair at least for a while despite all the committees and negotiations. Still, there is now a substantially higher level of industrial integration of arms production in Western Europe than until the mid-1980s. The industrial foundations for a common arms production and arms export policy in the EU have been created.

At the same time, the national legal prerogative over arms exports has eroded. The exercise of national controls has become more difficult to justify and more costly and has already been suspended without explicit political agreements to do so. A few aspects can demonstrate this point:

Co-operation of Companies. In the past, the major problem arose out of government-government co-production projects. Whose export laws should be applied? Should each participating government have right of veto? This issue has been largely settled. It is now common practice to agree beforehand that each partner state can export within its own legal framework to wherever it wants.[22]

International Sourcing. With increased co-operation of companies outside narrow co-production agreements, the issue of selling components and technology has become more prominent. Most governments treat such exports as intra-European, even when it is known that the final destination is outside of Europe. An arms producer can avoid national controls by assembling a weapon system from components from several West European countries.

Single Market. Border controls have been largely eliminated among the major continental EU members. That raises the temptation to ignore export controls and simply ship the goods to the foreign destination. Also, many companies are producing both civilian and military goods. Differing legal frameworks are now operative in these two areas. Because bureaucratic burdens are higher in the military field, there is a great temptation to declare as many products as possible to be civilian.

Efforts to Harmonize Export Policies

The opportunities to form a political framework for arms production in Western Europe have been passed over by decision-makers, mostly because some were afraid to loose sovereignty over this sector. They have not done much better with respect to arms export policies despite some strong political pressure to do so.

Interests and Interest Groups

A rather unusual orchestra of interest groups has been clamouring in the recent past for more harmonized policies on the exports of military groups: Europeanists, industry and arms export control advocates.

> Those favouring a more important role for EC institutions on grounds of principle are unwilling to accept an exception in an area as visible as the arms trade. The most vociferous group in this respect has been the European Parliament.[23] For the EP, the aim was to get both EC sovereignty over arms export and a role for itself.
>
> Lobbying activities by companies producing weapons and dual-use goods in favour of a common export policy increased markedly in the early 1990s. While ostensibly this was a joint effort from all member countries, German companies seem to have taken a leading role. They argue that German regulations, especially on the export of dual-use goods, put them at a disadvantage compared to companies in other West European countries. Through the call for a Europeanization of arms export controls they also hoped for a partial reversal of the strict German regulations. Companies in other countries stressed the need to limit paperwork and time delays. For them, the export issue was closely linked to the issue of a larger, more competitive European defence market.[24]
>
> Many critics of arms exports also were in favour of a more harmonized, EC-wide policy for arms exports. Especially those from countries with rather lax regulations hoped for more stringent European rules. Also, many arms export controllers feared that without the wider legal framework, companies would slip through existing regulations, especially with respect to dual-use goods.[25]

The differences in expectations were linked to perceived differences among member governments. Those in favour of a strict West European arms export regime hoped for Germany, the Netherlands and Denmark; those wanting more exports thought in term of the smallest common denominator, or a solution on the level of French regulations.[26]

Beyond specific arms export peculiarities, governments also had another interest to consider, namely that of clinging to sovereignty over a policy area with great domestic and foreign sensitivies. It was here where the greatest differences lay between member governments. Some, including Germany, were quite prepared to shift responsibility for (often unpopular) decisions to the EC level, while others, most notably the British government were very unwilling to cede any sovereignty to a multinational authority.

Negotiating Arms Exports

Arms exports were an issue in the pre-Maastricht negotiations on a possible elimination of Art. 223.[27] Without Art. 223, the EC would automatically become responsible for the regulation of arms exports. Member states' representatives discussed differences in current regulations, possible criteria for arms exports, but most of all what degree of EC sovereignty over arms export decisions would be acceptable and in what framework. Soon it became clear that there was a widespread reluctance to have the Commission and/or the EP involved. France and Germany formally proposed that arms exports be treated in the framework of the CSFP in the future. The Dutch government supported this position, calling for 'true coordination in an EPC framework'. The British government opposed any role for intergovernmental decision-making, proposing instead a closer co-ordination of member governments on the question of armaments on an informal basis. Luxembourg, in the presidency at the time, presented a two-tier concept in a draft treaty: informal co-operation on matters of 'general interest' and joint action on matters where the Council had explicitly decided on subject and objectives.[28] Towards the end of the negotiations, arms exports were low on the priority lists and not more than the mentioning as prori.[29] In a protocol annexed to the Maastricht Treaty, member governments agreed to implement joint action on the control of the transfer of arms exports and military technology as soon as the Treaty came into force (1 November 1993). Like most provisions in the Maastricht Treaty, this was a mere statement of intent to be made practical through later decisions. A unanimous vote will be necessary to decide on objectives after which further decisions could than be taken with qualified majority (article J.3).

Despite this failure to agree on substantial matters in Maastricht, one of the discussed aspects survived. Because of the strong criticism of national governments on arms export policies in a number of member countries and the need felt to develop a common viewpoint for the various multilateral fora on arms transfer reduction, member governments decided to give weapons proliferation a prominent place in the Communiqué of the Luxembourg Summit of 28–29 June 1991. The European Council – the meeting of the heads of state – adopted a list of seven criteria on which they promised to base their national arms export policies.[30]

A High Level Ad Hoc Working Group on conventional arms exports set up in late 1991 has discussed a wide range of issues, from individual cases of arms transfers to the co-ordination of embargoes. Judging by what is known about the confidential meetings, practical matters such as the design of a common transfer document for weapons take much more time than efforts to harmonize policies. Most participants seem to be highly sceptical of more harmonized West European arms export policies. They judge the High Level Working Group as a focal point for urgent multilateral action, for instance in the case of embargoes. Efforts to turn the Group into a clearing house of information on planned or ongoing arms exports from individual member states have been frustrated. Especially France and Britain are unwilling to share information with other member states on a regular basis.[31]

Negotiating Dual-Use Exports

While – with Art. 223 in force – efforts to arrive at common arms export policies could stagnate, the same 'wait and see' attitude seemed not possible for dual-use goods. Still, the Commission was reluctant to take the initiative because of the known reservations of some member governments.

It was not until 1990 that the Commission, more specifically the General Directorate III responsible for Single Market issues under Vice-President Martin Bangemann, began to start working on EC-wide regulation of dual-use good exports. After commissioning an external study on dual-use good production in the EC,[32] an inventory of national export regulations for dual-use goods was compiled by consulting member governments. Delayed by the pre-Maastricht negotiations, it took the commission until January 1992 to adopt a common position which it duly reported to member governments and the EP.[33]

The commission saw the urgent need for a common EC regulation reinforced by events surrounding the second Gulf War. Member governments were increasingly aware of the dangers of dual-use exports and therefore willing to extend controls. There was a clear danger that the differences in the degree of control would become more pronounced, with some EC countries strengthening their already rather restrictive regimes and others keeping their more lax regulations. That would encourage 'licence shopping', the illegal but increasingly simple transfer of goods to the country with the lowest legal export barrier. The EC had the legal competence to regulate this area and with the coming of the Single Market there was no practical alternative to EC wide control anymore. With the Single Market in place, there should be no question anymore that goods and technologies not expressly mentioned under article 223 should move freely between member states. As a *sine qua non* for the elimination of controls on intra-EC trade, all members states would have to establish effective controls, based on common standards and trusted by the other member states. The commission would help with improvements where necessary. The EC institutions would have to agree on common lists for goods and destinations, and on criteria that would have to be applied by the export licence agency.

Following the presentation of the Commission's position, the EC Council appointed, during a meeting in Lisbon, an Ad Hoc High Level Working Party to work on the issue that now had become an urgent matter. The group could build on some of the work done earlier, such as the discussion of criteria, lists of goods and countries. But it also inherited the major problems: how much sovereignty were member governments prepared to yield and to what EC institution, what role for national legislation versus EC regulations, how to avoid 'licence shopping' while providing for the free movement of goods within the EC?

Some progress was made over the spring and summer of 1992. It became clear that there would be no decision-making process on the West European level. Britain and Denmark opposed any transfer of sovereignty to EC institutions. The most they would yield to the EC was the role of an informal clearing house. The German representatives' preference for an early transfer of sovereignty to the EC Council or some other, possibly newly established EC institution had little chance of adoption. In addition, popular sentiments on the EC shifted in several member countries in 1992. After the Danish Maastricht referendum of June 1992, the Commission was on a hasty retreat with respect to claiming responsibilities.

Thus it became clear that the EC would not provide more than a framework for continued national regulation of dual-use exports. Intra-EC trade would be free, except for a short list of some goods with special character,[34] while for exports outside of the EC licences would be granted by one member state and be valid for all. Common lists of goods and countries, as well as standardized licensing procedures would guarantee common scopes of control but ultimate authority on whether to licence a transfer or not would remain with national governments. The lists of criteria agreed on earlier would be guidelines, but not more.

Although numerous issues were still outstanding, the Commission tried to increase the member states' sense of urgency by issuing the 'Proposal for a Council Regulation on the control of exports of certain dual-use goods and technologies and of certain nuclear products and technologies' (COM(92)/317final) on 31 August 1992. Reflecting the state of negotiations in the High Level Group, it left licence authorization to member governments, on the basis of common lists of goods, including technologies, and countries.[35] Reflecting German and British legislation, a 'catch all' clause was incorporated, requiring licences for goods not on the list, if the exporter knows of their military destination. The Commission reduced its own role to co-operating in the exchange of information. After a transitory period, during which licences would have to be sought in the country of origin of the goods, applications could be sent in by any legal owner of the good in any member country. The regulation contained the list of criteria adopted in Luxemburg in June 1991[36] that governments should consider when reviewing licences.

As standard procedure requires, the regulation was sent to the EC Council for approval. The High Level Working Group continued to negotiate on many of the issues, even the ones the Commission had hoped to have settled with its proposal. Disagreements included the scope of the list of goods and technologies, the country list, the catch-all clause, the question of where licences would have to be sought and the length of the transitory period during which intra-EC transfer would still require a licence. At the same time, national governments had the regulation discussed at the appropriate national levels.

None of the remaining issues seemed to be of overriding importance and positions were not very far apart by the summer of 1992. Still, negotiations went on. Because of the difficulty to come up with a list of proscribed countries, it was agreed by end-1993 that there should be a 'positive' list of those countries where simplified licencing procedures should apply.[37] This list contains those states that are members of relevant export control regimes.[38] The catch-all clause was limited to goods useful for the construction of weapons of mass destruction. The status of the criteria was reduced by having them in an appendix instead of in the text of the regulation. Sentiments on where licences should be sought shifted. The British government, supported by the Germans, pointed out the dangers of allowing licence applications by any legal owner.[39] It was decided that there should be a consultation process between the authorities in the countries where the licence application is sought and where the good are located. For a transitory period, member states can require companies to apply for licences whenever they know that goods are leaving the EU.

The few remaining differences, for instance on the length of the transition period, were ironed out by early 1994. Still by early summer 1994 it was not clear whether and when a regulation would be adopted by the EC Council. Even though it is now clear that the regulation will not be more than a common formal framework and leave decision-making power to national governments, some members find even this difficult to accept.

Prospects for Arms Exports from Western Europe to the Middle East

No explicit common arms export policy for the EU is in sight, neither with respect to the Middle East nor to any other region. There is limited willingness among the governments in Western Europe to give up national sovereignty in this core area of security. The chances for a common approach by Western European states towards a possible arms control regime for the Middle East are not very high. Each of the major states continues to follow its own foreign policy and arms-industrial interests, despite a long-standing project of harmonizing foreign policies in the framework of the European Political Co-operation and some more recent efforts at negotiating more co-operative arms industrial and arms export policies.

At the same time, there is a growing gap between political willingness to consolidate policies towards the production and export of arms and dual-use goods and actual integration of production occurring at the company level. Co-operation and consolidation at the industrial level advanced substantially in the late 1980s and early 1990s, and is on a much higher level than ever before despite the continuing lack of a political framework.

At least some EU member governments, such as Britain and France, seem to see advantages in continuing the current course of non-integration, for a number of reasons. An important one is that they judge the trend towards commercialization of the arms market as basically beneficial both from an economic and a political standpoint. For a short time in the early 1990s, these government seemed to be willing to strengthen the control element of arms transfer policies, for instance when they agreed to the criteria for arms transfers at Luxembourg and Lisbon. But this attempt at more control was soon abandoned when the images of Iraqi super-guns, built from components supplied from Britain, and Iraqi Scuds protected by French AA-systems and armed with chemical weapons, produced with German supplied equipment, faded. Difficult economic times, coupled with the drastic decrease in arms orders after the end of the Cold War have increased pressures on governments to deregulate arms export control in order to save national industrial capacities. At the other end of the political spectrum, support for more harmonization has dwindeld. The EC Commission and EP are marginalized in their attempts to make arms transfers a European issue. The German government seems more reluctant than before to press other member governments, and there is a powerful lobby for less restrictions on arms transfers.

The probability for a higher degree of political harmonization at the EU level has actually decreased since the negotiations leading to the agreement at Maastricht. True, there have been some diplomatic successes. Western European states are in a better position now to agree on joint arms export restrictions on 'outcasts'. The High Level Ad Hoc Working Group on conventional arms transfers agreed on procedures as well as criteria for arms embargoes. Also, it was possible to arrive at a consensual wording of a regulation for the export of dual-use goods. But these accomplishments are on the margin of policy. Embargoes will only come about when all members agree and the dual-use regulation allows each member to continue to pursue its own export policy. Agreement has been possible where interests of participants coincided, but not beyond.

The growing gap between economic integration and institutional capacity for control produces problems for arms transfers from Western Europe. One difficulty is the lack of a political framework for the industrial management of the build-down after the end of the Cold War. The pressure to export is increasing, not least because of the lack of common policy to counter this pressure.

A second problem is that arms-producing companies increasingly doubt the rationality of government policies. Many company managers trusted politicians and bureaucrats promising a more competitive and open arms market in Western Europe and were deeply disappointed. One expression of growing disappointment may be increased readiness to ignore export controls. The creation of the Single Market, with reduced custom controls, makes it much less likely that illegal inter-community transfers of dual-use goods will be detected. Industrial disillusion with policy-makers further erodes the basis for control of such goods that are already difficult to control because of their identity or similarity with civilian goods.

Third, the company-led integration of arms production at the West European level tends to pressure governments to lower control levels, first to the level of lowest control within the EU and possibly even beyond. Within the EU, companies can fairly easily shift production away from countries with higher levels of regulation to countries with lower levels of regulation. As this process occurs, governments exercising control over arms transfers come under pressure to deregulate controls in order to save jobs and technology in their countries. In those countries to which arms producers migrate, they increase their lobbying powers as economic dependence in arms production grows. A government that already exercises little control is most likely to become even better disposed towards arms production and arms exports.

Fourth, the chances of constructive participation by Western European governments in a possible arms control regime are decreasing. The problems of finding West European consent have already limited the West European contribution to the P-5 (Permament Members of the UN Security Council) and G-7 (group of members of the International Monetary Fund with the seven largest economies) deliberations on the limitations of arms transfers. In the rounds of P-5 talks, Britain and France stayed in the shadow of the other three participants, letting the United States and China take the dominant opposing roles. In the framework of preparing G-7 work, initiatives from Western Europe were limited to specific areas, such as the British proposal to support the UN Arms Trade Register and the German (together with the Japanese) plan to stress the links between arms exports and development issues. The one exception was the creation of the Arms Transfer Transparency Register in the United Nations. EC member countries and Japan were instrumental in bringing the Register about.

Though in discussions within the EU on arms export matters the Middle East was hardly ever mentioned, these general trends influence future arms transfers to the Middle East. First, although *de facto* differences in exports between arms producers in West Europe will most probably be smaller in the future, declaratory policy may not change. Britain and France will remain the more important Western European suppliers to Arab Middle Eastern states, but British and French weapon systems can increasingly be expected to contain components from other Western European countries, for instance Germany. Israel may expect to have access to technology from Britain and France if it can find another Western European government, such as Germany, to supply weapons containing such technology, even if Britain and France themselves remain unwilling to supply. In the future, weapon systems originating from Western Europe will be assembled from more or less the same sources of technology from within the EU, although they may differ in outer shape, location of final assembly, and, most importantly, availability to differing countries in the Middle East. Official statistics of arms exports from Western Europe to the Middle East may not look much different in the future and will continue to reveal political preferences, but they will be increasingly misleading as to where components are coming from.

Second, Western Europe is unlikely to play an active role in the control of arms transfers to the Middle East, neither as a whole nor through joint action of its major powers. Political integration is too slight and economic interests in arms production are too important. The conservative states on the Gulf and Egypt will continue to be preferred customers for weapons because they are increasingly important to the well-being of the shrinking and more concentrated arms industries in Western Europe. The exception will be arms embargoes targeted at specific states, such as Libya, but even here Western Europe is more likely to follow others, such as the United States, than to be an active proponent of sanctions.

Third, as no common policy of arms exports from Western Europe to the Middle East is likely to emerge, outside actors trying to set up an arms transfer regime for the Middle East will have to cope with a number of players from Western Europe. These include the major member governments, but also the EU Commission and to some extent those major arms-producing companies capable of evading national control because of their high level of internationalization. Western European actors will most probably not be the most difficult to draw into arms control efforts in the Middle East, but they will also not be as forthcoming and helpful as might be expected from their arms control rhetoric.

NOTES

1. I wish to thank participants of the conference 'Middle East Arms Control and the European Experience', Bar-Ilan University, Ramat Gan, Israel, 8–10 November 1993, for comments. Financial support from the US Institute of Peace is gratefully acknowledged.
2. Defined in the US data as the arc of countries from Morocco to Iran. For the sake of consistency, the same country grouping has been used for the SIPRI data presented in Table 1.
3. See Richard F. Grimmett, Conventional Arms Transfers to the Third World, 1985–1992, CRS Report for Congress 93–656F, 19 July 1993, pp. 56–7
4. This trend has been especially pronounced in the supply of weapons to warring states. See Stephanie G. Neuman, *Military Assistance in Recent Wars: The Dominance of the Superpowers,* The Washington Papers, No. 122 (New York: Preager with the Center for Strategic and International Studies, Georgetown University, Washington, DC, 1986)
5. Generally on small arms see Edward C. Ezell, *Small Arms Today,* 2nd. ed. (Harrisburg: Stackpole Books, 1988); for data on licensed production see Michael Brzoska and Thomas Ohlson (eds.), *Arms Production in the Third World* (London: Taylor and Francis, 1985) and United States Congress, Office of Technology Assessment (OTA), *Global Arms Trade* (Washington, DC: US Government Printing Office, 1991).
6. See François Chesnais (ed.), *Compétitivité internationale et dépenses militaires* (Paris: Économica 1990).
7. See Michael Brzoska and Peter Lock (eds.), *Restructuring of Arms Production in Western Europe* (London: Oxford University Press, 1992).
8. See Michael Brzoska, 'Behind German Export Scandals', *Bulletin of the Atomic Scientists* (July/Aug 1989), pp. 30–33 and Thomas C. Wiegele, *The Clandestine Building of Libya's Chemical Weapon Factory* (Carbondale: Southern Illinois University Press, 1992).
9. See Herbert Wulf, 'The Federal Republic of Germany', in Ian Anthony, *Arms Export Regulations* (London: Oxford University Press, 1992), pp.72–85.
10. Two exceptions were submarines for Israel in 1972 and submarines for South Africa in 1983. In both cases, though, drawings and parts for the production of submarines were exported: in the case of Israel, to Vickers in Britain which then built the three Gal Class submarines; and in the case of South Africa, to Sandock-Austral in Durban. Regarding the submarines for Israel, the German government under Chancellor Schmidt secretly sanctioned the delivery of plans and spare parts; as for the submarines for South Africa, a parliamentary investigation committee unsuccessfully tried to establish a similar claim made by the opposition parties. In the end, the relevant legal authorities ruled that the export of plans and parts did not violate the export law because they were not complete. The law was amended in 1990 to include incomplete deliveries to proscribed destinations.
11. The periodical intra-NATO controversy over the scope of standardization and co-operation is not treated here, see for instance Egon Klepsch, *Two-Way Street: USA-Europe Arms Procurement* (London: Brassey's, 1979), and Ron Matthews, *European Armaments Collaboration. Policy, Problems and Prospects* (London: Harwood, 1992).
12. In addition to NATO, with its Conference of National Armament Directors with several Working Groups, co-ordination was the objective of the Eurogroup (NATO members in Europe), FINABEL (a group of the original WEU members without Britain and Germany), IEPG (NATO members in Europe plus France) and Western European Union (WEU), all

with sub-groups, not mentioning bi- and multilateral *ad hoc* groups. In the late 1980s, there were over 250 multinational committees working on arms standardization and co-operation projects in Western Europe, according to one stressed participant, Wolfgang Ruppelt, 'Internationale Rüstungskooperation', *Wehrtechnik* (May 1992), pp.19–22.

13. See, for instance, Keith Hartley, *NATO Arms Co-operation: A Study in Economics and Politics* (London: Allen and Unwin, 1983) or Martyn Bittleston, *Co-operation of Competition? Defence Procurement Options for the 1990s*, Adelphi Papers No. 250 (London: International Institute for Strategic Studies [IISS], 1990) and Andrew Moravcsik, 'Armaments Among Allies: European Weapons Collaboration, 1975–85', in Peter Evans, Harold Jacobsen and Robert Putnam (eds.), *Double Edged Diplomacy: Interactive Games in International Affairs* (Berkeley, CA: University of California Press, 1993).

14. See, for instance, Trevor Taylor, 'The British Restructuring Experience', in Brzoska and Lock, *Restructuring of Arms Production.*

15. On restructuring in the West European arms industry see the annual overviews in the *SIPRI Yearbooks*; Brzoska and Lock, *Restructuring*; Elisabeth Sköns, 'Western Europe: Internationalization of the Arms Industry', in Herbert Wulf (ed.), *Arms Industry Limited* (London: Oxford University Press, 1993); and Laurent Carroué, l*es Industries européennes d'armements* (Paris: Masson, 1993).

16. Originally founded by European NATO countries and including France in 1975 in order to counter US pressure to buy more US equipment, the IEPG had little weight until the early 1980s.

17. Independent European Programme Group (IEPG), 'Towards a Stronger Europe. A Report by an Independent Study Team Established by Defence Ministers of Nations of the IEPG to Make Proposals to Improve the Competitiveness of Europe's Defence Equipment Industry under the Chairmanship of Henk Vredeling' (Brussels, 1986).

18. Its functions were transferred to the Western European Union. The WEU formed a new committee, largely identical to the IEPG group, to study improved armaments co-operation at the WEU summit in Rome in May 1993, now called the West European Armaments Group.

19. Reprinted in Klepsch, *Two-Way Street.*

20. See Agnès Courades Allebeck, 'The European Community: from the EC to the European Union', in Wulf, *Arms Industry*; and Harald Bauer, 'Institutional Frameworks for Integration of Arms Production in Western Europe', in Brzoska and Lock, *Restructuring.*

21. But see as an early measure the (unpublished) report by David Greenwood, Report on a Policy for Promoting Defence and Technological Co-operation Among West European Countries for the Commission of the European Community,' Doc. III–1499/80, Brussels.

22. European Parliament (EP), Report on the Community's Role with Respect to the Control of Arms Exports and the Arms Industry by Glyn Ford, PE 200.329/fin, 23 July 1992 and Jannis Sakellariou and Norbert Schöbel, 'Die Europäische Gemeinschaft auf dem Weg zu einer gemeinsamen Rüstungsexportkontrolle?', *Sicherheit und Frieden* (Jan. 1992).

23. Earlier, some governments, most notably the German, tried to negotiate rights of veto. In some cases, such as French-German anti-tank missiles, the German government failed because companies threatened to withdraw from the co-production projects. In other cases, such as the MRCA Tornado, the government succeeded, but gave up its veto right in 1983. British Aerospace was then negotiating major sales to a number of Middle Eastern countries and the German government was quite happy to shed any official responsibility while still profiting from the export business.

24. The EP has adopted numerous resolution and reports, see for instance European Parliament, 'Report on the Community's Role'.

25. See Lord Inglewood and Quentin Huxham, *The Defence Industry after the IGC's. A Bow Group Paper* (London: The Bow Group, 1991) and European Round Table of Industrialists (ERT), *Toward a Single European Export Control System: Harmony or Chaos? An Industry Viewpoint* (Brussels, 1991).

26. See Saferworld Foundation, *Arms and Dual-Use Exports from the EC: A Common Policy for Regulation and Control* (Bristol, 1992) and Harald Müller, 'The Export Controls Debate in the "New" European Community', *Arms Control Today* (March 1993).

27. The following sections are partly based on interviews. See also previous note.
28. Saferworld, *Arms and Dual-Use Exports*, pp. 91–3
29. In addition, in a declaration later appended to the Maastricht Treaty, the nine WEU member countries declared, under the heading of 'proposals that will be examined further': 'enhanced co-operation in the field of armaments with the aim of creating a European armaments agency.'
30. They range from the respect of international obligations, such as UN sanctions, to the observance of human rights in the country of final destination, the preservation of regional peace, security and stability, the danger of diversion of exports to unwanted recipients, such as terrorists, and the recipient's observance of international law. An eighth criterion was added at the Lisbon summit, June 1992: arms exports should be compatible with the technological and economic capacity of the recipient country.
31. All West European countries have willingly supplied information to the UN Arms Transfer Register, though. See Edward Laurance, Siemon Wezeman and Herbert Wulf, *Arms Watch: SIPRI Report on the First Year of the UN Register of Conventional Weapons, SIPRI Research Report 6* (London: Oxford University Press, 1993).
32. 'Eurostrategies 1991: Dual-Use Industries in Europe. Study Carried out for the Commission of the European Communities DG III', Brussels, April 1991.
33. European Community (EC), 'Export Controls for Dual-use Products and Technologies and the Single Market, Communication to the European Parliament EC Doc III/2305/91Rev.1', 17 January 1992; see also Jörg Wenzel, 'The European Community's Approach to Export Controls', in Kathleen Bailey and Robert Rudney (eds.), *Proliferation and Export Controls* (Lanham: University Press of America, 1993).
34. For instance, cryptographic equipment, highly secretive underwater sensors, plutonium, etc.
35. Neither country nor list of goods were attached to the proposal at that time. But it was made clear that technologies as well as goods should be included.
36. But not the additional Lisbon criterion, see note 30.
37. Bundesregierung, 'Bericht der Bundesregierung zum Stand der EG-Harmonisierung des Exportkontrollrechts für Güter und Technologien mit doppeltem Verwendungsweck (Dual Use Waren), Stand Ende Oct.1993', Unterrichtung an den Deutschen Bundestag, Drucksache 12/6187 vom 18.11.1993.
38. The Nuclear Suppliers Group, the Australia Group, set up to control exports of chemical and biological weapons, the MTCR and COCOM until its dissolution.
39. A company could, for instance, transfer goods legally to a daughter company in another member country, and have the daughter company apply for a licence and then ship the goods.

Russia and a Conventional Arms Non-proliferation Regime in the Middle East

YITZHAK KLEIN

Introduction: Regime-Formation from a Non-Hegemon's Perspective

Writing in this volume, Robert Leiber has raised the issue of whether America's emergence as the sole superpower will enable it to play a hegemonic role in the establishment of non-proliferation regimes. He warns that the ultimate effect of the transition from a bipolar to a 'unipolar' system may be counter-intuitive, and has written elsewhere that 'the very factors that have led to the emergence of a one-superpower world may also make it more difficult for America to play the ... leadership role which is widely expected of it'.[1]

This essay addresses the issue of regime formation in the specific conditions of the post-bipolar world from a somewhat different perspective: how willing are other international players to accede to a regime, should the supposed hegemon attempt to establish one? The player we focus on is Russia, the primary successor state to the former Soviet superpower, and the issue we concentrate on is the prospect of establishing a conventional arms non-proliferation regime in the Middle East.

Our conclusions reinforce Leiber's scepticism. A workable non-proliferation regime must include Russia, but it would be difficult for the United States to induce Russia to join such a regime. Obstacles include both systemic factors and Russian domestic political factors.[2] The alleged 'transition' from a bipolar to a unipolar world has not been as sharp or as unequivocal as it is sometimes represented. This is reflected both in fact – such as the disproportionate size and capacity of the Russian arms industries, compared to other 'non-hegemonic' powers – and in the attitudes which form Russian foreign policy. Russian–American relations exist in a kind of twilight, transitional stage where the roles of the two countries are not clear. This imposes special burdens on international co-operation between the two, notwithstanding the high expectations that have been raised in this regard.

Uniquely among the industrialized nations, Russia views its armaments industry as its most important industrial export sector, and it intends to remain a leading player in the international arms market. Thus no non-proliferation regime can long survive without Russian co-operation. At the same time, broad elements of the Russian elite have inherited attitudes formed during the Soviet period. Such elites are not prepared to concede to the United States the role of hegemon. They continue to lay claim in Russia's name to former Soviet interests among the Commonwealth of Independent States (CIS), Central Europe and the Third World. They persist in viewing Russia as a power in the same class as the United States, and are apt to view American efforts to exercise policy leadership in issue-areas such as non-proliferation as directed against Russian interests.

An additional factor tending to complicate the establishment of regimes is Russian resistance to the isolation of issue-areas; they tend to view all issue-areas as linked, so that friction in one issue-area casts its shadow over the prospects for progress in other areas. This is not to say that Russia has exhibited no interest in the establishment of non-proliferation regimes. It does mean, however, that the United States and other Western nations are likely to find the task of incorporating Russia into an international non-proliferation regime long and difficult. Both success and failure will entail significant costs, and these costs will increase as time goes on.

The rest of this chapter is divided into three parts. The first part concerns the domestic context of Russian arms-transfer policy. The second concerns the policy itself, considered as an aspect of Russian foreign policy. The third is devoted to some concluding remarks on Russia's role in the formation of an international arms-transfer regime.

The Domestic Context of Russian Arms Transfer Policy

The Triumph of an 'Illiberal' Agenda?

A common view of arms control in the Middle East in the post-Soviet era was expressed recently by a respected student of the regional arms balance:

> Superpower-level obstacles [*sic*] to the application of arms control in the Middle East became largely irrelevant following the end of the Cold War and the breakup of the Soviet Union. Indeed, the end of the Cold War created general international support for limiting further proliferation ...[3]

Reality is more complex. For most of the period since Russia achieved independence in December 1991, its foreign policy was the product of a delicate balance of forces between conservative and liberal elements, with the Foreign Ministry being the chief advocate for the latter perspective. The elections of December 1993 upset this balance, putting conservative elements associated with the Prime Minister, Viktor Chernomyrdin, firmly in power. Russian 'liberals' are now out of power, and President Yeltsin must rely on the influence of 'moderate' conservatives like Chernomyrdin, whose Parliamentary supporters include an element of the Communist Party, and the power of the armed forces. While Russia's neo-Fascists, the Liberal Democratic Party under the leadership of Vladimir Zhirinovskii, have failed so far to acquire a foothold in the government, President Yeltsin must rely chiefly on 'establishment' conservatives such as Chernomyrdin and Defence Minister Pavel Grachev to keep them in check.

Conservative elements in Russia are associated with the armed forces and with parts of the military-industrial complex which served them, the Interior Ministry (which controls its own armed forces), and the Internal Security establishment (the domestic half of the former KGB). Among these elements nationalist feeling is very strong, and it is frequently coupled with attitudes toward the West ranging from reserve to outright hostility.[4] Though the Soviet Union and its empire have for the time being collapsed, members of these groups look forward to re-establishing Russian influence over the former republics of the Soviet Union and even to re-establishing Russia's influence in Central Europe.[5] It is important to realize that this latter sentiment is very widely shared in Russia; in this respect even President Yeltsin is a conservative. One of the events that strengthened Yeltsin greatly in the weeks leading up to his anti-Parliamentary coup, and which probably contributed to his decision to go ahead with it, was his success in forcing the Ukraine and the Central Asian republics of the former Soviet Union into humiliating surrenders of sovereignty in favour of Russia.[6] The use of Russian troops to intervene in the affairs of other republics, such as Georgia and Moldova, are part and parcel of the same policy. As conservative influence over policy-making has increased, friction has arisen between Russia and the West over a broad range of issues: Russian military intervention in other states of the CIS, Russian opposition to the extension of NATO influence in Central Europe, Russian attempts to revise the terms of the treaty on Conventional Forces in Europe (CFE), Russian reluctance to support military intervention in Bosnia and sanctions against former Soviet client states such as Libya, Iraq, and North Korea.

Some conservatives view attempts to establish conventional arms non-proliferation regimes in the same light: a Western initiative directed primarily against Russian interests. Consider an article on arms sales which appeared in the conservative, strongly anti-Yeltsin journal *Pravda* early in 1993. Provocatively entitled 'Russian Hara-kiri, Kozyrev Style' (Kozyrev is Yeltsin's foreign minister), the article accuses the Russian government of sacrificing Russian interests in order to curry favour with the West. It alleges that arms sales abroad could bring Russia an income of up to $20 billion a year; however the policy of the Yeltsin government, which adheres to UN sanctions against Libya and Iraq, two of the former Soviet Union's leading arms clients, prevents this.[7]

The article just cited is not an isolated example, nor are the sentiments it expresses of recent vintage. During the Gulf crisis of 1990–91 as well, many voices were raised to oppose the Gorbachev government's support of UN-imposed sanctions against Iraq. According to this school of thought, regimes such as those existing in Iraq, Libya and Serbia are traditional allies of Russia. They deserve Russian support against Russia's traditional enemies in the West.[8]

The article is an extreme example of the polemic used in Russia since 1992 concerning foreign policy in general and arms sales in particular. Since the elections of 1993 this polemic has largely disappeared from official government sources. The conservatives have won, and the Foreign Ministry, from Kozyrev down, has slipped smoothly into a more conservative tone. For example, since the December 1993 elections Kozyrev has said that Russia 'should not withdraw from those regions which have been the sphere of Russian interests for centuries [the former Soviet republics including the Baltic states]; we should not fear the words "military presence",'[9] and that 'Russia sees the [states of Central Europe—Poland, the Czech Republic, Slovakia and Hungary] in its sphere of vitally important interests',[10] both statements he would not have made during 1993.

The elections of 1993 have thus caused a sea change in Russian attitudes toward the West. As Georgii Arbatov, former head of the USA and Canada Institute and an influencial commentator on Russian relations with the West has argued, a Cold War may be re-emerging between Russia and the West on a broad range of foreign policy and military issues.[11] Were this to happen it would not bode well for prospects of Russian participation in an American-brokered arms control regime, particularly considering the emphasis Russia continues to place on arms sales as a source of cash and international influence.

Economics and Russian Arms Trade Abroad

The arms industry of the Soviet Union had enormous capacity and Russia has inherited most of it. Estimates of the proportion of former-Soviet productive capacity located within Russia run from 65 to 75 per cent; the Ukraine is a distant second, at about 15–20 per cent.[12] Most of the productive infrastructure required to produce the innumerable components that make up weapon systems is located within Russia, and Russian officials have expressed the view that Russia can in principle undertake all the arms production it currently desires without recourse to manufacturing facilities located in other republics of the CIS.[13] Unlike Russia, none of the other successor states to the Soviet Union possesses the manufacturing infrastructure to produce complex weapon systems independently, though collaboration between arms manufacturers in the different republics of the CIS remains one of the better-functioning subsystems of the former Soviet economy.

The Russian arms industry is currently in dire straits. The armed forces are shrinking precipitately in size, and huge inventories of unneeded and largely obsolescent weapons are distributed about the country. The government hovers on the edge of bankruptcy, and such sums as are allocated to military procurement are withered by runaway inflation. According to official figures, arms procurement declined 38 per cent in real terms between 1990 and 1991; 1992 saw a further decline of 68 per cent.[14] In 1994 the military establishment has obtained, for the first time since 1991, a modest 10 per cent rise in procurement funds,[15] but this hardly redresses the damage done in previous years. The military budget authorized for fiscal 1994 (37 trillion rubles) was less than half the Ministry of Defence's request.[16]

Large-scale conversion of Russia's military industry would require massive infusions of capital which simply are not available. In recognition of this fact Russian policy has changed; conversion no longer tops the agenda. The military-industrial establishment is concentrating on pre-serving and extending its technological capacity.[17] R&D and the production of high-technology items are receiving priority. Most other production will be allowed to die on the vine.

The preservation of military-technological capacity is viewed as crucial to the future of the national economy as a whole. In the words of Andrei A. Kokoshin, first deputy defence minister in charge of the arms industry,

> There is a danger that a large part of military production will disappear. And it is the chief resource in our ability to compete with the developed nations, due to the quality of engineers, scientists and workers employed, their work discipline, and especially dual-purpose technology.[18]

In other words, rather than dismantle the cream of the arms industry, a policy which would lead to the dissipation and loss of its unique resources, leading military industries are to be preserved in their present form. Eventually, when the Russian economy recovers, they will form the core of its technological base. The new policy was expressed succinctly in an interview by one of President Yeltsin's advisers, Mikhail Malei:

> [There is] a new approach toward the conversion of the Russian

military production system, the crux of which is that the government will no longer destroy the complex but feed it ... thanks to the export of arms and military technology. [19]

Arms exports represent an integral part of this strategy. Russia can sell off its inventory of surplus weapons – a T-72 tank goes for a song at $500,000 – but in doing so it competes with other republics, particularly the Ukraine, where the surpluses are smaller but more modern. The funds to maintain R&D and the production of advanced systems must come from the sale of advanced systems. Thus arms sales are seen as necessary, not only for the preservation of military productive capacity, but for the survival of Russia as a modern technological power. That is a very powerful incentive to sell arms, one not present to the same degree in any other major arms-exporting country. While Soviet-Russian arms sales have declined precipitately in the 1989–93 period, they remain Russia's primary export after energy, and its primary manufactured export.

The Russian government has formed international commitments to limit conventional arms sales; these will be discussed below. Despite this, encouraging the sale of arms and military technology is official policy. In February 1992, soon after the dissolution of the Soviet government, President Yeltsin promised the military establishment to encourage arms sales abroad.[20] In early 1993, according to press reports, Yeltsin scolded his ministers for not doing more to promote arms sales, particularly to India.[21]

Regulatory Environment and Controls on Arms Transfers

The Russian government's attempts to establish a regulatory framework for the control of arms transfers have had to contend with the chaotic conditions created within the country in the wake of the Soviet Union's collapse. From 1989 onward, the capacity of the Soviet government to exercise control over the areas and the resources within its nominal purview eroded. This was as true of control over the armed forces and its armaments stockpiles as of other aspects of Soviet life. The depths to which the process reached is indicated in an interview given in 1993 by the Russian defence minister, Pavel Grachev, who claimed that in January 1991 military units were given permission to sell surplus military equipment in their possession and to maintain themselves on the proceeds.[22] Clearly, no very close control could be maintained over what was sold, to whom, and where it eventually ended up. Other reports speak of entire SAM missile complexes abandoned without guard, the missiles or their components available for the taking.[23]

The internal and external borders of the CIS are extremely porous. Customs controls do not function over large stretches of the CIS periphery.[24] To illustrate the consequences, an entire Russian army, the 14th, maintains itself and conducts what amounts to a private foreign policy in the trans-Dneistrian region of Moldova, drawing supplies in some fashion from Russia across the entire breadth of the Ukraine. Similarly, the numerous ethnic and political conflicts in Central Asia and the Caucasus draw supplies quite freely from the enormous stockpiles of weaponry distributed throughout Russia.[25]

'Rogue', unofficial weapons transfers, while dangerous, represent mostly one-off deliveries of low-tech weapons and/or ammunition. The situation is different with complex, high-technology weapon systems which significantly enhance a nation's war-making capacity, such as radar systems, air-defence complexes, and combat aircraft. Such systems require continuing maintenance and replacement, which in turn require a stable contractual relationship with a particular supplier. They cannot simply be smuggled abroad, and attempts to purchase them must go through official channels. Russian regulatory efforts to date have largely been concerned with such transactions.

Russian domestic arms control policy originated in a decree by President Yeltsin dated 22 February 1992, which prohibited the export of certain categories of goods, including arms and 'strategic materials', without a license.[26] The existing Russian regulatory regime originated in a presidential decree dated 12 May 1992.[27] An inter-ministerial committee for Military-Technical Co-operation (Russian jargon for the arms trade) is in charge of determining policy regarding proposed arms transfers, and it reviews every official proposal to export armaments. The Foreign Ministry participates in this committee, and presumably tries to impose limitations on arms exports in accordance with Russia's international commitments. The technical aspects of licensing an arms transfer are handled through the Ministry of Foreign Economic Relations' Main Administration for Military-Technical Co-operation.

The Ministry originally worked only with its officially licensed, government-owned trading companies. Pressure from the military establishment forced the ministry to agree to issue licences to additional companies, and about six or eight additional firms are reported to be working in the official arms export trade; most are affiliated with the Ministry of Defence or various service arms. In the aftermath of the December elections these firms gained the right to solicit potential customers and sign export agreements independently of the Ministry of Foreign Economic affairs or the Foreign Ministry.[28] It is unclear what degree of control over arms exports government ministries retain.

The ambiguity of Russia's regulatory environment for the arms trade is the result of an ongoing conflict between civil and military authorities for control over this trade and its proceeds.[29] Even though known Russian arms sales have declined sharply compared to the Soviet period, the $2–4 billion annually in foreign currency receipts in 1992 that they represent is enormously important to the Russian economy.

The military establishment's position is that the proceeds from sales of 'its' arms are to be used to build housing and provide relief for discharged officers, and it believes it has a commitment by the government to that effect. Its representatives frequently object that the government, and particularly the Foreign Ministry, block valuable arms sales in the name of adherence to Russia's international obligations such as UN-imposed sanctions and other arms transfer limitations.[30] Naturally, the government would like to use precious foreign exchange earned by the sale of government property abroad for its own, national economic purposes.

In June 1992 it became known that the Ministry of Defence, which is controlled by serving officers, had established a special welfare administration to take care of the needs of serving and discharged soldiers.[31] The director of this administration claimed his organization was authorized to sell arms abroad and dispose of the proceeds. South Africa and Taiwan were mentioned as nations ostensibly negotiating arms purchases from this organization. At the time this claim was made South Africa was under a UN arms embargo and the People's Republic of China was the single biggest purchaser of arms from Russia.

A sense of the perspective in which the Ministry of Defence official viewed arms sales can be gathered from the following statement:

> Profits [from sales] must be divided so that the present actual possessors [of arms to be sold] will be interested in selling. Otherwise we will get nothing. 50 per cent and sometimes more must be set aside for the various service arms and regions from which arms are taken …the rest may be used centrally, for the entire army.[32]

This quotation gives one a window on an arms sales environment entirely different from that portrayed by the official government regulations. Arms 'belong' to the units possessing them, not the Russian government. The service arm of the unit 'making the sale' and local civilian authorities get their cut. The rest goes to the Ministry of Defence. An official department of the Ministry of Defence exists to make the sales, negotiate the pay-offs, and turn the proceeds over to the Ministry of Defence without reference to the state budget or the Finance Ministry or Russian foreign policy constraints.

Russian Arms Transfers to the Middle East

Selling Russian Arms in the Middle East

The Middle East is viewed by Russian authorities as a market of opportunity.[33] During 1993 the Russians invested considerable efforts in selling in the region. Their most prominent effort came in the form of extensive participation in the 'Idex '93' arms fair at Abu Dhabi. The Soviet delegation was headed by Viktor Glukhikh, head of the defence ministry's military industry directory; over 370 weapon systems were exhibited.[34] Simultaneously Russian defence minister Grachev paid a visit to Kuwait.[35] In May 1994 Turkey was reported to be examining Russian SS-21 surface-to-surface missiles with a view to purchasing them.[36] These missiles are far more sophisticated than the Iraqi and Syrian Scuds they are intended to counter, and transferring them to Turkey may constitute a violation of the international Missile Technology Control Regime (MTCR).

The Soviet Union used to transfer huge volumes of arms to Soviet clients in the Middle East. Unfortunately for the Russian arms industry, circumstances have made it impossible for this activity to continue at anything like its former volume. The Soviet Union's most important arms clients in the Middle East used to be Iraq, Libya and Syria; Iran and Egypt were potential clients to a lesser extent, Iran because the Soviets hedged their bets in the first Gulf War and Egypt because the Egyptian armed forces retain some Soviet-manufactured systems. Of the leading three clients, Iraq and Libya are under UN sanction. Syria is not; but Syria, like many Soviet clients, received many of its arms at nominal prices and under very favourable credit terms. Both Iraq and Syria owed billions to the Soviet Union for arms deliveries; these debts essentially are uncollectable now. Much of the Russian arms trade in the region must consist of small change: spare parts and ammunition for Soviet-made systems already in the recipients' possession. This is also consistent with the reported dollar value of Russian arms sales worldwide in recent years, sales to the Middle East being a significant component thereof.

TABLE 1

SOVIET/RUSSIAN ARMS TRANSFERS, 1988–92
BILLIONS OF DOLLARS

1988	1989	1990	1991	1992
14.658	14.310	9.724	4.448	2.043

Source: SIPRI Yearbook, 1993, Table 10.10, p.444.

Information on Russian arms sales is sketchy and incomplete. One thing is clear: a drastic decline has taken place, though the incomplete nature of available figures may overstate the case. Table 1 presents SIPRI's estimates of Soviet/Russian arms sales. Russian sources put arms sales for 1993 at $2.15 billion in 1993[37] and a prospective $2.2 billion for 1994.[38] Table 2 presents information, from a Russian source, of the distribution of Soviet arms deliveries in 1991. Deliveries to the Middle East, presumably excluding Iraq, are more numerous than deliveries to all the rest of the world put together. If this pattern has continued in subsequent years, that would make the Middle East presumptively Russia's largest arms market. Of course the table gives no sense of the dollar value of these deliveries.

Prior to the elections of 1993 Russia seemed to be concentrating on arms sales as tool of economic policy rather than as an instrument of political influence. An important exception may have been the transfer of three submarines to Iran in 1993. Since the 1993 elections the Russian government has once more made an attempt to use arms sales as a tool of influence rather than merely a source of income. The chief beneficiary of this policy is Syria. In April 1994 it was reported that Syria and Russia had signed an arms agreement worth $1.6 billion. The deal included 14 SU-27 fighters, 30 SU-24 attack aircraft, 54 MiG-29 fighters, 450 T-72 and T-80 tanks, and infantry weapons.[39] It is clear that this is a concessionary deal; nearly 100 modern combat aircraft and 450 tanks for $1.6 billion represents tremendous value for money. The aircraft alone should have fetched far more on the open market – provided Russia could find a buyer. Of course, if the aircraft represent equipment that the cash-starved Russian military establishment can no longer operate or maintain, it makes sense for Russia to sell them at almost any price rather than let them rust away in hangars at home. Another report in May 1994 mentioned a Syrian-Russian deal for $500 million;[40] it is not clear whether this report refers to a component of the April deal or an additional sale.

TABLE 2

SOVIET ARMS DELIVERIES, BY REGION, 1991

Near East	Middle East	Europe	Africa	Latin America	Asia
8	61	12	1	1	17

Source: Nezavisimaia Gazeta, 29 Sept. 1992.

An interesting aspect of the deal is the treatment accorded Syria's existing $10 billion debt to the former Soviet Union for previous arms sales. Russia agreed to forgive $9 billion of this debt if the Syrians paid Russia the remaining $1 billion. This sum, which presumably Russia would never otherwise have realized, must be added – tentatively, for the Syrians have yet to pay – to Russian receipts from the deal.[41]

Russian Attitudes toward Arms Sales and Arms Limitations

The official stance of the Russian government is to favour arms limitations at every level and to co-operate with existing international arms control regimes. The Soviet government participated in the London Meeting of the five permanent members of the Security Council in October 1991 and subscribed to the 'Guidelines for Conventional Arms Transfers' issued on 18 October.[42] The Russian government considers itself to have inherited the standing and obligations of the former Soviet government, and the Russian Ministry of Foreign Affairs has referred to the Guidelines as obligating Russia.[43] At the US–USSR summit of 31 May–3 June 1990, President Gorbachev delivered to President Bush the Soviet Union's commitment to abide by the terms of the MTCR.[44] While Russia is not formally a member of MTCR, it officially has adopted the MTCR guidelines. The Russian government formally has committed itself to observing UN-mandated arms embargoes; these apply to Libya and Iraq, two of the former Soviet Union's primary customers for arms in the Middle East.

As the domestic context of Russian arms sales has made clear, however, this official policy stance is under siege, and the government of Russia is probably neither able nor interested in adhering to it strictly.

Publicly expressed Russian views of the arms trade are, not to put it too strongly, practical. The chairman of one of the official trading companies assured an interviewer that Russian arms sales to the Middle East did not upset the balance of power in the region or make aggression more likely. On the other hand, 'We cannot assume that if we refuse to sell combat hardware to someone, they will not buy it from our competitors – nature abhors a vacuum.'[45] In defence of Russia's policy of frankly supporting arms sales, the Russian press often cites the United States' rise to the position of the world's largest arms exporter.[46] The force of the argument is hard to deny.

Was there ever an opportunity in the past for Russia to be incorporated into an international arms transfer control regime? Quite possibly. In February 1993 Russian foreign minister Kozyrev suggested that Western nations allocate to Russia a share in the Middle East arms trade as an alternative to direct economic aid.[47] This indicates that Russia might have adhered to such a regime, as well as the sense in which Russia would view its participation in the regime. Kozyrev's concern was to ensure Russia an equitable slice of the arms-trade pie, a natural reaction to the precipitate decline in the volume of Russia's arms trade.

Kozyrev's tentative offer was not taken up by anyone in the West. Since it was made the motives behind Russian policy in the region have evolved further. It is likely now that Russia would attempt to include among the ground rules of such a regime explicit recognition of its 'right' to certain markets, and at least partial rehabilitation of those of the former Soviet Union's clients which are under international sanction today, such as Libya and Iraq. The demand would have an economic dimension, of course – Russia wants these countries to become paying customers – but it would have a political dimension, and for the United States a political cost, as well.

Conclusion: Some Reflections on Regime Formation

While regime theory is a tool of inestimable value in analysing certain phenomena in international relations, one must take care lest too formal an approach to real problems concerning real issue areas render theory sterile. It is valid to raise the question whether the power of an alleged hegemon will be adequate to permit it to isolate an issue area and impose a regime to solve a problem. The answer to the question cannot be pursued at such a level of abstraction. One must take into account the historical experience and perceptions of the various players, and not just the hegemon; note how shifts in domestic politics translate into changes in agendas and perceptions; and take due note of the possibility that, in some countries and to some elites, it is not obvious that the hegemon wears a label identifying it as such and granting it the right to define the terms of international intercourse. Our discussion of Russian policy has been informed by this perspective.

Russian domestic politics have been evolving since the Soviet Union was dissolved in December 1991, and this evolution has accelerated since the Russian elections of December 1993. The influence of conservative and nationalist forces has grown steadily, and they have gradually increased their influence over Russian foreign policy. As time goes on, Russia is less and less willing to concede to the United States the presumptive status of hegemon, more and more concerned to secure recognition for the international interests that were the Soviet Union's. As a direct result, the cost to the United States of establishing international regimes in issue areas such as arms transfer limitations has grown. This is a secular trend arising out of the evolution of Soviet domestic politics and is independent of any 'objective' calculus of the relative power of Russia and the United States.

The future of Soviet–Western co-operation depends very heavily upon Russian policy toward the other republics of the former Soviet Union, toward Central Europe, toward the CFE accord and the response to these policies in the West. For both Russia and the West these issues are liable to loom far larger in their calendar of international concerns than arms control in the Middle East. To the degree that Russia has the potential to be a significant supplier of arms to the Middle East, a stable arms control regime in the region depends on events that will take place far away and without much reference to the regional issues at stake. The probability that Russian–Western relations will indeed break down has risen significantly in the aftermath of the Russian elections.

At present, Russia's potential to serve as one of the leading suppliers of arms to the region are limited. Even though Russia hopes to become a major exporter of sophisticated weapon systems, the kind that produce quantum leaps in a nation's strategic defence capability, its ability today to produce such systems at the technological level required and to maintain them reliably is questionable. Most nations of the region interested in such systems have made their choices and committed their funds already, chiefly choosing rival Western systems. As the Russian economy improves during the 1990s, this situation may change.

Nonetheless, Russian co-operation is required today if any non-proliferation regime is to be established and survive. Its armaments are quite adequate in terms of cost, quality, and availability to upset, if Russia so desires it, any attempt to establish a regional arms balance. Russia, too, has traditional client states in the region whose ability to procure sophisticated arms from other sources is practically non-existent. As Russian arms sales to Syria show, Russia is willing to be much more aggressive today in attempting to re-establish its international presence in the region by means of arms sales.

The Russians feel that they have been hurt badly by their adherence to UN-imposed arms embargoes on some of the former Soviet Union's best arms clients. They will take even harder any Western attempts to limit future arms sales to the region – especially if they perceive that Western interest in regional arms control has arisen after the Gulf states have placed their orders and the quarterly dividends of major Western arms manufacturers have been guaranteed for a number of years to come. Securing Russian adherence to any international regime of arms transfer limitations will become more costly to the West in both political and economic terms even as it becomes more necessary.

Should relations between Russia and the West break down over events in the Ukraine or Georgia or the Baltic states, the effects on arms control in the Middle East region will be profound. Voices calling for unlimited arms sales to the region, including to Iraq and Libya, will grow much stronger. No arms control regime can succeed if the Russians are actively engaged in trying to thwart it. A policy of unbridled Russian arms sales to the region will remove any interest other powers have in pursuing restraint. Other nations may still make most of the sales, but Russian non-cooperation will be the trigger that frustrates the hope of regional arms control.

NOTES

1. Robert J. Leiber, 'American Hegemony, Regional Security and Proliferation in the Post-Cold War International System', see pp.1–13 of this volume.
2. The discussion here and in the conclusion to this article is informed by Manfred Zorn's thought-provoking paper on domestic politics as a variable in determining prospects for regime formation. See Zorn, 'Bringing the Second Image (Back) In: About the Domestic Sources of Regime Formation,' in Volker Rittberger (ed.), *Regime Theory and International Relations* (Oxford: Clarendon Press, 1993), pp.282–311.
3. Shai Feldman, 'Arresting Weapons Proliferation,' in *The Middle East Military Balance 1992–1993* (Tel Aviv: Jaffee Center for Strategic Studies, 1993), p.93.
4. Yitzhak Klein, 'Soviet Policy During the Gulf Crisis,' in Gad Barzilai, Aharon Kleiman, and Gil Shidlo (eds.), *The Gulf Crisis and its Global Aftermath* (London: Routledge, 1992), pp.192–3.
5. See, for example, Pavel Grachev's statement that conditions are ripening for the reunification of the former republics of the Soviet Union, cited in Pavel Felgengauer, 'Stariie granitzi i "noviie" bazi; strategicheskoe otstupleniie armii okanchivaetzsia' (Old Borders and 'new' Bases; the Army's Strategic Retreat Ends), *Segodnia,* 16 Sept. 1993, p.3; or the statement by Yevgenii Primakov, director of the Foreign Intelligence Service (heir to the foreign operations of the KGB) that if the Central European states accede to NATO, 'the need would arise for a fundamental reappraisal of all defence concepts on our side,' *International Herald Tribune,* 29 Nov. 1993.
6. On 6 August 1993 Russia, Kazakhstan and Uzbekistan signed an agreement reintegrating the economies of the two Central Asian republics into the ruble zone. The terms of the agreement were such as effectively to subordinate their economies to Russia's. On 3 September, as the Ukrainian economy collapsed under the burden of hyperinflation, President Kravchuk met with President Yeltsin of Russia and promised to hand over to Russia Ukraine's half of the former Soviet Black Sea Fleet in return for the cancellation of the Ukraine's $2.5 billion debt to Russia. The blow to Ukrainian prestige was significant, even though the Ukrainians later welched on the deal.
7. *Pravda,* 24 Feb. 1993.
8. Klein, 'Soviet Policy,' p.200.
9. Kozyrev address to Russian ambassadors, 19 Jan. 1994, reported by ITAR-TASS.
10. Reported by Interfax news agency, 14 Feb. 1994.
11. Arbatov, in *Nezavisimaia Gazeta,* 14 April 1994.
12. Peter Almquist, an authority on the former Soviet military-industrial complex, puts the figure at 75 per cent. See Almquist, 'Arms Producers Struggle to Survive as Orders Shrink,' Radio Free Europe/Radio Liberty Research Report, Vol. 2, No.25 (1993), pp. 33–4. Other estimates run to 65–70 per cent; see Ian Anthony, Paul Claesson, Elizabeth Sköns and Siemon T. Wezeman, 'Arms Production and Arms Trade', in Stockholm International Peace Research Institute, *SIPRI Yearbook: World Armaments and Disarmament,* 1991, p.449.
13. Vladimir Khrustov, in *Rossiskiie Vesti,* 25 Feb. 93, p.7.
14. A. A. Kokoshin, interview, *Izvestiia,* 18 Jan. 93.
15. *Christian Science Monitor,* 15 Oct. 1993.
16. Reuters, 16 March 1994.
17. A. A. Kokoshin, 'Contradictions of Formation and Pathways of Development of Russian Military-Technical Policy,' *Voennaia Mysl'* (Military Thought), Feb. 1993. Trans. JPRS-UMT- 93–005-L, 18 May 1993, pp. 1–7.
18. A. A. Kokoshin, interview, *Rossiskiie Vesti,* 18 Jan. 93.
19. Malei, interview, *Izvestiia,* 28 Jan. 93. Actually, the language is that of Malei's interviewer,

which Malei immediately confirmed.
20. *Nezavisimaia Gazeta,* 2 Feb. 1993.
21. *Izvestiia,* 5 Feb. 1993
22. Interview on 'Rossia' television network, 22 Feb. 1993. Reported in BBC *Summary of World Broadcasts* (henceforth SWB), SU/1622, p. C1/1, 25 Feb. 1993.
23. Moscow TV, Channel 1, Broadcast. Reported in FBIS-SOV–93–129, 8 July 1993, p.28.
24. Pavel Felgengauer, 'The Arms Trade–How Much to Sell, to Whom, and for How Much,' *Nezavisimaia Gazeta,* 7 Nov. 1992.
25. Ibid.
26. Ian Anthony *et al.,* 'Arms Production and Arms Trade,' p.466.
27. Felgengauer, interview with Deputy Foreign Minister Vladimir Shibaev, in 'The Arms Trade How Much to Sell, to Whom, and For How Much', *Nezavisimaia Gazeta,* 11 July 1992.
28. Interfax, 19 May 1994.
29. Stephen Foye, 'Russian Arms Exports After the Cold War,' Radio Free Europe/Radio Liberty *Research Report,* Vol. 2, No.13, 26 March 1993.
30. Interview with Gennadi Yanpol'ski, general director of military production in the Russian Ministry of Production, *Krasnaia Zvezda,* 29 Aug. 1992.
31. Pavel Felgengauer, 'Apartments for Arms.' Interiew with Aleksandr Temerko, chairman of the Committee for the Social Protection of the Serviceman in the Russian Defense Ministry. *Nezavisimaia Gazeta,* 23 June. 1992.
32. Ibid.
33. Interview with Viktor Gluhkikh, head of State Committee for Defense Industry, TASS, 15 Jan. 1993. Reported in BBC SWB SU/1593 p. C2/3, 22 Jan. 1993.
34. Vladimir Khrustov, in *Rossiskiie Vesti,* 25 Feb. 1993, p.7.
35. *Nezavisimaia Gazeta,* 19 Feb. 1993.
36. UPI, 15 May 1994.
37. Khrustov, *Rossiskiie Vesti.*
38. *Nezavisimaia Gazeta,* 5 April 1994, p.7
39. Interfax, 19 May 1994
40. *Arms Transfer News.* Bradford, UK: Dfax Associates/Farndon House Information Trust, 15 April 1994, p.6.
41. Ibid., 20 May 1994, p.7.
42. Stockholm International Peace Research Institute, *SIPRI Yearbook: World Armaments and Disarmaments* (1992), pp. 304–5.
43. Felgengauer, 'The Arms Trade.'
44. Stockholm International Peace Research Institute, *SIPRI Yearbook: World Armaments and Disarmament* (1991), p.334.
45. Interview with Maj. Gen. Sergei Karaoglanov, Chairman, 'Oboroneksport', *Izvestiia,* 9 Feb. 1993. Trans. FBIS-SOV-93–027, 11 Feb. 1993, pp. 6–9.
46. See, for example, ibid.; Glukhikh interview, TASS, 15 Jan. 1993.
47. *Financial Times,* 16 Feb. 1993.

The International Agenda

.

The Nuclear Issue in the Middle East in a New World Order

AVNER COHEN

The post-Cold War world makes the problem of nuclear proliferation more difficult and challenging. The very possession (or the lack of it) of nuclear weapons was central in defining the Cold War world order; the making and the relative success of the Non-Proliferation Treaty (NPT) was, to a large extent, an outcome of Cold War nuclear bipolarity. The non-proliferation regime – that is, the entire edifice of treaties, norms, safeguard mechanisms and international organizations that embody the ideal of nuclear non-proliferation – grew out of that order. But now the very international order is in transition. One global order has been replaced by another, and though the old one is gone the rules of the new one are not yet in place. The United States is still the world's only superpower, it is still the most devoted custodian of the non-proliferation regime, but its commitment is tested in an increasingly fragmented world as its own orientation becomes more inward-driven. Can the non-proliferation regime survive the post-Cold War circumstances?[1]

While it is apparent that the end of the Cold War has given rise to new challenges to the non-proliferation regime, it is less clear in the United States and elsewhere how to face those challenges. There are many difficult and new questions: are the traditional tools of the non-proliferation regime, such as technology denial, the safeguard system and other means of security assurances and arms control, adequate, or is there a need to supplement them with a new and bolder policy of 'counter-proliferation' to deal with new proliferation threats, such as North Korea and Iran?[2] How to deal with the new former Soviet nuclear weapons states? What about the three old *de facto* nuclear weapons states – India, Pakistan and Israel? How, if at all, could the non-proliferation regime effectively distinguish between the 'old' proliferators and the 'new' ones? How could the global non-proliferation regime become compatible with new regional nuclear arrangements? Answers to these questions will no doubt shape the landscape of international security in the next decade.

The Middle East is an especially interesting and important region in which these questions can be explored. Given the fundamental political changes that are now shaping the region, one wonders what the impact of those changes will be on the nuclear issue: could the old Arab–Israeli impasse that prevailed in the nuclear situation in the Middle East be resolved along with the peace process? Are there circumstances under which Israel, the only *de facto* nuclear state in the region, could be brought into the non-proliferation regime? What about the Iranian-Iraqi part of the nuclear equation? Could new global approaches be reconciled with the complexity of the nuclear situation in the Middle East? Is there a way to marry arms control with the counter-proliferation approach? Could such a marriage be useful to the cause of non-proliferation in the Middle East?

The future of nuclear proliferation in the Middle East depends primarily on two broader and opposing regional developments: progress toward the establishment of a new regional order built upon the political settlement of the Arab–Israeli conflict, and on political, social and technological developments in states (e.g. Iran) which are outside the peace process, even acting to undermine it. Other global developments, such as the outcome of the North Korean nuclear challenge, and decisions about the future of the NPT in 1995, will also have an important impact. The present situation, therefore, is a mixture of good and bad possibilities.

On the good side, the difference between the situation in July 1990 and today is striking. If in July 1990 the region was about to be engulfed in the most dangerous nuclearization spiral it had ever faced, now most of the region is captured by anticipation of the end of the Arab–Israeli conflict. While in summer 1990 Iraq was escalating the Arab–Israeli conflict (and other Arab–Arab rivalries) to the nuclear level, posing a potential existential threat to Israel of the kind that that nation had never before encountered, four years later the Arab–Israeli conflict seems to be approaching a point of peaceful resolution. In the wake of global and regional sea-changes – the end of the Cold War, the collapse of the Soviet Union, and most significantly, the defeat of Arab radicalism in the Gulf – the region has embarked on the road to peace. After a century-long quarrel, the Palestinian–Israeli dispute, at the heart of the Arab–Israeli conflict, seems to be moving into a phase of historical reconciliation. If the peace trend prevails, the Middle East may follow the denuclearization path that we have witnessed in other parts of the world, from South Africa and Latin America to the United States and Russia. Peace and non-proliferation inevitably go hand in hand.

But there is ominous news, too. The region's most determined and advanced proliferators, Iran and Iraq, are not parties to the current peace fever, each for its own reasons. Between the two, Iraq is now the lesser problem. For one thing, Iraq is no longer a regional power, politically or militarily, and as long as Saddam Hussein remains in power it is not likely to break its geopolitical isolation within the Arab world. Iraq has a marginal impact on the Arab–Israeli peace process, let alone a capacity to disrupt it. For another, Iraq's nuclear aspirations are indefinitely under the toughest internationally managed control any modern state has ever faced. Though the monitoring UN Special Commission on Iraq (UNSCOM) is not an absolute guarantee that Iraq could not renew its nuclear programme, it is still the best one could hope for in an imperfect world. As long as the international community is determined to keep Security Council Resolution 687 to the letter, it would be difficult for Iraq to rearm itself with weapons of mass destruction. However, a reduction in the future effectiveness of UNSCOM could bring Iraq back into the nuclear weapons business. According to a recent International Atomic Energy Agency (IAEA) report, notwithstanding UNSCOM's long-term monitoring plans, on the basis of its acquired technical knowledge Iraq might be able to conduct an experimental weapons programme, including calculations, simulations and design work, with a low probability of its being discovered.[3] Long-term monitoring in Iraq is essential to keep its nuclear ambitions in check.

The Islamic Republic of Iran is a different story altogether. Iran is not under a tight monitoring regime; on the contrary, despite economic distress and political divisions among its leadership, post-Khomeini Iran is still an Islamic Republic committed – for reasons of ideology, geopolitics or both – to regional hegemony. Learning the lessons of the two Gulf wars, the Iranian military has undergone a major military build-up and modernization. Though this build-up is not unrelated to Iran's internal divisions, one cannot ignore its potential to destabilize the Gulf and the entire Middle East. Especially worrisome are the reports of an Iranian purchase of North Korea's most advanced ballistic missile, the No-Dong (with an estimated range of 1,000 km), as well as Iran's interest in developing naval-denial capabilities.[4]

Though less politically dominant now, the Revolutionary Guard and its religious leaders use the rhetoric of Islamic defiance of the West – and Israel – in promoting an active interventionist foreign policy, in Bosnia, Lebanon and even in Gaza. Of all Islamic states, Iran is the most hostile to the peace process in the Middle East; Iran continues to train and finance the Hizbollah in Lebanon, a terrorist organization that has vowed to make Lebanon an Islamic Republic and to confront Israel.

This explains why Iran's renewed nuclear ambitions, especially the purchase of the two big research reactors from China and other military equipment and reactor components in Europe, appears to Western intelligence organizations suspicious and worrisome despite Iranian claims that its nuclear programme is purely peaceful. These concerns are reinforced by rumours about Iranian efforts to purchase nuclear weapons or fissile material from sources within the former Soviet Union. The fact is that Iran has strong and obvious motivations to acquire nuclear weapons.[5] Nuclear weapons can be the key for Iran to achieve its vision of regional dominance and the ultimate symbol of Islamic defiance; it would also deter the Gulf states, and the United States and Israel, from responding to an assertive Iranian policy in the Gulf and in the Middle East. Iran's own lesson of its humiliating defeat at the end of the Iran–Iraq War, as well as Saddam's fateful miscalculations before and during the 1991 Gulf War, probably reinforce these views.

Of course, there is no UNSCOM-type organization to monitor Iran. Iraq is a signatory of the NPT, and thus far the IAEA has found no incriminating evidence that Iran has violated its Treaty obligations. This was also the judgment of the IAEA in Iraq prior to the establishment of UNSCOM. The fact is that the NPT/IAEA safeguard system could not prevent countries from acquiring and developing most of the infrastructure needed for a weapons programme; on the contrary, as long as the activity is declared the IAEA allows, even helps, states to acquire nuclear technologies.

The lessons learned from dealing with both the Iraqi and the North Korean nuclear programmes highlight these concerns regarding Iran. The prime Iraqi lesson is that a clandestine nuclear programme of the magnitude that was revealed can happen again. Iraq taught us how difficult it is to deny a determined proliferator state, especially a state which is a signatory of the NPT. States with a limited industrial and technological base can obtain sufficient access to bomb-making technology and know-how to initiate a large-scale nuclear weapons programme and can largely conceal such a programme from both national technical means of intelligence-gathering and the IAEA safeguards regime. While after the Gulf War the IAEA insists on its right to conduct a 'special inspection', its effectiveness in the real world has not yet been demonstrated. In fact, the IAEA clearly failed to enforce the precedent of 'special inspections' in the North Korean case.[6]

The intelligence failure in the case of the Iraqi nuclear programme shows not only that mistakes can be made in the allocation and evaluation of intelligence collection efforts, but also how profoundly imperfect the whole enterprise of nuclear intelligence is. The recent revelations that the United States may have underestimated the former Soviet nuclear arsenal by about a third only highlights that realization. The vast uncertainty regarding the North Korean bomb effort – on the issue of whether and how much plutonium was processed thus far as well as on that of how advanced the North Koreans are in their design work – is another stern reminder of the intrinsic limitations of nuclear intelligence. Given what is at stake, this uncertainty forces us to think of the possible threat in terms of a worst-case scenario.[7]

The success or failure of the non-proliferation regime in both the Iraqi and the North Korean cases is bound to have an impact on the Iranian nuclear effort. Iranian nuclear ambitions are, to a large extent, a reactionary replica of the Iraqi nuclear programme. If Iran is to be persuaded not to go nuclear, it must be convinced that an Iraqi nuclear programme will not re-emerge sometime in the future. While it is likely that the international community will carry out tight monitoring of Iraqi activities as long as Saddam is in power, it is doubtful whether such a tight inspection regime would continue once a new leadership takes power in Baghdad. For the long run, the only solution to the Iraqi–Iranian nuclear race would be a bilateral Iranian–Iraqi agreement (possibly modelled on the Argentinean–Brazilian bilateral agreement) for the establishment of a Nuclear-Weapon-Free Zone (NWFZ) in the Persian Gulf, possibly in the entire Middle East. Whatever the outcome of the current North Korean challenge of the NPT – and it is probably the most severe test of international security in the post-Cold War era – it will have an enormous impact on the Iranian case. If North Korea wins, Iran is most likely to be the next challenger; if the credibility of the NPT is preserved in this case, it is unlikely that Iran would dare to test it again.

The Iranian nuclear issue highlights both the uncertainty of the situation and the interconnection between these two opposite trends in the Middle East. The fate of Iranian aspirations for hegemonic dominance in the Middle East depends, to a large extent, on whether a new regional order of peace succeeds or fails. If Arab–Israeli reconciliation succeeds, the Iranian ideological cause weakens, and vice versa. In return, if Iran is getting closer to the bomb, this could radicalize the Middle East and harm the cause of Arab–Israeli peace. In short, Iran's nuclear ambitions are intimately connected with the fate of the peace process.

Iran's ambitions have led for the first time to a shared and visible concern on the part of most Arab states and Israel about the dangers of nuclear proliferation and the need to deal with it on a regional and international basis. Under the surface of Arab rhetoric, there is little doubt that moderate Arab states, in particular in the Persian Gulf, are more concerned about Iranian/Iraqi nuclear ambitions while becoming quite complacent about Israel's quarter-of-a-century-old 'nuclear option'. Some Arabs, especially Palestinians, even perceive the Israeli undeclared nuclear deterrence as playing a *positive* and *stabilizing* role in promoting the cause of Arab–Israeli peace, giving Israel the courage to make painful territorial concessions from a position of strength while knowing that it faced no existential threat; Iranian/Iraqi nuclear weapons are the region's nightmare.[8] In general, below the common Arab public rhetoric demanding that Israel sign the NPT and place its nuclear facilities under IAEA safeguards, lies a good deal of flexibility and political realism.

In Israel, too, behind the official secrecy the Gulf War has forced a quiet reappraisal of the nuclear issue in the context of regional war and peace. It is now increasingly recognized among Israeli strategists that both twin pillars of Israeli nuclear policy for the last three decades – ambiguity about Israel's own programme and a commitment to prevent Arab nuclearization – ought to be revisited. First, at this point the entire Arab world is convinced that Israel is a nuclear power, regardless of whether Israel acknowledges it or not; this is a political fact. Second, and more significantly, Israel no longer has confidence in its ability to detect and destroy a nascent hostile nuclear threat unilaterally, as it did in 1981 in Iraq. While Israel sees itself as the first nation to apply the use of non-diplomatic means to counter hostile proliferation – the Israeli precursor of the 'counter-proliferation' doctrine – co-operation in this regard with other states, particularly the United States, has now become a necessity for Israel.[9]

The concern about Arab and Iranian nuclearization is central to the geopolitical thinking of Israel's Prime Minister, Yitzhak Rabin. He sees the intimate linkage between peace and nuclearization in a vivid way. He believes that the Gulf War has given Israel a window of opportunity of perhaps five to ten years to minimize the threat of hostile nuclearization. During this period Israel should contribute to a vigorous nuclear denial strategy via enhanced political and intelligence co-ordination with friendly states, and more fundamentally, it should make peace agreements with all its direct neighbours to reduce incentives and support for nuclearization in the Arab world and Iran. For Rabin and Peres, the concern over nuclear proliferation is one of the strongest motivations for his peace strategy.[10]

To sum it all up, after the Gulf War the concern over the danger of nuclear proliferation became one of the shared incentives for peace for many, both in the Arab world and Israel. In particular, both sides have recognized that a vision of future regional security and arms control in the Middle East must involve dealing with the nuclear question. This recognition is at the core of the multilateral Working Group on Arms Control and Regional Security (ACRS) that was founded in the wake of the Madrid Peace Conference in October 1991. But it is one thing to recognize an issue, and another to come up with mutually acceptable ideas and modalities for dealing with it. The nuclear issue, as all parties fully recognize, is the most difficult and complicated among all the issues of regional arms control, conceptually and practically, politically and technically.

Negotiating regional arms control, and especially discussing nuclear matters, is new to the states of the Middle East. In the not-too-distant past there was no regional forum to negotiate such issues; the context of the

Arab–Israeli conflict did not permit the existence of such a forum. The idea that Israelis and Arabs should sit together and talk to each other on issues of regional security and arms control was for years unthinkable; it meant *de facto* recognition of the legitimacy of Israel, which was anathema for the Arabs.

This does not mean, of course, that states of the region have not called for proposed general and nuclear disarmament before. Certainly they did; endless speeches on disarmament were made by Arab and Israeli diplomats at the UN and other international forums. Arabs usually stressed the nuclear issue, pointing their fingers at Israel, while Israel in return called for peace to be followed by general disarmament. Those calls were made primarily within the context of scoring points and counter-points in the Arab–Israeli propaganda battle. But talking *at* each other is quite different from talking *to* each other on regional security and arms control in a shared forum. One well-advertised disarmament idea that was circulated over the years was the notion of establishing the Middle East as a NWFZ. Both Arabs and Israelis publicly professed to endorse this idea for years; Egypt and Iran initiated such a proposal at the UN in 1974, and Israel has proposed its own version since 1975. In the past, however, this apparent consensus went nowhere and meant little. The formal preconditions that each side stipulated in its proposal for NWFZ were patently unacceptable to the other. The Arab states stipulated all parties' adherence to the NPT as a condition for the establishment of a NWFZ; Israel, which refused to sign the NPT, insisted that the question of NWFZ in the Middle East must be addressed only through direct negotiations among all the regional parties, and in direct relation to the whole question of regional security and arms control in the Middle East. Behind the appearance of consensus there was an impasse built upon conflicting interests.

In the past, the impasse over NWFZ was politically immaterial. While both sides could claim the moral high ground for their proposals for NWFZ, they knew that the whole exercise was futile, no more than diplomatic posturing. As long as the Arabs were not ready to recognize Israel and to deal with it directly in a context of regional security, Israel had no difficulty in proposing NWFZ, recognizing only too well that nothing practical would be achieved by such a proposal, and that it would not suffer any restrictions on its freedom of action in this field. Certainly such a position was compatible with Israel's policy of nuclear opacity. For the Arabs, their proposal, linking NWFZ with signing the NPT, aimed to embarrass Israel and highlight Israel's refusal to sign. In a sense, the impasse over the NWFZ proposals was convenient for the rhetoric of both sides.

While some of the formal reasons for the impasse have recently been removed – the establishment of the ACRS meant satisfying the Israeli regional approach – it is far from being overcome. For one thing, not all the region's states are parties to the ACRS; in fact, some of the most relevant states in this regard are missing. Neither Iran nor Iraq is a party to the ACRS; Syria, while negotiating peace and security with Israel at the bilateral level, decided not to attend the multilateral forum until it saw significant progress on the bilateral channel. This absence alone makes it highly unlikely that any substantive agreements can be negotiated at the ACRS in the foreseeable future. For another thing, and even more importantly, on the nuclear issue Arabs and Israelis have opposite approaches, priorities and agendas. This fundamental difference has become evident in all the ACRS rounds held thus far. The apparent consensus on the visionary objectives of the process – the establishment of a zone free of all weapons of mass destruction – disguises the reality that these objectives are not likely to be translated into action.

Why is the nuclear issue so intractable? The difficulties are intrinsic to the special character of the nuclear situation in the Middle East. First, there is a vast asymmetry in nuclear capabilities between Israel and all its Arab neighbours; Israel has established a situation of nuclear monopoly. Naturally, it is this monopoly that Israelis, believing it has helped them to achieve peace, want to keep – at least until peace is expanded and firmly established; Arabs, on the other hand, want to dismantle this Israeli advantage as soon as possible. Such asymmetry did not exist when the United States and the Soviets were conducting nuclear arms control negotiations in the 1960s; nor did it exist in the less structured and more rudimentary cases of India and Pakistan or Argentina and Brazil.

The result of this asymmetry is a clearcut divergence of interests and agendas between the parties. Arabs, and especially the Egyptians, seek to highlight the nuclear issue and isolate it from the rest of the security agenda; they insist on entering into negotiations on a zone free of all weapons of mass destruction as early as possible. For them, an end to Israeli nuclear superiority is the most important single item on the arms control agenda. Along these lines, Egypt conceives of the establishment of such a zone through a pre-determined and relatively autonomous time sequence, including both activities and declarations. Some Egyptians have even proposed, in private communications, that such a time sequence could last fifteen or even twenty years, but in the end 'all Israeli nuclear weapons must be dismantled'.

Israelis, on the other hand, want to keep the nuclear card in play until the peace-making process is complete, insisting that the establishment of NWFZ ought to be the last stage of the arms control negotiations, linked to other issues of regional security and arms control, it will symbolize the end of the entire arms control path.[11] In general, Israel insists that the nuclear issue cannot be isolated from the rest of the arms control package, the way the NPT does; on the contrary, discussion of steps toward the establishment of a NWFZ must be linked with political progress on the peace front, as well as with progress in other areas of arms control, both conventional and non-conventional. Since the parties do not start the bargaining process from positions of relative equality, Israel has a clear edge, and will want as many gains in peace and security as possible before it gives up its nuclear option.

This issue of nuclear asymmetry is compounded by another sort of difficulty, from the arms control perspective: Israel's long-standing policy of opacity regarding its nuclear capability, which is expressed by the three-decades-old formula, 'Israel will not be the first to introduce nuclear weapons to the region'. A certain basic transparency is required for the very possibility of arms control, as proved since the early arms control negotiations between the United States and the Soviet Union some thirty years ago; in order to negotiate such agreements the negotiating parties must know and openly communicate what is on the table. Opacity, or lack of transparency, makes it very difficult for the parties even to agree upon the appropriate vocabulary that forms the basis of discourse through negotiation. For example, while the Arabs insist on 'a full accounting of Israel's nuclear arsenal' as a necessary step in order to establish a NWFZ, the present Israeli official discourse will not allow any reference to 'weapons'. In order to 'eliminate' or 'dismantle' weapons those weapons need first to be 'introduced', but thus far Israel claims it will not be the first to 'introduce' them. As long as they are not 'introduced', they are not within the ontology of the discourse. The most that Israel will currently allow to be said about its 'nuclear option' is to refer to it in terms of a 'capability' consisting of 'unsafeguarded nuclear facilities'. Under the present circumstances, it is unlikely that Israel would be ready to admit to owning anything beyond unsafeguarded fissile material.

The present impasse is likely to remain as long as both sides continue to stake too much on the declared long-term objectives of the arms control process: the establishment of a zone free of all weapons of mass destruction, especially nuclear weapons. The substantive reason for this is known by all but openly acknowledged by none: until Israel feels secure in the new Middle East, it will continue to regard its unacknowledged nuclear deterrent as an essential ingredient for its national security, and will not readily relinquish it. In fact, many Israelis, especially on the Left, believe that Israel's 'nuclear option' has been thus far instrumental in persuading the Arabs to choose the peace path: the way the Israeli bomb has manifested itself, both as a symbol and as a perception in the Arabs' mind, was tacitly an important factor in what brought the Arabs to accept Israel's existence. As noted earlier, many Arab strategists half-openly share this view.

Therefore, it is the idea of *lasting* peace, for some Israelis defined in terms of peace among *democratic* regimes, that is at the heart of the Israeli proposal for a NWFZ.

Furthermore, as long as Iran, Iraq and Syria are not among the core states in the discussion of ACRS it would be futile for Israel to discuss the establishment of NWFZ. Without the relevant partners around, there is no point for Israel in discussing nuclear matters. In any case, as a matter of national strategy Israel will continue to insist on linking progress on the nuclear issue with substantial political progress on the peace front, as well as on linking the nuclear issue to visible progress in other areas of arms control, both conventional and non-conventional.

Realistically, then, it should be clear that Israel will not hasten to establish a NWFZ. No Israeli cabinet could be expected to preside over dismantling the nation's 'nuclear option'; on the contrary, Israeli defence sources have already made clear that a leaner, peacetime Israeli army must have an even stronger strategic deterrent component, and that it is Israel's 'nuclear option' that will preserve the peace. Israel's new partners for peace, as well as Israel's remaining foes, must not question Israel's commitment to maintaining its deterrent strength.

This does not mean that Israel should now abandon its long-time support of a NWFZ in the Middle East, but it means that as a practical reality a NWFZ cannot be foreseen for the immediate future. While it is important to define and discuss a long-term vision of arms control, it should also be recognized that such a vision is only heuristic, not a blueprint for immediate action. Implicit in this view is a certain criticism of both Egypt's and Israel's declared positions on the NWFZ.

In the case of Egypt, the country that most persistently presses the Israeli nuclear issue; its overemphasis on this question is self-defeating: pushing Israel into a corner on this highly sensitive issue has the potential to jeopardize and paralyse the whole arms control discussion. Egypt must realize politically that Israel is not ready to negotiate the NWFZ issue, especially when it is simultaneously negotiating the return of the Golan Heights to Syria and asking the United States for an enhanced security package.[12] Egyptians and other Arabs must understand, and accept, Israel's insistence on basic linkages between the NWFZ and the establishment of lasting peace in the region. The nuclear issue cannot, and will not, be isolated from the rest of the regional security agenda, including matters of restructuring conventional forces in the region.

As for Israel, long years of taboo and secrecy have resulted in a mind-set that resists the very practice and theory of arms control negotiations. Israel, too, invested too much in its NWFZ proposal: a proposal that may have had its day when scoring points in a propaganda war could stir accusations of 'bad faith' in the context of regional arms control negotiation. Though there are seeds of readiness to rethink the issue, the burden of the past makes fresh thinking difficult. The fear of 'the slippery slope' still dominates Israeli thinking on these sensitive matters, perhaps more than it should, but it is a fact to reckon with.

If the arms control process means educating oneself about the other's security and threat perceptions, Israel must explain why it developed its nuclear option in the first place and the Arabs must learn to see this from the Israeli perspective. By the same token, if Israel wishes to legitimize its right to a nuclear shield as its ultimate insurance policy until true peace comes, it must be ready to explain more openly and honestly to its Arab interlocutors why it went nuclear in the first place.

Israel's early decision to develop a national nuclear option, but without escalating the conflict to the nuclear brink, can be defended on both political and moral grounds. Israel's nuclear project was not launched for the sake of national glory or prestige. Rather, Ben-Gurion's decision that Israel should develop a nuclear option was taken as a sacred matter of national survival, the ultimate way to offset the fundamental asymmetry in conventional power between Israel and the Arab world. Developing the nuclear option was meant to provide Israel with the margin of security that would ensure its survival as an island in a big and hostile Arab ocean, it was Israel's ultimate insurance policy: placing Israel in a position to inflict a holocaust to prevent another Holocaust. Polls taken during the Gulf War indicated that this view was overwhelmingly supported by the Israeli public. In fact, not only in Israel itself but in the Western world virtually no one questions the moral and political legitimacy of Israel's nuclear option. For this reason alone a true NWFZ in the Middle East will not be a politically feasible in the near future.

There are also other reasons to be suspicious about investing too much energy in the final objective of establishing a NWFZ. The experience gained in South America, the only continent to have made a serious effort to establish NWFZ and the case that Israel cited as a regional approach to non-proliferation, reveals the enormous difficulties involved in that approach. A comparison of the South American and the Middle Eastern cases shows that those difficulties would be compounded in the latter.

Though the Treaty of Tlatelolco for the Prohibition of Nuclear Weapons in Latin America and the Caribbean, establishing the framework of a NWFZ in the South American continent, was opened for signature in 1967, over twenty-five years of complex negotiations and amendments have followed to bring the Tlatelolco Treaty close to realization. Notably, while on the

Latin American continent there was nothing comparable to the enmity which prevailed in the Arab–Israel conflict, rivalry and suspicion between its two most advanced nuclear nations – Argentina and Brazil – for many years made the Tlatelolco Treaty mostly a vision, as these two nations refused to sign it. Only now, and primarily due to fundamental domestic changes in both countries, the Treaty of Tlatelolco is on its way to becoming a political reality.[13]

In July 1991 Argentina and Brazil signed a bilateral agreement establishing a Joint System for Accounting and Control of Nuclear Materials, jointly administered by the Argentine–Brazilian Agency for Accounting and Control of Nuclear Materials (ABACC). Following the establishment of the ABACC, a Quadripartite Agreement among Argentina, Brazil, the ABACC and the IAEA set up a structure for applying IAEA full-scope safeguards, on the model of the EURATOM/IAEA safeguards agreement. In the wake of these agreements, the Presidents of Argentina and Brazil proposed in February 1992 a series of amendments to the Tlatelolco Treaty which, once adopted, would eventually lead to their nations' full adherence. The main purpose of these amendments was to change the verification procedures of the Treaty, transferring the inspection responsibility to the IAEA. It was only on 18 January 1994, after a lengthy amendment process, that Argentina and Chile ratified the Treaty and put it into force in their territories; though it is expected that Brazil will follow suit soon, as of this writing (May 1994) it has not yet completed the ratification process. A NWFZ will come fully into force in the continent of Latin America and the Caribbean only when Brazil and Cuba have joined the other 27 signatories.

The Latin American case, complex and lengthy as it is, pales by comparison to the complexity of the Middle Eastern situation. Politically, no state in the South American continent has ever faced the kind of existential threat that Israel did; nor does the South American situation of relative nuclear symmetry and equality between the two advanced nuclear states, Argentina and Brazil, fit the Arab–Israeli conflict, though it does fit somewhat the Iranian–Iraqi rivalry. Realistically, given the difference in nuclear development between Israel and the Arab states, the ABACC is probably not applicable to the Arab–Israeli context *per se*; though it may become more applicable once it combines the Middle East and the Persian Gulf into one geographical package. More significantly, while in the Latin American case the NWFZ stands on its own as a strictly nuclear matter, in the Middle East any attempt to establish NWFZ must be linked to a full array of other security and arms control agreements and arrangements, in particular a reduction in the size of conventional standing armies. Again, due to the essential asymmetry of nuclear capabilities in the region, no separate and isolated nuclear deal can be made.

There is another reason why a Tlatelolco-type treaty would not easily fit the Middle East nuclear situation. Nuclear weapons were never developed in Latin America; nuclear weapons design know-how, nearly equivalent to actual possession of the weapons themselves, was never fully gained there. A country that exercises its national sovereignty over the ownership of fissile material and the know-how to produce nuclear weapons will continue to be only a step from possessing the bomb. The application of NWFZ to states which preserve these two elements raises questions that were never considered by the framers of the Tlatelolco Treaty.

But this is not the case in the Middle East. Israel does possess this knowledge, as the late Prime Minister Eshkol openly acknowledged as early as in 1968, and such knowledge will not simply go away. While the control of nuclear facilities through safeguard procedures is conceptually straightforward, this is not the case concerning the control of nuclear weapons *knowledge*. There is no precedent for an international system to control such knowledge, and it is doubtful if it is possible at all; nor is there an historical precedent of applying NWFZ to regions and states where advanced nuclear weapons capabilities have already been developed. The terms and procedures of a NWFZ on the Tlatelolco model do not apply to the heart of the situation in the Middle East. If this issue can be addressed at all, it must involve a broader, more visionary, discussion of the concept of a nuclear-weapon-free world. The difficulties concerning establishing the Middle East as a true NWFZ are not very different from those of establishing a nuclear-weapon-free world.

For the reasons just mentioned, at the present time a NWFZ in the Middle East is not feasible. In general, to place too much political and intellectual emphasis on the *final* nuclear arrangements would probably be a political mistake for all parties, almost certainly generating stalemates, impasses, accusations and counter-accusations inimical to the whole process of arms control. However, this does not mean that the alternative is to leave the nuclear issue untouched until a lasting peace is established. For reasons that tie together regional and global interests – among them the very interests that first gave rise to the arms control discourse in the Middle East – it is clear that the nuclear issue in the Middle East will not go away. Though the visionary objective of making the Middle East free of all weapons of mass destruction cannot be reached just yet, some interim measures should be discussed.

What measures are both achievable and constructive? At the present time, it is unlikely that a realistic initiative on this issue can come from the region's states. For one thing, it is over precisely this issue that an impasse exists between Israel and its Arab partners in the ACRS. The Arabs, especially the Egyptians, continue to insist on the priority of the nuclear issue, contending that they will not join the Chemical Weapons Convention (CWC) unless Israel signs the NPT; the latter issue is, of course, a non-starter for Israel. Israel, on the other hand, is quite comfortable with the nuclear impasse, especially if it is kept opaque and in low profile; it sees no need to deal with this highly sensitive issue during its delicate political negotiations with the Palestinians and the Syrians. Israel has always been inhibited on this issue, and there is no reason for this to change now. For another thing, the regional parties are not the custodians of the non-proliferation regime. Their calculations *vis-à-vis* the regime are based almost entirely on their own national interest; global considerations concerning the future of the non-proliferation regime play a limited role in shaping their national policy on these matters.

It is the custodians of the non-proliferation regime, and most particularly the United States, that are the most likely candidates to try to break the impasse. For the United States, a nuclear agreement in the Middle East has important extra-regional implications: it must be consistent with the United States global non-proliferation and counter-proliferation policy for the post-Cold War era. If the non-proliferation regime is to survive in the post-Cold War environment, it is mostly responsibility of the United States to lead the way. Preventing the spread of weapons of mass destruction, either by traditional non-proliferation means or by the less traditional means of 'counter-proliferation', is the most important global job that remains for the United States, the only post-Cold War superpower.

This, at least in theory, is also the view of the Clinton administration. There are currently six areas, or sets of problems, in which the United States global commitment to non-proliferation is being exercised, shaped and tested: (1) the continuing confrontation with North Korea over its NPT obligations (is a test case for the credibility of the NPT and the regime as a whole); (2) relations with the new nuclear weapon states in the territories of the former Soviet Union; (3) an effort to negotiate a region-specific denuclearization arrangement for the Indian sub-continent; (4) policy preparations for the NPT Extension and Review Conference to be held in May 1995; (5) negotiations to complete a Comprehensive Test Ban Treaty (CTBT) by the time of the NPT Extension and Review Conference; and (6) negotiation of a global convention to prohibit further production of fissile material for the use in nuclear weapons (the so-called 'cut-off' proposal). The first three issues are dealt with primarily at the bilateral or the regional level; the last three are multilateral in nature and linked directly with United States global policy. For our purposes I will focus here on the last issue, first on the general idea of the 'cut-off' proposal, and later on its relevance and usefulness to the Middle East

In his address to the United Nations on 27 September 1993, President Clinton set the framework under which his administration would act to prevent the proliferation of weapons of mass destruction and their ballistic delivery means. A key component in that policy was a comprehensive approach to the problem of fissile material, centred on an effort to ban where possible the stockpiling of fissile material for weapons worldwide. In terms of the non-proliferation regime, this effort means extending the regime one step further: dealing with the problem of nuclear proliferation not only at the level of prohibiting the weapon itself, as the NPT does, but at the previous stage of production of fissile material. A White House fact sheet released in connection with Clinton's address stated that under this approach the United States will:

- seek to eliminate where possible the accumulation of stockpiles of highly enriched uranium or plutonium, and to ensure that where these materials already exist they are subject to the highest standards of safety, security and international accountability.

- propose a multilateral convention prohibiting the production of highly enriched uranium or plutonium for nuclear explosive purposes or outside of international safeguards.

- encourage more restrictive regional arrangements to constrain fissile material production in regions of instability and high proliferation risk.

- submit United States fissile material no longer needed for our deterrent to inspection by the IAEA.

- explore means to limit the stockpiling of plutonium from civil nuclear programs, and seek to minimize the civil use of highly enriched uranium.[14]

This is, no doubt, an ambitious approach, which includes both domestic and international aspects. Of particular interest to us is the second item on this list, perhaps the most ambitious part of it all, that commits the United States to seek a multilateral convention to end the production of fissile material for weapons worldwide, the so called the cut-off proposal. Unlike the discriminatory character of the NPT, this proposal calls for a non-discriminatory, universal, multilateral convention, modelled on the CWC. If the NPT provides legitimacy for the nuclear arsenals of the five nuclear weapon states and delegitimizes nuclear weapons for the rest of the world, the proposed cut-off convention would delegitimize future production of fissile material for weapon anywhere. Such a treaty would not be a replacement for the NPT but rather an important addition to it; in fact, except for details, it appears that the cut-off treaty would place no additional legal constraints on non-nuclear weapons states already parties to the NPT; rather, it would be a way to extend the non-proliferation regime particularly to the three current *de facto* nuclear weapon states – India, Israel and Pakistan – who never signed the NPT.

While negotiations on the details of such a treaty have hardly begun, its essential idea is shaped by a certain political realism. Such a treaty would provide implicit recognition of the special status of the three *de facto* nuclear weapons states – possibly others as well – by acknowledging the existence of a second tier of nuclear weapon states. Viewed thus, the cut-off proposal is a sensible way to rewrite the old boundaries and rules of the non-proliferation regime: it expresses the political recognition that there must be a way to distinguish between these old *de facto* nuclear states and new proliferators such as North Korea and Iran (both signatories to the NPT) Though the cut-off proposal, like the NPT, is *status quo* oriented in the sense that it accepts the reality of a second tier of nuclear weapon states, yet it is also not *status quo* oriented in the sense that it calls for a worldwide moratorium on the future production of fissile material for weapon.

In a way, the cut-off proposal addresses the phenomenon of 'opaque proliferation' as a by-product of the non-proliferation regime. Since the NPT was introduced in 1968, no state has openly declared its desire to possess nuclear weapons. It was Israel (which presumably had already possessed nuclear weapons before 1968) that created the pattern of going nuclear opaquely: while resisting American pressure to sign the NPT, it never openly defied the non-proliferation regime. India, Pakistan and South Africa followed suit (the last is the only state that decided to roll back its nuclear weapons programme and join the NPT). While a cut-off treaty would 'grandfather' their unsafeguarded past stockpiling – granting them a legitimacy of sorts by default – it would also invite them to shape a new, and more equal, non-proliferation contract. Under this contract no country could produce fissile material for weapons, an interim measure leading to the objective of world free of nuclear weapons.

Notwithstanding the commitment of the Clinton administration to a multilateral cut-off convention, it is clear that it will be a long time before a formal treaty can be signed. There are many complex issues involved in negotiating such a treaty: what should be covered, verification procedures, its relation to the NPT, etc. Due to this complexity, negotiations could drag on for years. The more ambitious the proposal, the more difficult the negotiations. It is also apparent that although it is exploring the issue, the United States has no intent to start serious negotiations on it before the 1995 NPT Extension Conference. At the moment the focus at the Conference on Disarmament (CD), the global forum in which such negotiations takes place, is on the question CTBT, not the cut-off proposal.

Realizing that achieving a formal global treaty may be long and difficult, it has been suggested that such a treaty should be thought of as the end of a process starting with weaker arrangements concerning fissile material cut-off – that is, informal, declaratory, non-intrusive, etc. – to be established on regional, bilateral or even unilateral terms. This helps interpret the third item on the White House fact sheet, 'restrictive regional arrangements' on the matter of fissile material. Indeed, the suggestion to place a moratorium on the production of fissile material was made by the Bush administration shortly after the Gulf War. The Bush plan for arms control in the Middle East included a direct reference 'to implement a verifiable ban on production and acquisition of weapons-usable nuclear material'.

Notably, the Bush plan was only a loose framework of regional arms control arrangements in the Middle East. It was announced shortly after the Gulf War, and since then it has been 'on hold' pending further progress on the peace front and within the newly established ACRS forum. Nevertheless, this was the first time that the United States made some effort to incorporate the highly sensitive nuclear issue into a broader context of regional arms control. How viable is this notion?

Since Israel is the country most directly affected by a cut-off proposal, it is almost entirely up to Israel to determine whether such an idea is viable. Nevertheless, it should be remembered that Israel would be unlikely itself to initiate a proposal for action on this issue (except perhaps as a way of pre-empting other proposals); Israel might reject certain ideas, or negotiate them, but is hardly expected to propose them. Nor is it likely that Israel's Arab partners at the ACRS would seek a cut-off deal; their concern is to press Israel on the NPT as a condition for establishing a NWFZ in the region, not to legitimize Israel's past nuclear activities. The only country that can press Israel to consider the issue is the United States, whether as an issue within the ACRS or as a global treaty. Hence, the fate of a cut-off proposal would be determined ultimately more in the context of Israeli–American rather than in Arab–Israeli relationship.

At present Israel rejects any effort to focus on the nuclear issue at the ACRS. For Israel, it is the bilateral political processes – further progress on the issue of Palestinian self-rule and in the negotiations with Syria – that should drive all other developments on the front of regional arms control, not the opposite. At this point, Israel is testing the political and security implications of the self-rule agreement it signed with the Palestinians while peace talks with the Syrians on withdrawal from the Golan Heights are still at a rudimentary stage. Furthermore, until the Syrians are a full party to the ACRS it is nearly certain that no substantial progress – more than declaratory – could take place there. Thus far the Syrians insist on joining the ACRS only after substantial progress is made in its bilateral negotiations with Israel.

It is only within the context of a comprehensive peace agreement with Syria, including a substantial bilateral package on security and arms control, that Israel might agree to consider a nuclear component, probably along the lines of the cut-off proposal, which could be sold as an interim measure toward the establishment of a zone free of all weapons of mass destruction in the Middle East. Whatever Israel might agree to do on the nuclear side would have to be linked to Syrian undertakings in the whole area of weapons of mass destruction and means of delivery, as well as other means of demilitarization in the conventional field. For less than a comprehensive deal it is very unlikely that Israel could make concessions on the nuclear issue in a situation when it gives up strategic territorial assets in the Golan. Notwithstanding the strategic issues involved, for any Israeli government it would be difficult to make concessions on the nuclear issue, the existential issue, without a tangible *quid pro quo*.[15]

Another Israeli concern would be the inclusion of both Iraq and Iran in any regional nuclear regime. Just as reaching an agreement with these states would be a strong incentive for Israel to accept the cut-off proposal, their absence, especially Iran's, would be a disincentive to full Israeli particip-ation. Israel may accept such an agreement in principle, may even sign it, but would postpone formal ratification until Iraq and Iran joined the regional framework.

The extra Israeli caution in dealing on this matter goes deeper than geopolitical considerations. It is rooted in a culture evolved around the nuclear issue for over thirty-odd years during which Israel fought hard to maintain total control and absolute secrecy over all its nuclear activities. It never placed its Dimona nuclear facility under IAEA safeguards, nor has it since 1970 allowed any other type of inspection visits to that site. Even if Israel could live with the direct implications of the cut-off proposal *per se*, and it appears that this might be the case, it would be very cautious about placing Dimona under any on-site verification procedures. Some of this concern may be driven by a worry that the verification system could reveal more than would the cut-off itself; some of it may be driven by a general concern about the implications of such an arrangement for Israel's freedom of action in this area (the 'slippery slope' argument). As to the latter, Israel would almost certainly insist on reaching private understandings with the United States before agreeing to any regional or global nuclear cut-off. Such understandings would prevent Israel from falling into further pressures on this matter (the 'slippery slope' concern), as well as co-ordinating efforts of both countries to deny proliferation in the region.

But as the saying goes, the devil is in the details. Whether as a global cut-off convention, or as a regional nuclear arrangement negotiated through the ACRS, the negotiation of cut-off verification protocols for both Israel and the Arab states is certain to be a complex and lengthy undertaking. The difficulty is rooted not only in the verifying procedures themselves, but also in deciding who would be the appropriate body for that. For example, if Israel insists on verification measures similar to the Argentinean–Brazilian verification agreement it would mean that Israeli, Arab, and possibly Iranian, inspectors would visit each other's nuclear facilities. Would Israel agree to a verification system built on the principle of 'managed access' which would allow others to inspect the entire Dimona facility and other sensitive sites?

In general, any attempt to negotiate formal agreements demanding degree of nuclear transparency beyond the *minimum* required to verify non-production is unlikely in the foreseeable future. Another mode of action could be along the informal path of a unilateral national undertaking, possibly a declaration, with no intrusive on-site verification procedures of at all. For example, at an appropriate political moment Israel could declare the Dimona reactor to be shut down, and invite verification through non-intrusive measures.

Much of this discussion, however, is only theoretical. At this point no party in the region has shown an interest in pursuing the cut-off proposal, nor has the Clinton administration shown any great desire to move beyond the declaratory statements that it has made thus far. For one thing, the multilateral cut-off convention is not yet on the global agenda; for another, the United States has left matters of regional arms control to the ACRS. In general, the United States seems to agree with the basic Israeli approach on this issue, in particular with the Israeli view that an attempt to deal with the nuclear issue now would serve no useful purpose but only cause further tensions and disagreements. Though the United States has by no means abandoned its interest in the cut-off idea for the Middle East, at this point it has tested it – thus far unsuccessfully – in the somewhat easier context of the Indian subcontinent, presumably in the belief that if the cut-off idea were workable there it would be more difficult for Israel to reject it outright.[16]

However, if any interim nuclear arrangement is possible for the Middle

East, it is difficult to think of a conceptual structure different from the cut-off idea. This proposal is realistic because it takes embraces the two most important features of Israel's nuclear opacity. First, the cut-off idea is a future-oriented bargain, explicitly ignoring the past while implicitly acknowledging its reality. Second, it makes no generic or specific reference to nuclear weapons as such; instead, it bans only fissile material for weapons.

In the past, nuclear opacity in the Middle East was as a substitute for discussion and negotiation, but it need not be that way in the future. Indeed, just as opacity helped to create constructive ambiguity in the past, it could also contribute to creating constructive ambiguities for future arms control.

NOTES

1. On the issue of the theory of nuclear proliferation in the post-Cold War world see Zachary S. Davis and Benjamin Frankel (eds.), *The Proliferation Puzzle* (London: Frank Cass, 1993).
2. The new term 'counter-proliferation', as a conceptual addition to the traditional term 'non-proliferation', reflects a certain post-Cold War attitude in the United States toward proliferation. The term originated was by defence intellectuals around the United States Department of Defense in the period after the Gulf War and it reflects a basic recognition – a lesson of the Iraqi case – about the inability of ordinary non-proliferation mechanisms to prevent proliferation of 'hostile' states like Iraq or North Korea, states that go nuclear from within the NPT. Counter-proliferation means here a broad spectrum of non-diplomatic options to try to deny proliferation in such states. Indeed, Ashton Carter's new title is Assistant Secretary for Nuclear Security and Counterproliferation. .

  This new attitude is also evident in recent reports on proliferation produced by various United States defence intellectuals. For example, the authors of a report, *Proliferation, Theater Missile Defense, and United States Security*, commissioned for the Institute for Foreign Policy Analysis, say the following:

  > The Working Group recognized that current non-proliferation techniques embodied in such arms control regimes as the Non-Proliferation Treaty, the safeguards regime of the International Atomic Energy Agency, and the Missile Technology control Regime, are important and valuable. By themselves, however, they are insufficient to halt weapons proliferation, a fact underscored by Iraq's surreptitious nuclear program...Iraq's nearly successful nuclear weapons program, combined with North Korea's current efforts to avoid IAEA inspections, reinforces still further the notion that non-proliferation efforts require supplemental measures.

  As the conceptual tension between these two phrases (non-proliferation and counter-proliferation) and their bureaucratic constituencies became apparent, the NSC issued a memorandum that included 'agreed definitions' of both terms:

  > Nonproliferation is the use of the full range of political, economic and military tools to prevent proliferation, reverse it diplomatically or protect our interest against an opponent armed with weapons of mass destruction or missiles, should that prove necessary.
  > Nonproliferation tools include: intelligence, global nonproliferation norms and agreements, diplomacy, export control, security assurances, and the application of military force.
  > Counterproliferation refers to the activities of the Dept of Defense across the full range of US efforts to combat proliferation, including diplomacy, arms control, export controls, and intelligence collection and analysis, with particular responsibility for assuring that US forces and interests can be protected should they confront an adversary armed with

weapons of mass destruction and missiles.
These definitions were brought to my attention in a note (#429) by Amende Dory of the Carnegie Endowment at the NNN network.

3. The reference to the IAEA Fact Sheet of January 1994 appears in the *Programme For Promoting Nuclear Non-Proliferation Newsbrief*, No. 25 (1st Quarter 1994), p.11.

4. Douglas Jehl, 'Iran Is Reported Acquiring Missiles', *New York Times*, 8 April 1993; Knut Race, 'Iran Buying 150 'Terror Missiles', *Long Island Newsday*, 11 April 1992; Christopher Walker, 'Iran Submarine Purchase Tilts Gulf Power', *The Times* (London), 5 Oct. 1992.

5. See Geoffrey Kemp, *Forever Enemies? American Policy & the Islamic Republic of Iran* (Washington DC: Carnegie Endowment for International Peace, 1994), pp.57–60. Kemp makes particularly references to Sharham Chubin, *Iran's National Security Policy: Intentions, Capabilities and Impact* (forthcoming).

6. Indeed, the issue of the right of the IAEA to conduct 'special inspections' in undeclared facilities was at the heart of the early confrontation between the IAEA and North Korea. The IAEA demand to conduct 'special inspections' in waste sites was flatly denied by the North Koreans, and when the IAEA brought the issue to the Security Council North Korea announced its decision to withdraw from the Treaty altogether.

7. David Albright, 'North Korea and the 'worst case' scare-nario', *The Bulletin of the Atomic Scientists*, Vol. 50, No. 1 (January–February1994), pp.3–6; Michael R. Gordon, 'North Korea Said to Have A-Bomb Fuel', *New York Times*, 8 June 1994, p.A7.

8. There are many indications, albeit tacit, that the perception of Israel as a full nuclear power helps to bring Palestinians to the painful realization that they must make a deal with Israel on terms much less favorable than they ever hoped; this recognition was at the background of the historical recognition between Israel and the PLO that was struck through the Oslo agreement. I formed this impression through many personal communications with Arabs, and especially Palestinians, strategists during the last few years. See this author's 'Did nukes nudge the PLO?', *The Bulletin of Atomic Scientists* (December 1993), pp.11–13.

9. Yitzhak Rabin, 'Only the United States Can Prevent Proliferation', *Davar* (in Hebrew), 17 January 1992; Ze'ev Schiff, 'Race Against Time', *Politika*, No. 44 (March 1992), pp.14–17.

10. This point was apparent in Rabin's inaugural speech to the Knesset on 13 July 1992. In that speech he stated: 'Already in its initial stages, the Government, possibly with the cooperation of other countries, will give its attention to the foiling of every possibility that any of Israel's enemies should not get hold of nuclear weapons'. See also his article, 'Taking Advantage of the Time-Out', *Politika*, No. 44, (March 1992), pp.28–9.

11. This kind of posturing was already evident during in the first two rounds of the bilateral talks on arms control in Moscow in January 1992 and in the Washington 'seminar' in May 1992. See Ruth Sinai, 'Mideast Arms Talks', The Associated Press, 11 May 1992.

12. Steven Greenhouse, 'Israelis Offering to Leave Golan, Negotiators Say', *New York Times*, 18 May 1994.

13. For an update on the Argentine-Brazil situation *vis-à-vis* the Tlatelolco Treaty see John R. Redick, 'Argentina-Brazil Nuclear Non-Proliferation Initiatives', *Programme for Promoting Nuclear Non-Proliferation*, Review Issue, No. 3 (January 1994).

14. The White House, Office of the Press Secretary, Fact Sheet, 27 September 1993.

15. Indeed, Israel may feel less secure in the immediate period after it trades land for peace, and some will argue that a nuclear deterrent is the ultimate guarantee of a smaller Israel.

16. See John F. Burns, 'India Resists Plan to Curb Nuclear Arms', *New York Times*, 15 May 1994, p.19A.

Israel and the Changing Global Non-Proliferation Regime: The NPT Extension, CTBT and Fissile Cut-Off

GERALD M. STEINBERG

Over the past three decades, a global set of norms and rules of behaviour has been developed in the area of non-proliferation of weapons of mass destruction. These norms and rules can be viewed in terms of a global regime, consisting of the Nuclear Non-Proliferation Treaty (NPT), the activities of the International Atomic Energy Agency (IAEA), the Chemical Weapons Convention (CWC), and various supplier agreements.[1]

However, the global regime is currently under challenge and in the process of significant change. The 1995 NPT Review Conference will determine whether this pivotal agreement will be extended, and if so, under what conditions and for how long. Simultaneously, negotiations have finally begun on a Comprehensive Test Ban Treaty (CTBT), and discussions are taking place on a proposed cut-off on the production of fissile material. Each measure is of major significance, and they are closely interlinked.

For the Middle East, in general, and Israel in particular, these measures and proposals, and the future of the global nuclear non-proliferation regime are of major importance. Although Israel has never acknowledged the possession of nuclear weapons, the reactor in Dimona has been producing plutonium for many years, and Israel is generally credited with a nuclear option. Other states in the region, including Iraq, Iran, Algeria and Libya, are widely suspected to be pursuing nuclear weapons, and, unless checked, this will eventually lead to a Middle East with many nuclear powers. This article is designed to examine the Israeli position in response to the changes and initiatives in the global non-proliferation regime, and to explore the growing role of a regional approach to supplement and reinforce the global regime in areas where this regime is particularly weak.

Israeli Policy on Nuclear Proliferation

Israeli policies and interests with respect to the NPT are mixed. On the one hand, the national interest is served by a robust NPT and the strengthening of obstacles to proliferation. Israeli national security and regional stability would be severely threatened if a number of states in the Middle East acquire nuclear weapons. To the extent that the NPT and other elements of the regime have served to slow or prevent this process, these factors have contributed to the Israeli national interest.

At the same time, Israel is a major NPT 'holdout', along with India and Pakistan. Given continued threats to national survival, Israeli decision-makers view the maintenance of an ambiguous nuclear option as necessary for deterrence. In addition, the verification framework, based on the International Atomic Energy Agency (IAEA), is seen as inadequate to ensure that the other states in the region do not obtain nuclear weapons.

Nuclear Deterrence and Israeli Security

The Middle East is still a region characterized by a high level of conflict and warfare. Although the Arab–Israeli peace process has produced some possibilities of change, the potential for conflict remains high. The Arab states maintain a major advantage in the quantity of conventional weapons, and, in the past decade, have been able to increase the qualitative level of these forces. Israeli conventional strength is generally judged to be sufficient to deter most potential attacks from individual Arab states. However, this is not the case regarding 'worst case' scenarios, consisting of a large-scale combined attack, led by Iraq and Syria, and, potentially, including additional forces and advanced platforms from the Saudi inventory. In the event of a major change in the Egyptian regime, the rise of a fundamentalist or radical state, and the renunciation of the 1979 Peace Treaty, Egyptian participation in such an attack cannot be ruled out.

For four decades, Israeli military and political leaders have viewed an indigenous nuclear response as the best means of deterring such threats to national survival. Israel is a small and narrow state, with no strategic depth, and highly vulnerable population centres. A full scale conventional attack, particularly before reserve troops are mobilized, could readily overrun the state, and reach the major cities in a few hours. This geographic reality led Ben-Gurion to initiate the development of a nuclear option and 'weapon of last resort' against full-scale attacks that threatened the survival of the state.[2]

A number of Arab states have also developed or are seeking to develop non-conventional capabilities. Chemical weapons were used in the 1960s by Egypt in the war in Yemen, and by Iraq in the war with Iran, while Syria, Libya, and Iran have also produced large inventories of chemical weapons. Iraq, Syria, and Iran have acquired ballistic missiles capable of delivering both conventional and non-conventional warheads. Most importantly, the rate of nuclear proliferation has increased. Iraq was within grasp of a nuclear weapons capability when the United States attacked and destroyed many of the Iraqi nuclear facilities in the 1991 Gulf War, but the Iraqi programme could re-emerge as soon as international sanctions are lifted. Iran has also sought to accelerate the development of a nuclear infrastructure, and Algeria has sought to acquire the technology necessary. Most recently, theft of fissile material from sites in Russia and the former Soviet Union (FSU) may provide Iran, Iraq or Libya with a short cut to nuclear weapons. Thus, the Israeli nuclear option is now also seen as a deterrent against Arab non-conventional weapons.

As long as these conventional and non-conventional capabilities and threats remain, Israeli leaders will continue to see the nuclear option as a necessary deterrent and guarantee of national security. Shalheveth Freier, who was head of Israel's Atomic Energy Agency, describes the policy of nuclear ambiguity as providing 'a sense of reassurance to Israelis in times of gloom' and 'to serve as possible caution to states contemplating obliterating Israel by dint of their preponderance of men and material'.[3] In other words, the nuclear capability remains a necessary 'weapon of last resort'.

Inadequate Verification and Response

Beyond the issues of deterrence and national security, Israel has always viewed the international non-proliferation regime as inadequate and even counterproductive in the Middle East. The lack of confidence in the verification system operated by the International Atomic Energy Agency was clearly demonstrated in the 1981 attack on the Iraqi nuclear reactor complex. When Israeli representatives and officials voiced concerns regarding the Iraqi nuclear weapons programme, they were told that Iraq was a signatory to the NPT, and that there was no cause for concern.[4] From the Israeli perspective, the NPT and IAEA provided legitimacy and a cover for Iraqi efforts to acquire nuclear weapons.

The Iraqi experience demonstrated that the IAEA safeguard system is unable to ensure 'timely warning' of a nuclear weapons programme. Although some improvements in the safeguard system have been announced, the IAEA is still limited both technically and politically. As long as most states in the Middle East are non-democratic and largely closed societies, verification will continue to be particularly difficult. As became clear in the case of Iraq, and seems to true for Iran as well, under authoritarian regimes, with large areas, it is possible to hide major weapons development programmes, both internally and from outside inspectors and even overhead reconnaissance.

In addition, the structure and political activities that take place within the framework of the IAEA are a source of concern. The Arab and Islamic states exploit the IAEA and other international organizations for political purposes, demanding support for anti-Israel resolutions. While many Arab states (including Iraq and Libya) have been elected to membership on the Board of Governors, and their representatives play a major role in the IAEA structure, Israel has been blocked from such activities.[5] This factor has served to reduce the confidence of Israel in the IAEA even further.

Israel and NPT Extension

Despite the continued reliance on a nuclear option, the weaknesses of the safeguards system and the reactions to violations, the Israeli government views the NPT and the related regime as important factors in slowing or blocking proliferation in the Middle East. While not an NPT signatory, the indefinite extension of the Treaty is in Israel's national interest. However, for the reasons cited above, there is no reason to expect any change in the Israeli position in the next few years.

In contrast, Egypt and other Arab states have sought to link support for NPT extension to Israeli acceptance of this agreement. The Egyptian Foreign Minister, Amre Musa, embarked on a major public campaign designed to create pressure on Israel. This issue was a major agenda item in Musa's visit to Israel in September 1994, and he sought support in meetings of the Arab League and the United Nations General Assembly.

As a result of this campaign, some analysts have suggested that the US should pressure Israel into signing the NPT.[6] Although Israel receives substantial aid, both military and civil, from the United States, over the past thirty-five years (since US spy planes first detected construction of the reactor at Dimona), Israel has not yielded to pressures in this area, and this policy is likely to continue. Some American decision-makers have sought to pressure Israel into accepting limitations on its nuclear programme, but these pressures have been consistently resisted, and this situation is not likely to change.[7]

Alternatively, there has been some discussion of Israeli acceptance of the NPT, but as a nuclear weapons state. Bundy, Crowe and Drell argue that most countries in the Middle East tacitly view Israel as a nuclear weapon power, and the rest of the international community should do the same. In turn, they argue that such recognition would lead Israel to be more open and transparent regarding its nuclear capability. This proposal, however, is unlikely to be acceptable to Israel, other states in the Middle East, or to the United States government.[8]

The security assurances that have been discussed in the context of NPT extension are also insufficient to meet Israeli security concerns. Such assurances are described as attempts to provide states that view nuclear weapons as essential to their national security with alternatives. In 1968, as part of the efforts to gain ratification the NPT, United Nations Security

Council Resolution 255 specified that the nuclear weapon states would assist non-nuclear states that were threatened with attack.[9] (These are known as 'positive assurances', in the sense that they require positive action by the NWS, in contrast to 'negative assurances', in the form of pledges not to use or threaten to use nuclear weapons.) Recent post-Cold War discussions have also considered collective security assurances involving the five nuclear powers, and the US, in particular, including the possibility of an broader UN Resolution or international treaty. In addition, there have been discussions of expanding the 'no first use' pledges of some of the nuclear powers.[10]

In considering the value of security assurances, both positive and negative, Israeli leaders recall the past cases of failure of security guarantees, even from the United States, particularly during the events preceding the 1967 war. Then, despite the Egyptian blockade of the Red Sea and the perceived threat of imminent invasion from Egypt and Syria, the United States and the other major powers took no action. After the Iraqi invasion of Kuwait in August 1990, the US did act, but only after six months of domestic and international negotiations to gain support, and this reinforced this emphasis on self-reliance. Analysts such as Dore Gold have also questioned the reliability and desirability of such security guarantees in other situations, such as the Golan Heights.[11] Unless vital and immediate US interests are at stake, promises of American military involvement and security assurances are not considered to be sufficiently credible, and not an acceptable alternative to an independent deterrent. (Quester and Utgoff note that the American commitment to the defence of Israel is linked to the 'persistent rumors that Israel had "a bomb in the basement".'[12] From this perspective, if Israel were to relinquish its nuclear option, the credibility of American security guarantees would actually decline.)

In the effort to reconcile the interest in the long term or infinite extension of the NPT regime with a refusal to sign this agreement under current conditions, the Israeli government has signalled a willingness to include limitations on nuclear weapons in a broader Middle East peace settlement. The centrality of a Middle East Nuclear-Weapon-Free Zone (MENWFZ), including all the states in region, and based on a dedicated system of mutual inspection and verification, has been re-emphasized.[13] In addition, Israel has taken an active role in, and expressed support for, a number of new initiatives, including the proposed Comprehensive Test Ban Treaty.

The CTBT: A Modest First Step?

The concept of a global Comprehensive Test Ban Treaty (CTBT) has been discussed for decades. Indeed, the proposal for a complete ban on the testing of nuclear weapons was considered in the 1950s, and at the time, the 1963

Partial Test Ban Treaty (PTBT), which banned testing in the atmosphere and under the sea, was considered as a first step towards a CTBT. However, the verification of very low yield tests (one-tenth of a kiloton and below), as well as the Cold War and continued weapons development, blocked progress for many years.[14]

With the end of the Cold War and the steady reduction in nuclear stockpiles, the possibilities for negotiating a CTBT have increased. In July 1993, after many years of debate, the US government announced a full moratorium on nuclear testing, and the US Congress has set a goal for completion of negotiations by 30 September 1996. On 10 August 1993, the 38 nation Conference on Disarmament (CD) in Geneva gave its Ad Hoc Committee on a Nuclear Test Ban a mandate to begin negotiations, and intensive negotiations began in January 1994. China, which is attempting to close the technological gap with the US and Russia in this area, and continues to test, has opposed a rapid agreement. In addition, the French government is under pressure from the military to resume testing.[15] Other sources of conflict result from the proposed prohibitions on simulations and hydronuclear tests, complex verification issues and questions regarding peaceful nuclear explosions (PNEs). While a draft 'rolling text' was tabled in September 1994, it is heavily bracketed and many disputes remain to be resolved.

Substantively, the CTBT is not strongly linked to the issue of horizontal proliferation and the NPT. A number of states, including Israel and Pakistan, are generally credited with having a nuclear weapons capability, even though they have never tested a weapon. Testing is not considered to be a necessary requirement for the development of first-generation nuclear weapons, and a ban on testing would therefore not pose a significant obstacle for states seeking to achieve the status of nuclear powers.

However, the CTBT is indirectly and politically linked to NPT extension. Article VI of the NPT states that the signatories agree to 'undertake to pursue negotiations in good faith on effective measures relating to cessation of the nuclear arms race at an early date and to nuclear disarmament and on a treaty on general and complete disarmament under strict and effective international control'. For many years, the non-nuclear weapon states, led by India and Mexico, have demanded that the nuclear powers meet their obligations to limit 'vertical proliferation' under the NPT, and make substantive progress towards nuclear disarmament. This was a major issue of contention in the Fourth NPT Review Conference that took place in 1990. Critics argue that the continuation of testing and the production of new weapons worked in the opposite direction, increasing the gap between the NWSs and the NNWSs.[16] In addition, supporters of the CTBT have argued that an end to testing would provide moral support for efforts to pressure NPT holdouts to adhere to the global non-proliferation regime. It follows that agreement on a CTBT would, to a limited degree, support the viability of the NPT.[17] Indeed, initial negotiations on the preamble to the CTBT have included discussion of a specific reference to this measure as 'a step towards a nuclear free world'.[18]

Israeli Interests and the CTBT

For Israel, consideration of the CTBT is based on both procedural and substantive issues. Although the Israeli government has sent observers to the negotiations in the CD, Israel has been denied membership of this organization.[19] In addressing the Conference on Disarmament (CD) on the issue of the CTBT, Israel's Ambassador Itzhak Lior noted the hope that in the future, 'Israel will be able to address the CD in the capacity of a full member.'[20] Without active participation in the negotiation process, Israeli officials will find it difficult to approve the final product. Acceptance of Israel within the CD would clearly improve the potential for Israeli ratification of the Treaty. The political importance of acceptance as a full partner and participant in international organizations and institutions, particularly those involving security issues, is a central factor in Israeli foreign policy, and outweighs the substantive impact of specific measures, such as the CTBT.

Substantively, Israeli officials support an 'effectively verifiable' and universal ban on 'nuclear test explosions'.[21] Israel has signed and ratified the 1963 PTBT, and its policy of 'deliberate ambiguity' with respect to the existence of a nuclear deterrent does not require testing.[22] (Indeed, testing would mark a radical change in policy and the end of this carefully developed policy, while creating numerous political problems.) At the same time, a comprehensive test ban would not have an impact on the Israeli nuclear capability.

However, for much the same reason, the benefits of a CTBT are also limited. The pace of proliferation and the nuclear programmes in Iraq, Iran, Algeria or Libya will not be affected. The impact of a CTBT on regional norms, and as a means of strengthening of the application of the global non-proliferation regime in the Middle East, is also likely to be minimal.

The verification systems that are being proposed for the CTBT, in general, are also unlikely to have an impact on Israeli policy. Israeli representatives at the CD have supported 'the establishment of a verification regime aimed at assuring compliance', including a system for global monitoring, detection, and identification of nuclear explosions, and 'non-routine event-triggered consultation'.[23] However, efforts to include intrusive and challenge inspections to verify proposed bans on test simulations and other activities are problematic, and lead to fears of abuse.

Here, as in other cases, challenge inspections can be used to gain access to sites that are unrelated to verification of the specific terms of the treaty. Thus, Israeli policy favours relegating such inspections to very rare cases under very precise conditions.

In addition, the institutional and organizational aspects of the CTBT are important from the Israeli perspective. As noted above, the structure and operation of the IAEA have created significant political and substantive difficulties. The Swedish draft of the CTBT proposed that the IAEA become the agency for implementing and verification, and Mohammed El Baradei argued that CTBT verification would be 'fully in line with the Agency's statutory objectives'.[24] Israel, however, would be more likely to agree with the American and Chinese positions that call for the creation of a new and independent agency for this purpose. The Israeli position states that 'the prospective CTBT organization should be…professional and impartial. Its structure should enable each State party to exercise its rights in the various organs, on an equal and non-discriminatory basis'.[25]

Finally, the Israeli position on the CTBT will also be influenced by the degree to which acceptance and ratification are seen as 'opening the door' for increased pressure on Israel to sign the NPT. As noted, ratification of the PTBT did not have a measurable impact on Israeli policy or external pressures with respect to the NPT. However, the PTBT was negotiated in 1963, well before the NPT. In contrast, the CTBT is designed to strengthen the NPT regime. To the degree that Israeli political and military decision-makers perceive the CTBT as closely linked to the NPT process, they may seek to avoid creating expectations of a change in policy.

The Fissile Material Production Cut-Off

In July 1992, the United States government announced a halt to the production of fissile material for nuclear weapons, and other countries were asked to adopt this policy. President Yeltsin responded that Russia intended 'to proceed with the program for the cut-off of weapon-grade plutonium production' and to open discussions with the US 'concerning the cut-off of fissionable materials production for weapons'.[26]

In a speech to the United Nations on 27 September 1993, President Clinton proposed the negotiation of an international agreement to halt fissile material production. This initiative was discussed further in the context of the annual meeting of IAEA Board of Governors and endorsed in a unanimous decision of the United Nations General Assembly.[27]

Supporters of this initiative claim that a 'legally enforceable, multilaterally negotiated, and credibly verifiable' prohibition on the production of fissile material would be of major importance to the global non-proliferation regime.[28] Paul Leventhal argues that such a cut-off agreement is the best way to prevent proliferation.[29] Rauf argues that a fissile material cut-off, together with a CTBT, could provide unprecedented international oversight over the nuclear weapon states, and demonstrate their commitment to Article VI of the NPT.[30]

In January 1994, the Conference on Disarmament appointed Canadian Ambassador Gerald Shannon as 'special co-ordinator on the issue of A Ban on Production of Fissile Material for Nuclear Weapons or other Nuclear Explosive Devices'. In March 1994, the CD issued a progress report which concluded that states 'are favorable to negotiations', and are interested in proceeding even before a CTBT agreement is reached.[31]

However, the initiative is still quite vague; fundamental questions and disputes remain regarding the scope of such a ban, as well as the status of existing stockpiles. In a report issued in August 1994, Ambassador Shannon noted that preliminary discussions in the CD had failed to produce an agreed mandate or the establishment of a negotiating committee.[32] A number of states, including Egypt, Algeria, Iran and Pakistan, have demanded that the proposed cut-off include provisions for declaration and verification of existing stockpiles,[33] but this is opposed by the US and other Western states. This position would require participating states to reveal the extent of their capabilities and place them under a system of international inspection. The 'threshold nuclear states' (India, Pakistan, and Israel) are unlikely to accept these requirements, so that any potential benefits from the cut-off proposal for non-proliferation would be erased.

Mechanisms for international monitoring and inspections are also under discussion, and Feiveson notes, 'without verification, the prospective Parties to the cut-off would have little confidence that the other nuclear weapon states or threshold countries had actually halted production'.[34] Remote 'national technical means', such as satellite based infra-red sensors, could be used for some verification tasks, and could determine whether plutonium production reactors are in operation. In cases where the information is ambiguous or there appears to be evidence of attempts to interfere with the remote systems, on-site inspections would have to be authorized.

Alternative routes to the production of fissile material would be more difficult to detect and monitor, particularly for states that operate civil nuclear facilities. Uranium enrichment facilities, such as centrifuge plants, and plutonium reprocessing plants, would require onsite monitoring, but this could also be based on sensors and video devices broadcasting continuously to external monitors. However, as the experience of the IAEA in Iraq has demonstrated, detection of undeclared facilities is difficult, and this problem is likely to limit the effectiveness of a fissile material cut-off agreement.

In addition, the lack of an effective response to violations and the threat of 'breakout' will continue to limit any international regime. The problems of enforcement demonstrated in the cases of Iraq and North Korea with respect to the IAEA will be no less complex with respect to a fissile material cut-off agreement.

Israeli Perspectives

As in the case of the NPT and the CTBT, Israeli policy on the proposed cut-off on the production of fissile material is based on an assessment of how this measure is likely to affect the Israeli nuclear option, and on the question of verification. No official public position has been taken, but according to press reports, Israeli officials did not reject the Clinton initiative and are considering its potential impact as part of a large package which includes 'explicit reference to parallel search for secure, just, and stable peace in the Middle East'.[35] One anonymous source was quoted as saying that 'Israel does not have a problem with the initiative and can live with it'.[36]

Indeed, Cohen and Miller, among others, have urged Israel to endorse the fissile material cut-off proposal.[37] This initiative would allow the undeclared nuclear states – India, Pakistan, and Israel – to maintain existing capabilities and stocks of weapon-grade fissile materials. In contrast to the NPT, which would require Israel to give up its nuclear deterrent, a cut-off would leave this capability intact for a number of years, until the effectiveness of the weapons is eroded. In this way, Israel would maintain its nuclear advantage over the Arab states for a number of years.[38]

Israeli officials are likely to reject the proposals of Cohen and Miller that 'Israel should cap its production of weapons-usable nuclear materials, while the Arab states and Iran should reinforce their declaratory commitment not to produce nuclear weapons by accepting the authority of the IAEA to make special inspections at both declared and suspected nuclear facilities'.[39] Declaratory commitments from Iran and Iraq are dismissed as worthless, and credible verification in these states is difficult to envisage.

There is also concern that by agreeing to an unverifiable fissile material cut-off, Israel would be establishing a dangerous precedent. Former Science Minister Yuval Neeman, who is also a prominent member of the Israeli scientific and technical community, warned that Israel must avoid a process that will require dismantling of its power. In commenting on the cut-off, Neeman argued that, 'We must be careful not to enter into an atmosphere of Messianism ... and not to lose our protection with a single unnecessary signature'.[40] From this perspective, a cut-off is seen as a step 'down the slippery slope' leading, in the longer term, to the end of the strategic deterrent, and endangering the survival of the state.

Israel will also pay close attention to the institutional mechanisms created to monitor and verify compliance with the cut-off. As noted above, the IAEA is viewed as a political organization, in which the Arab and Islamic states, and their allies, can successfully bloc Israeli participation in governing institutions and can gain support for anti-Israel resolutions and actions. If the IAEA is a central player in monitoring the cut-off, or a similar institution is created, this will not inspire confidence in Israel, or lead to a willingness to take major risks. If a cut-off agreement is accompanied by an entirely new institutional structure for verification and enforcement, in which Israel has the same rights as other states, and which is immune to the political manipulation that has characterized the IAEA, the Israeli view may be more favourable.

Global versus Regional Approaches

Beyond the direct implications of the CTBT and cut-off, these initiatives are designed to strengthen the NPT-based global non-proliferation regime. However, for Israel, this global regime and the international organizations that are central to its operations are problematic. Reflecting the importance of this issue, Freier notes that 'Israel is especially wary of initiatives and interferences by international organizations. These lift preferred issues out of context and pass resolutions by majority votes...'.[41] The creation of new global institutions, or granting of new powers to existing ones, such as the IAEA, is anathema to Israeli national interest.

As a result, since the 1970s, Israeli policy-makers have favoured regional approaches to arms control and non-proliferation, and the government has supported the development of a Middle East Nuclear-Weapon-Free Zone (MENWFZ).[42] Regional agreements and regimes can be tailored to local conditions and requirements, and verification procedures would be based on mutual and direct inspections by each of the parties. In addition, a regional framework would be able to encompass limits on both conventional and non-conventional capabilities, in contrast to the global regime.[43]

Following the 1991 Madrid conference and the beginning of the Arab–Israel peace negotiations, Israel and a number of Arab states have participated in the multilateral negotiations on Arms Control and Regional Security (ACRS). In addition to bi-annual plenaries, the ACRS process includes frequent intersessional activities, workshops, and demonstration projects. These meetings focus on a wide range of issues, including confidence and security building measures (CSBMs) and verification (for limitations on conventional as well as non-conventional weapons).

The ACRS, in which arms control is linked directly to progress in the overall peace process and to Israeli national security, has become the focus of Israeli arms control policy.[44] In contrast, the proposed CTBT and fissile material production cut-off are part of and designed to strengthen the global regime and the NPT system, and are not linked to the ACRS agenda.

As Israeli policy-makers seek to shift the focus of activity from the global regime to regional frameworks, these new global initiatives are steps in the wrong direction. From an Israeli perspective, the benefits of a CTBT and fissile-material cut-off will be minimal, the costs, at least for the cut-off, will be high, and the overall thrust of both is misdirected. Although forced to respond to these initiatives by external political considerations, that have more to do with maintaining good relations with the United States and other powers than with the substance, the primary hope for Middle East arms control lies in the negotiation of regional measures. Such measures, under discussion in the ACRS, are not focused exclusively on nuclear weapons or any other isolated issues, and can encompass the broad security concerns that are essential to any effective arms limitation regime. Thus, whatever the outcome of the NPT Review Conference, and the CTBT and cut-off negotiations, the major direction for Middle East arms control will continue to be towards development of regional regimes.

NOTES

1. For an overview of regime theory, see Robert Jervis, 'Security regimes', *International Organization,* 36 (Spring 1982), pp.357–78; Charles Lipson, 'International Cooperation in Economic and Security Affairs', *World Politics,* 37 (Oct. 1984), pp.1–23; and Janice Gross Stein, 'Detection and Defection: Security "Regimes" and the Assessment of International Conflict', *International Journal,* Vol.40, No.4 (Autumn 1985), pp.599–627. For an application of regime theory in arms control, see Gerald M. Steinberg, 'US Non-proliferation Policy', *Contemporary Security Policy,* Volume 15, No. 3 (Dec. 1994).
2. The limitation of the nuclear option as a 'weapon of last resort' is widely recognized, even by critics of Israeli policy. For example, Bundy, Crowe and Drell note that, 'the underlying motivation for the Israeli bomb is clearly the reality of vastly outnumbering unfriendly neighbors. The fact that the Israeli bomb is not for casual use is evident both in the desperate conventional battles that have been fought without its use and in the intense Israeli commitment to conventional strength.' McGeorge Bundy, William J. Crowe Jr. and Sidney D. Drell, *Reducing Nuclear Danger: The Road Away from the Brink* (New York: Council on Foreign Relations Press, 1993), p.84.
3. Shalheveth Freier, 'A Nuclear-Weapon-Free Zone (NWFZ) in the Middle East and its Ambience', unpublished manuscript (revised 14 July 1993).
4. Freier, ibid.
5. The exclusion of Israel from the decision-making process is inconsistent with the assumption that in international security regimes decisions are collective and all participants play a role in creating norms and rules of behaviour. See Stein, 'Detection and Defection: Security "Regimes" and the Assessment of International Conflict,' p.604.
6. See, for example, Bundy, Crowe and Drell, *Reducing Nuclear Danger: The Road Away from the Brink.*
7. Yitzhak Rabin reports that in 1965, the US first sought to make the supply of conventional weapons conditional on Israeli nuclear restraint. Similarly, in 1968, the US sought to link the supply of F-4 combat aircraft to an Israeli agreement to resume American inspection of all

military research and development installations. The implication is that the primary focus of the American demand was the nuclear installation in Dimona. See Rabin, *Pinkas Sherut* [Hebrew] (Tel Aviv: Ma'ariv), pp.129, 236–43.

8. Bundy *et al., Reducing Nuclear Danger,* p.67. A similar option is considered and rejected by Molander and Wilson, who note that such a policy would stimulate the nuclear programmes of the Arab states and Iran. Roger C. Molander and Peter A. Wilson, 'The Nuclear Asymptote: On Containing Nuclear Proliferation' (Santa Monica: RAND/UCLA Center for Soviet Studies, 1993), pp.42–5.

9. George Bunn and Roland M. Timerbaev, 'Security Assurances to Non-Nuclear-Weapon States', *The Nonproliferation Review,* Vol. 1, No. 1 (Fall 1993).

10. George H. Quester and Victor A. Utgoff, 'No-First-Use and Nonproliferation: Redefining Extended Deterrence', *Washington Quarterly,* Vol. 1, No.2 (Spring 1994), pp.103–14.

11. Dore Gold, *US Forces on the Golan Heights and Israeli-Syrian Security Arrangements* Memorandum no. 14, Jaffee Center for Strategic Studies, Tel Aviv University, August 1994.

12. George H. Quester and Victor A. Utgoff, 'U.S. Arms Reductions and Nuclear Nonproliferation: The Counterproductive Possibilities', *The Washington Quarterly* (Winter 1993), p.131.

13. The Israeli government initially endorsed the concept of a MENWFZ in the 1970s, but this was considered a very distant and unrealistic goal under the conditions that existed at that time. With the peace process and the meetings of the working group on arms control and regional security, the importance of the MENWFZ has grown. See Israeli Foreign Minister Shimon Peres, Address at the Signing Ceremony of the Chemical Weapons Convention Treaty, Paris, 13 Jan. 1993. For a detailed history of Israeli policy, see Daniel Mustacchi, *Can a Nuclear-Weapon-Free Zone be Established in the Middle East? If so, under what conditions?* (MA Thesis, Department of International Relations, Hebrew University, Jerusalem, 1992).

14. In 1974, the US and Soviet Union agreed on the Threshold Test Ban Treaty, setting a limit of 150 kilotons on underground tests, but ratification was blocked by the absence of reliable verification techniques.

15. The French position is that universal acceptance of the NPT must precede the CTBT, for as long as small states and regional powers are able to acquire nuclear weapons, France must be able to expand its arsenal in order to stay ahead. Policy-makers argue that only when the nuclear efforts of other states are frozen will France be able to halt its own nuclear programme.

16. For a counterview, see Donald G. Boudreau, 'On Advancing Non-Proliferation' in *Strategic Review,* Vol.19, No.3 (Summer 1991), pp.66–7. Boudreau rejects the 'unproven nexus between testing and proliferation'.

17. For a strong presentation of this case, see Bundy *et al., Reducing Nuclear Danger,* and *SIPRI Yearbook 1990: World Armaments and Disarmament* (Oxford: Oxford University Press, 1990), p.548.

18. *Nuclear Proliferation News,* Vol. 94, No.5, 10 June 1994.

19. An August 1993 proposal submitted by Australian Ambassador Paul O'Sullivan to admit an additional 23 states, including Israel, was blocked by US, since this would also have admitted Iraq. In subsequent discussions, Iran has opposed admission of Israel. The US and Russia have indicated a preference for keeping membership limited in order to avoid creation of procedural problems resulting from a much larger group of participants. It should be noted that the CD operates by consensus, so that additional participants could complicate decision making. See *Nuclear Proliferation News,* Vol. 94, Nos.1 to 8, 1994.

20. Statement by Ambassador Itzhak Lior to the Conference on Disarmament, 2 June 1994.

21. Ibid.

22. In 1979, US early warning satellites detected a 'mysterious flash' in the South Atlantic near South Africa. This has often been attributed to a joint Israeli–South African nuclear test, but no evidence of this has ever surfaced, and the technical information does not indicate that the signal was caused by a nuclear explosion.

23. Ibid.

24. *Arms Transfer News,* Special Issue, 18 March 1994.

25. Ambassador Itzhak Lior, 2 June 1994.
26. Cited by Harold A. Feiveson, 'A Cut-Off in the Production of Fissile Material', in *Strengthening the Non-Proliferation regime: 1995 and Beyond* (Oxford Research Group, Current Decisions Report Number 13, Oxford, 1993), p.35. Feiveson notes that three Russian production reactors were still operating in 1994.
27. United Nations General Assembly Resolution 48/75L, 16 Dec. 1993.
28. Tariq Rauf in 'Should the NPT be Extended Indefinitely?: A Panel Discussion on Nuclear Non-Proliferation: The Challenges of a New Era', Carnegie Endowment for International Peace, Washington DC, 17-18 Nov. 1993, p.42–4.
29. Paul L. Leventhal, 'Plugging the Leaks in Nuclear Export Controls: Why Bother?' in *Orbis* Vol. 36, No.2 (Spring 1992), pp.174–5.
30. Rauf, pp.28–49.
31. *Nuclear Proliferation News,* 15 April 1994.
32. Gerald E. Shannon, Ambassador and Permanent Representative of Canada, 'Report of the Special Co-ordinator on Cut-Off to the Conference on Disarmament', Geneva, 4 Aug. 1994.
33. *Nuclear Proliferation News,* Vol.94, Issue 11, 16 Sept. 1994, p.2.
34. Feiveson, 'A Cut-Off in the Production of Fissile Material', p.35
35. *Ha'aretz,* 5 Oct. 1993, p.1.
36. Aluf Ben, 'Conflict in Israel regarding the Clinton Initiative to Freeze Plutonium Production', *Ha'aretz,* 28 Dec. 1993, p.1 [Hebrew].
37. Avner Cohen and Marvin Miller, ' How To Think About – And Implement – Nuclear Arms Control in the Middle East', *The Washington Quarterly,* Vol. 16, No.2 (Spring, 1993).
38. The have been a number of reports of minor radioactive leaks at the Dimona reactor, and the Israeli press has published allegations that cancer rates among Dimona are higher than the national average. Such problems are not deemed sufficient to lead to pressure to shutdown the reactor, or to provide a reasons for acceptance of a fissile material cut-off agreement. See *Ha'aretz,* 11 Jan. 1994; and *Ma'ariv,* 29 April 1994 (Musaf Shabbat, pp.2–4).
39. Cohen and Miller, p.110.
40. *Ha'aretz,* 18 May1993.
41. Freier, 'A Nuclear-Weapon-Free Zone'.
42. See Avi Beker, 'A Regional Non-Proliferation Treaty for the Middle East', *Security or Armageddon: Israel's Nuclear Strategy* (Lexington, Ma: Lexington Books, 1985).
43. See Gerald Steinberg, 'US Non-proliferation Policy', *Contemporary Security Policy,* Vol.15, No.3 (Dec. 1994).
44. Gerald M. Steinberg, 'Arms Control and Regional Security in the Middle East', *Survival,* Vol. 36, No. 1 (Spring 1994), pp.126–41.

Towards Understanding
Chemical Warfare Weapons Proliferation[1]

JEAN PASCAL ZANDERS

Introduction

Chemical warfare weapons (CWW)[2] proliferation began topping the security agenda during the past decade and was, in the words of one analyst, 'rapidly becoming the most serious threat to world peace'.[3] The newly perceived threat led to an explosion of learned and not-so-learned analyses. Yet, virtually nobody deemed it necessary to define what actually constitutes CWW proliferation. Such an observation is even more striking because these authors discuss the attraction of CWW under certain circumstances as well as the number and identity of states suggested by officials based on classified, and therefore essentially unverifiable, information. Moreover, they often propose policy alternatives to counter the developing threat. Must we therefore assume a common understanding or consensus of what proliferation is? The debate originated and evolved in a highly ideologized environment of growing political pressure as well as heavy opposition in the United States to resume CWW production. East–West relations had deteriorated significantly. US allegations of chemical and biological warfare (CBW) activities by the Soviet Union and its client states were either taken as proof of wilful Soviet deceit in international relations and disarmament negotiations or met with considerable scepticism. The coincidence of US allegations of CBW in Third World conflicts and the domestic debate to begin the production of binary chemical munitions was not lost on Europe either, resulting in much suspicion regarding Washington's agenda.[4] It is hardly conceivable that such a climate of opposing views could nurture any common understanding of the proliferation phenomenon.

Yet such an assumption appears to exist. CWW proliferation is usually understood to be a flow of precursor chemicals, high technology and expertise from North to South, from industrial to industrializing countries. The notion describes a lateral spread from one area to another, affecting new areas at an increasing speed.[5] Set in these terms, the word 'proliferation' is entirely consistent with dictionary definitions. The 1968 Nuclear Non-

Proliferation Treaty (NPT) demarcated the semantic field in international relations and security. Articles I and II defined the direction of the proliferation flow: from possessor states to non-possessor states. The preamble attached the negative connotation absent in dictionary definitions by stating that the proliferation of nuclear weapons 'would seriously enhance the danger of nuclear war' and therefore posed a serious risk to international security in general. Developing countries later complained that the nuclear powers displayed no serious intent to disarm as required by the NPT while they had to forswear the acquisition of such weapons and only had very conditional access to nuclear technology. This contributed to the further conceptual narrowing down of the direction of the flow from industrial to industrializing countries, from North to South. The rational has since been extended by the Missile Technology Control Regime (MTCR) which explicitly wishes 'to limit the risks of nuclear proliferation by controlling transfers that could make a contribution to nuclear weapons delivery systems other than manned aircraft'. A US statement of 16 April 1987 announcing the agreement stressed that 'adherence of all states to these guidelines [is] in the interest of international peace and security'.[6]

The notions and concepts from the NPT have been transposed to the CWW proliferation debate without much critical appraisal as to whether the two processes are in fact comparable. This conceptual leap is clear from the ways in which Western governments have imposed export controls on key chemical compounds from 1984 onwards, gradually expanding the list, and later extending the restrictions to dual-use technology and even materials required for biological weapons programmes. In 1985, some industrialized countries also organized themselves into a suppliers' club, the so-called Australia Group. Despite some initial efforts towards modelling it after the London Nuclear Suppliers' Group (NSG),[7] the Australia Group has remained an informal consulting and co-ordinating platform whose members had to enact new legislation individually. This policy choice to stem the spread of chemical weaponry in analogy with CoCom and NSG export controls carries a strong suggestion that the processes involved are similar. But, are they?

The present paper argues that if CWW is viewed as a lateral spread, then different moments in the CW history will reveal different processes, different actors, different political motives, and different policy choices. Today's predominantly supply-side discussion of the phenomenon explains much of its perception. Proposed policy options to counter the threat – essentially self-imposed restrictions on the supply – confirm the existing analytical bias and actually contribute to reinforcing threat perceptions emanating from proliferation. An alternate approach focusing on the demand side allows to define proliferation as a domestic armament dynamic in which the importation of strategic commodities is but one way for a country to build up an unconventional capability. Such a definition brings the debate within the scope of existing theories regarding international relations and armament dynamics, thus demystifying proliferation as a novel or different threat. Moreover, it will bridge the conceptual gap between the policy goals of anti-proliferation and disarmament regimes. The Chemical Weapons Convention (CWC) can certainly be portrayed as aiming at deproliferation.

CWW Proliferation as a Security Issue

CWW proliferation as it is discussed today is the outcome of more than two decades of issue creation. The spectre was first raised shortly after the signing of the Nuclear Non-Proliferation Treaty (NPT) as part of the opposition to the American use of chemical herbicides in South-East Asia.[8] Interestingly, speculation about nuclear weapons proliferation was also started by 'outsiders' after Hiroshima, although there was an immediate clear distinction between those who viewed the developments in apocalyptical terms and those who envisaged a desired stable situation based on mutual deterrence in a world of nuclear powers.[9] It thus seems that the present debates on proliferation originated from a major event that prompted intellectual polemic even before the development took place or policy makers and other 'insiders' decided that it was a security issue. The debate's origin was instrumental to its further development. The original dichotomy in the nuclear discussion helps to explain why as late as the early 1980s nuclear proliferation could still be advanced as beneficial to world security[10] and why a decade later the ideological and theoretical polemic still rages on.[11] The NPT nonetheless framed the chemical and biological weapons proliferation debate: the spread was undesirable. Consequently, to our knowledge, no author – barring one exception[12] – has advocated the spread of CWW.[13]

During the 1970s a new dimension was added to the CWW proliferation debate. From within the US military establishment some were acting to reverse President Nixon's decision to halt CWW production. They developed multiple thrusts, three of which have a direct bearing on the present discussion. On the one hand, they claimed that the USSR was attaching growing importance to military operations in a chemically contaminated environment following the discovery that Soviet-made tanks captured during the 1973 Yom Kippur war had overpressurized crew cabins. Distrust was to rise as détente was crumbling. On the other hand, there were an increasing number of claims that Soviet proxies in the developing world, including Vietnam, Ethiopia and Angola, had obtained toxic substances from the Soviet Union and were actually using them. Even the Soviet Union itself was reported to have employed CW agents in Afghanistan. Whatever the veracity of these reports, they served those who had a vested institutional interest in renewed American CWW production well. Finally, the Reagan administration's great preoccupation with terrorism inevitably lead to scenarios in which subnational groups or individuals could pose a direct threat to US interests at home and abroad.[14] In fact, this was but a variation on a theme developed by Matthew Meselson in his Congressional testimonies between 1969 and 1971.[15] He then expressed fear that American troops in South-East Asia would be exposed to great peril if their continued use of CW agents would lead to less-sophisticated forces or guerrilla fighters acquiring and employing such weapons against them. Using the same incident to argue opposite views was not an uncommon phenomenon. Indeed, by the time the United Nations conclusively demonstrated that CW was an integral part of the Iran–Iraq War, both proponents and opponents of America's chemical rearmament programme had added proliferation-threat scenarios to their list of arguments. In essence, both groups departed from fundamentally different basic assumptions. Advocates of CW rearmament programmes believed – for ideological rather than factual reasons – that the Soviet Union and its client states were engaging in CW and concluded that they were weakening international constraints, a development that the West had to deter.[16] Opponents, on the other hand, questioned the validity of the allegations and feared that Western rearmament would lead to proliferation into regions as yet free of such weapons. They placed much greater faith in disarmament negotiations to avert the threat. Even if the allegations were true, a speedy conclusion of an international disarmament treaty would be a better safeguard against the erosion of international constraints than yet another arms race.[17]

The confirmation in 1984 of Iraq's systematic chemical attacks firmly established CWW proliferation as a separate security issue that required specific policy decisions not only in the USA, but also in other Western countries and even in the CMEA member states. Taking the precedent of the NPT, export controls – first on chemicals, later on dual-use technology, and most recently on components necessary for biological warfare (BW) – were the instruments of choice. The need for international co-ordination led to several Western industrial countries organizing themselves in what would later be known as the Australia Group. Within that framework they have since 1985 exchanged intelligence regarding actual and potential proliferators and suggested legislative measures. The deliberations remained informal so that each individual participating country still had to draft and enact the export controls, or indeed, retained the freedom to take no action. The major problems with such an arrangement are of course the limited number of participating countries and the virtual absence of representatives of the developing world. Moreover, as the considerable German involvement in the construction of a Libyan CWW production plant near Rabta and general Western embroilment in Iraq's chemical and biological programmes have shown, participation in the Australia Group does not exclude the possibility of Western industrialized countries playing an important role in CWW programmes of other states.

The Gulf War and the subsequent UNSCOM inspections amplified concerns regarding industrializing countries' advanced armament programmes. These have propelled missiles to the forefront of threats. Before the Kuwait crisis, the MTCR primarily wanted to deny countries with nuclear ambitions or capability advanced delivery means. The United States and some Western allies at best viewed it as an extra instrument for strengthening the nuclear non-proliferation regime. Countries only seeking an advanced conventional, chemical, or biological capacity, however, were technically legitimate purchasers of such technology according to the MTCR guidelines.[18] In unstable regions, such as the Middle East, advanced missile systems were viewed as promoting crisis instability because their enhanced counterforce and countervalue properties invited pre-emptive strikes. Moreover, the extending ranges of missiles risked expanding the geographic boundaries of any future conflict.[19] The petering out of the Cold War focused attention on so-called out-of-area threats to Europe and the USA. Besides terrorists, missiles were the only instruments of war that could strike at the Western heartlands. The demise of the Warsaw Treaty Organisation (WTO) and the Gulf War, as well as the ensuing shift of threat perceptions influenced both the content and the nature of the proliferation debate. The means of delivery had become just as threatening as the payload.

The non-use of CWW during Desert Storm appeared to have sealed their fate as totally obsolete in the face of modern technology. They became an adjunct to the ballistic missile threat. However, mated to missiles – especially after UNSCOM inspectors' confirmation that Iraq had constructed crude chemical warheads for the Al-Husseyn missile – CWW found a new lease of life as a weapon with high strategic potential. The images of the Israelis sheltering in their safe room every time the sirens wailed added credibility to such a vision.

At this point, the threat assessments of missiles with chemical payloads split in diametrically opposing views. Analysts working mainly on CW matters argue that the combination is fairly ineffective and probably holds its greatest value as a weapon of terror as long as it is not used. They add that conventional warheads would produce higher casualty rates especially if the attacked had provided chemical defences for the civilian population.[20]

Others defining missile proliferation as the central issue allocate a high strategic value to the combination with chemical warheads. Their conclusions can be very leading. Steve Fetter, in an article in *International Security*, concluded that 'it should not be surprising if the future of missile proliferation points in the direction of chemical and biological weaponry, since for many states these are the only weapons that could constitute a strategic threat or a strategic deterrent'.[21] With such a new line of reasoning it comes as little surprise that in the past two years a country such as Saudi Arabia suddenly features on the list of CWW proliferators.[22]

It is fair to state that at present the impact of analyses departing from missile proliferation is dominant. Perceptions in West Europe and the United States enhance it. Since the demise of the Soviet Union, NATO and the WEU are alliances in search of a threat. The only possible direct threat to the West can come from missiles or terrorists and both are currently seen as important vectors for chemical and biological warfare agents.[23] In other words, a large-scale CBW threat can only come from hostile developing countries with a sophisticated missile capability. However, given these countries' current technological abilities, missiles act as threat multipliers – euphemistically called 'force multipliers' – serving the institutional interests of some.

Different Times, Different Meanings

Military thinking on CW after the Second World War underwent the impact of the advent of the atomic bomb and when a CWW proliferation threat was perceived to emerge the debate did not escape the influence of the NPT discussion. However, modern CW predates the first nuclear explosion by three decades. Nations had to deal with the threat both in times of war and peace. If the general assumption of CWW proliferation, namely the lateral spread of precursor chemicals, technology, and expertise from possessor states to non-possessors, is applied to different eras in the history of CW, then some divergent underlying mechanisms emerge.

Historically, the development of chemical and nuclear armament was fundamentally different. Whereas early German and American research into nuclear energy was driven by the quest for the atomic bomb, modern CW agents were rather a derivative of a 100-year development in the chemical industry. Poisonous weapons are known to have been used since antiquity and novel strategies to exploit the toxic characteristics of some compounds were proposed at different times, especially when defences and fortifications posed a challenge to existing weaponry. CW as it is understood today, however, is a typical product of the second industrial revolution which originated from an increasingly utilitarian application of scientific principles driven by an economic rationale during the second half of the previous century. The foundations for this revolution were laid more or less simultaneously in several countries, including Great Britain, France, Germany and the United States, that then already belonged to the industrial centre. Some of the compounds that were to become notorious during the First World War had been discovered over a century earlier.[24] The real challenge was their production on an industrial scale once their utility in other processes had been established, a capability only achieved towards the end of the nineteenth century.[25] For diverse reasons – including access to overseas raw materials and the search for alternatives – the chemical industry developed at markedly different rates in those countries.

It comes as little surprise that new thoughts about military application of novel toxic compounds emerged in those countries with a fledgling chemical industry. Two British officers floated such ideas at different times in the last century.[26] The presentation of deadly gases as high-technology weaponry in many military science-fiction novels in different countries around the turn of the century – for instance, H. G. Wells' *The War of the Worlds* – reflected the chemical industry's growing impact on societies. Such developments occurred relatively independently in the different countries. The then theoretical possibility of employing novel toxic substances as a potentially decisive weapon of war, as well as past experiences, must have caused sufficient alarm for the powers to include prohibitions against such use in several international treaties and draft treaties.[27]

The First World War would of course prove to be the real stimulus for focused military-oriented research into chemical compounds with the prime purpose of exploiting their poisonous characteristics against humans or their habitat. However, it cannot be excluded that without the Great War there would have been no advancement towards CW capabilities. The French had tear-gas cartridges for riot control on the eve of the hostilities.[28] Gas defences also initially benefited from prior experiences in mining and the civilian industry, although the different conditions of CW would lead to a specific gas mask development process.

This brief overview shows that military considerations played little if any role in the development of chemistry and the chemical industry. Throughout the nineteenth century and the first years of the twentieth century scientific knowledge spread to a certain extent among the most advanced nations. It is less likely, however, that information about industrial production processes permeated the frontiers on any significant scale given the great rivalries between the leading powers and protectionist economic policies. Consequently, on the eve of the First World War some important preconditions for CW were present in the industrialized countries, although some marked differences in technological advancement and industrial expansion existed between the rival powers. Once those countries at the threshold of a CW capability moved to establish a research and production base dedicated to purposefully acquiring such weaponry and erected a bureaucracy and decision-making procedures with as prime purpose organizing CW employment and defence, proliferation began. Reviewing the history of modern CW, three generations of CWW proliferation can be distinguished (see Table 1).[29]

Characteristic of 'first generation proliferation' is direct and conscious governmental involvement in the dealings. The spread of CW capabilities must therefore be considered as an integral part of a government's foreign and security policy. As a consequence of the First World War, which involved the countries in the industrial centre, the proliferation process began immediately after the first large-scale German chlorine attack of 22 April 1915. The exchange of production capacity regarding chlorine and phosgene between respectively Great Britain and France was essential to their early CW efforts.[30] The pre-war commercial and industrial utility of the compounds under consideration for offensive CW meant that private firms initially played an important role in the Allied drive for retaliation. However, governmental and military bureaucracies almost instantly took over organizational control over the CW venture and, after the war, established a specialized research and production base under their authority.[31] During the last two war years when production capacity could finally meet military requirements, France and Britain were able to sell gas munitions to smaller powers such as Belgium to assist in its building-up of a retaliatory and later offensive capability. Such a capability can also be acquired or augmented if authorities decide to incorporate captured enemy dumps into their arsenals. Large sections on the use of German *T-Stoff* shells in Belgian field manuals of the time testify to such occurrences.[32] The spread of CW defences and the results of research and development followed similar patterns. Countries that lacked the ability to produce gas masks domestically or at short notice, such as Belgium and the United States, obtained them from France and Great Britain. Information and data on CW offense and defence were regularly transmitted to the Allies. Military and civilian representatives attended important field trials and both scientists, military specialists, and bureaucrats produced huge volumes of reports on CW which they sometimes shared at Allied conferences or on other occasions.

After the Armistice, a variation of these proliferation patterns occurred. On the one hand, the countries in the industrial centre transferred the production capacity to their immediate periphery. An example was the reported French delivery of an entire filling facility for CW agents to

TABLE 1

HISTORY OF CWW PROLIFERATION VIEWED AS A LATERAL SPREAD

1.	Emergence of a chemical industrial base in the centre	
2.	CWW proliferation within the centre	**1st Generation**
	⇨ Exchange of production capacity, knowledge, etc.	
	⇨ Direct sales or transfers of munition to other governments	
3.	CWW proliferation to the periphery	
	⇨ Transfer of production capacity to countries in the immediate periphery	
	⇨ Transfer of CWW to the colonies for use by the colonial powers	
4.	CWW proliferation in the periphery	**2nd Generation**
	⇨ Reproduction of the industrial base in the periphery	
	⇨ Trivialisation of technology	
5.	CWW proliferation within the periphery	**3rd Generation**

Melilla in Spanish Morocco before 1921.[33] France, however, refused to sell state-of-the-art agents such as mustard gas, for which Spain eventually turned to Germany. Dr Stoltenberg, who led his private company and whom the Allies had instructed to destroy German chemical munition, headed in close collaboration with the German military and diplomatic corps the enterprise to build the Fabrica Nacional de Productos Quimicos at La Marañosa near Madrid. The Germans reportedly had to provide skilled labour for the construction of the large-scale plant.[34] Such a venture was undertaken despite the Versailles Treaty and could not have escaped the notice of the French and the British. The interesting part to the story is that both Allies let the Germans carry on because it served their respective interests in their rivalries over colonies in Africa.[35] The episode foreshadowed Western acquiescence in Iraq's chemical attacks against Iran.

Spain was but one country in whose CW armament drive Germany was involved. From 1923 onwards, Germany exported technology, components and provided assistance to Italy, Yugoslavia, Turkey, Sweden, and countries as far away as Brazil, China and Japan. One of the largest collaborative efforts was with the Soviet Union, which allowed both countries to develop a domestic CW capability. The illicitness of Germany's actions resided solely in articles 170 and 171 of the Versailles Treaty, not in any particular prohibition on CW armament or a generally accepted norm against such activities. Both articles not only forbade CWW manufacture in Germany, but also their importation. Moreover, Article 171 distinguished explicitly between CW agents and their delivery means on the one hand, and the materials necessary for their production and storage on the other. The Allied victors deemed any reference to exportation unnecessary presumably because the article's basic objective – a comprehensive production ban – precluded such a probability.

The drafters of the Versailles Treaty of course had no intention of establishing a CWW non-proliferation regime. It was a condition imposed on the vanquished and did not affect the victors. Among Allied and neutral countries, such trading was apparently perfectly legal. Belgium, having declared itself neutral again, sought a limited CW capability in the 1930s and bought the thiodiglycol for mustard gas production from the French government. Moreover, some European powers may have promoted the proliferation of CWW among allies and neutral countries as part of a European security framework. Balancing the CW threat rather than dispensing with it was a major motive underlying the 1925 Geneva Protocol. When it became apparent that the League of Nations' conference 'for the supervision of the international trade in arms and ammunition and in implements of war' was heading for failure, a US proposal to prohibit all international trade in toxic weapons was rejected on grounds that it would discriminate against states unable to manufacture toxic weapons of their own.[36] The conference ultimately compromised over a ban on their use. Interestingly, during these negotiations in the late spring of 1925 France was aiding Spain's CW effort in its Moroccan war. Both countries were participants at the League of Nations' conference and eventually signed the Geneva Protocol.[37] The formal argument in favour of proliferation may therefore have legitimized an ongoing process or safeguarded particular economic interests.

Italy's colonial war in Abyssinia in 1935–36 points to a final variant of first generation CWW proliferation to the periphery: the introduction of CWW into the colonies and possible abandonment by the colonial power. After the First World War, gas was believed by some to be an effective weapon to control inaccessible rebellious territories. The British, for example, used or had gas at their disposal in Mesopotamia, Afghanistan and India. The Netherlands manufactured a mustard agent at Batujajar near Bandung on West Java in 1940 and 1941.[38] There are few indications that these powers left militarily significant stocks behind which were later incorporated in the arsenals of the independent country's armed forces. However, to our knowledge, no research has focused on whether peoples that were once subjected to chemical threats or attacks by their colonial rulers are today more open to acquire a CW capability. During the Yemen civil war in the sixties, the Egyptians reportedly used CWW retrieved from British stocks abandoned after the Second World War.[39]

Aspects of first generation proliferation have continued until today. For instance, the Canadian, British and US chemical warfare establishments, who had worked closely together during the Second World War, formalized their collaboration in the so-called Tripartite Agreement of 1947. This joint effort on offence and defence continued until the early 1990s.[40] The licensing by the US Department of State's Office of Munitions Control of export applications for tear gas guns, grenades, launchers, and launching cartridges to Israel is just one example of continuous first generation-like transfers, which happened to be noticed because of the Israeli Defence Force's (IDF) employment of CS during the *intifada*.[41]

'Second generation CWW' proliferation is the phenomenon of much of today's debate. Private companies rather than governments act as suppliers not of ready-to-fire chemical munitions or complete production and filling plants but of individual components, technology, and expertise. Most of those transactions were initially not illegal. However, after the UN confirmed Iraq's use of CW agents, Western governments began enacting legislation to prevent their nationals from participating in other countries' CW armament programmes. This led to the establishment of complex international networks to conceal the true nature of the transactions and circumvent export controls. On the one hand, supplying companies subcontracted other firms for specific parts of the project thus hiding their true purpose and set up false companies abroad as shipping addresses to fool customs. On the other, the proliferating country placed its orders with companies in different countries to limit the number of people fully aware of the regime's true intent. Reconstruction of the network Libya had set up for building its factory at Rabta showed that it sought expertise and technology from companies all over the world.[42]

The Japanese Steel Works (Nihon Seijo) supplied lathes and air guns for an equipment factory, and Toshiba an electrical power station in the belief the Libyans were constructing a desalination plant. VEB Stahlbau Plauen from the former German Democratic Republic furnished steel constructions. A computer was obtained from the Florida-based Harris Company. Thyssen and Karl Kolb, two West German firms at the time already being investigated for their part in Iraq's chemical warfare programme, also participated. Imhausen Chemie, however, played the pivotal role for installing the actual production system. It placed important orders with other firms that were apparently unaware of the final destination. Salzgitter Industriebau GmbH – a state-owned enterprise – initially denied having drawn up the plans for Rabta, but admitted to having delivered pipes and electrical equipment for a pharmaceutical production unit between 1984 and 1987. Imhausen had ordered the equipment for a subsidiary in Hong Kong. Later it emerged both companies had held several meetings, discussing the constructions in Libya. Teves GmbH, a subsidiary of the American multinational ITT that had supplied cooling equipment, also claimed Hong Kong was the final destination. So did many other firms involved.

In fact, Imhausen had set up a double project in Hong Kong and Rabta, both called Pharma 150. The German company actually built a factory on the Yeun Long Industrial Estate in Hong Kong, although it only served as a cover for other activities. An early important indication that the Rabta plant was indeed a chemical weapons production site followed from the declaration by the Frankfurt based company John Zink that it had exported an incinerator for superfluous gases ordered by Ishan Barbouti International Engineering to Hong Kong. Ishan Barbouti, who appeared to have close ties with Colonel Gaddafi, owned branches in most industrial countries, which were often nothing but letter box addresses. Between 1985 and 1987, Barbouti placed large orders with several German building companies, whose representatives were convinced these were intended for metal works. The materials were shipped to Rabta over Rotterdam and Antwerp. Especially in Belgium, weak transit regulations meant that Imhausen and its associates could easily defeat German customs by involving Antwerp-based shippers. Subsequent court cases in Germany have established that some companies were not aware of the true destination or purpose of the orders. Despite all the international attention drawn to the Rabta plant in 1989 and 1990, which according to some reports forced Tripoli to make the installation look more like a civilian pharmaceutical plant and at one point was said to have been destroyed by a mysterious fire,[43] efforts to construct another CW production facility at Tarhunah, 65 kilometres south-east of Tripoli, appear to involve non-Western expertise and labour.[44] If true, it suggests that developing countries no longer require major Western assistance for their CW programmes effectively defeating existing export control regimes. Although it attended the 1993 Paris signing ceremony Libya ultimately refrained from signing the CWC there. Analyses of Iraq's CW armament efforts show equally intricate acquisition endeavours.[45]

'Third generation CWW proliferation', finally, describes a process by which countries in the developing world expand their technological, R&D and industrial base into other Third World nations. In other words, the transfer takes place *within* the periphery. The industrialized world is no longer involved and can therefore exert only very limited – if any – control over the development. From a Western viewpoint, this would herald the final defeat of export controls. So far, no firm evidence exists about whether this type of CWW proliferation is occurring in any concerted form. Some transactions to suspected countries, mostly involving the shipment of precursors, have nonetheless surfaced. In one example, the Indian company United Phosphorous shipped 90 tons of trimethyl phosphite – a CWC schedule 3 precursor also figuring on the Australia Group Export Control

List with possible use in G-agent production – to the Setma Limited company in Syria. The first half had reached its destination in May 1992; the second half was intercepted by Cypriot authorities at Germany's request. The Indian company nevertheless declared it would not halt its shipments unless it received firm evidence that it was not used for its stated purpose of pesticide production. Bonn was here able to intervene because the German conveyors had not obtained a German export license, which is required even if they carry cargo from elsewhere.[46] This came two years after another Indian company's delivery of thionyl chloride, a precursor to mustard gas, to Iran using Dubai to avoid attracting international attention.[47] In another case, Singapore seized eight chemical reactor vessels bound for Libya in June 1993, which according to British and US intelligence officials could have been used to mix corrosive nerve agents in the plant at Tarhunah. Tripoli had ordered the reactors from Malaysia. Despite British warnings, Malaysian authorities were not persuaded that they had any military value. The seizure was possible because of the UN embargo on military goods against Libya for its presumed role in the 1988 bombing of the Pan Am airliner over Lockerbie.[48] In two of the cases special circumstances allowed the West to take action. The controversy surrounding the Chinese ship *Yinhe*, allegedly carrying thiodiglycol and thionyl chloride – respectively schedule 2 and 3 precursors to mustard gas – to Iran during the summer of 1993, points to the West's great dependence on accurate intelligence reports and limited scope for action. Washington had no legal basis for inspecting or seizing the vessel. Some countries in the Gulf, notably Bahrain, Kuwait and the UAE, refused *Yinhe* access to their ports because they did not wish to antagonize Iran by co-operating with US inspections. Eventually, Chinese and US assisted Saudi inspectors declared that the ship was not carrying any of the compounds. Although US officials later declared that under the CWC they would have been able to demand a challenge inspection,[49] it remains an intelligence mistake they cannot afford to make too often.[50]

This couple of as yet isolated cases reveal that the supplying states do not participate in existing international consultations to stem the spread of chemical weapons and at best have minimal export regulations, which, in any case, have not been co-ordinated with those of industrialized states. They are also largely immune to external political pressure. Moreover, such orders may constitute an important source of foreign currency, which only increases that country's protection of the trade. During the negotiations, the regimes often displayed much scepticism regarding the CWC for a variety of reasons. Countries such as China, India, Iran and Malaysia signed the convention at the 1993 Paris ceremony. A distinct possibility therefore exists that the new international regime may prove to be the best guarantee against any further nefarious developments.

Analytical Problems

Today's discussion of CWW proliferation as a lateral spread thus essentially deals with second generation patterns. The spectacular nature of new revelations and the preoccupation with strengthening export controls conceal that even in the worst case of US intelligence estimates only about 13 per cent of the world's independent nations are in one way or another *believed* to have engaged in some form of CW armament dynamic. This is still less than the 17 per cent reliably known possessors during the First World War and 19 per cent on the eve of the Second World War, but higher than most of the time since 1945.[51] These comparisons may be misleading because the intelligence reports in the public domain do not define CW capability. Such an approach, moreover, ignores that some nations may have renounced seeking an offensive CW arsenal. In other words, despite an apparently rising trend, the mix of CW capable states may vary at different times.

Second generation differs from first generation proliferation in that the supplying actors are no longer governments pursuing security or other national interests but private companies seeking profits. International security and domestic export-led economic growth together with liberalization of international trade have become national policy goals at odds with each other. Export controls are more or less the only means by which a government can regain some degree of control over transactions that affect its general foreign policy goals. However, one can surmise that to enforce restrictions going against a domestic agenda of job creation and a fundamental ideology of free trading, a government must define a serious threat to the country's national security interests. Reviewing the Imhausen-Rabta case, one can postulate that a right-wing administration advocating market economics must emphasise threat perceptions to legitimise controls,[52] whereas a left-of-centre government favouring more direct state intervention in economic policies can claim moral grounds for such restrictions. Similarly, countries with a global role and an interventionist tradition, such as the USA or the United Kingdom, will be more receptive to arguments about direct external threats, than countries that only see a limited overseas military role for themselves, such as the Federal Republic of Germany.

Thus, in the FRG's export-oriented climate high unemployment statistics during the first half of the 1980s increased pressure on the Federal Government to ease up on arms export restrictions. Budget constraints also led to a sharp decline of domestic orders for weaponry. The strict interpretation of the regulations under Chancellor Brandt during the 1970s was abandoned near the end of Schmidt's tenure in 1982.[53] The German arms industry, which became closely interconnected and thus more powerful and competitive after a series of take-overs, forced Chancellor Kohl to relax export controls even further. It mainly argued for the preservation of jobs and technological progress in key military areas. Federal ministers nevertheless still considered these laws to be very restrictive and in the interest of the West German economy:

> Our position is clear! We shall stick to our restrictive weapons export. This conforms to our historical responsibilities and the ethical foundation of our foreign policy and it conforms to our economic interests. An extensive weapons export policy – which means primarily arms transfers to the Middle East – would harm our international relations and would put jobs in Germany at risk. We are now the prime exporter of civil products to the Middle East. We would lose a part of these markets if we were to go into arms sales.[54]

The statement – made two years before the Rabta controversy came to a head – is illustrative of competing policy priorities in a government. Meanwhile, the Rabta case and UNSCOM inspections in Iraq have enlightened the world on the nature of much of the civil products the FRG has exported to the Middle East – indications of which the Federal Government conveniently chose to ignore for many years despite warnings from intelligence services.[55]

If export controls are but a means for a government to regain some control over a security development that negatively affects other foreign policy goals, then competing domestic priorities, as well as the fact that only a limited number of countries enforce such regulations, will ensure that they ultimately fail. The issue becomes even further complicated if a particular industrial sector succeeds in convincing policy-makers that their activities are in the national interest. In the worst of cases, this may lead to governments simply paying lip service to export controls and make them active actors in the proliferation.[56] Moreover, many developing countries acquire as part of their legitimate industrialization programmes growing levels of autonomous knowledge, expertise and technology. This implies that if such countries also wish to acquire a CW capability they are able to start their development and production processes at increasingly lower levels of specialization. As a direct consequence, the industrialized states will have to submit a growing number of materials and technology to an export licensing system if they wish to retain an equal effect, which in the long term will prove untenable (see Figure 1).

Area 1 contains precursors and key precursors for CW agents, as well as technologies with specific or possible application in their production. The export controls several Western states have enforced are at level E, of which it is hoped that the threshold for specialized applications to manufacture chemical munitions in Third World countries is sufficiently high. However, as a consequence of industrialization and other directly related societal aspects such as schooling, developing countries are able to expand their own industrial and technological base. They thus achieve the ability to develop the more specialized processes and intermediate materials indigenously. Regarding CWW production, this development (Δ D) means that, for example, Third World countries can produce precursors that figure on export control lists domestically and to this end import other chemicals with much broader civil applications in area 2. These chemicals will, moreover, trigger less suspicion in the exporting country because the direct link with an armament programme is less evident. A similar trend is possible with technology and knowledge. If an exporting country wishes to continue countering proliferation with export controls, then it must of necessity shift the threshold to E bringing more goods into the export licensing system. Such a move also broadens the base of the types of commodities a government must subject to export controls. Such a list-based policy will cause three different kinds of practical problem. First, the promulgation of new laws and export regulations only makes sense if the authorities are also prepared to augment the administrative cadres accordingly. The broader the base to be scrutinized, the costlier the implementation of an export control philosophy becomes. For many West European countries such an option runs counter to the imperative necessity to cut public spending, which, again, raises the question of long-term workability of export control policies. Second, such a course would affect a country's trade relations adversely, especially if its direct competitors maintain less stringent restrictions. The trend will therefore be a search for the lowest common denominator among supplier countries. The German chemical industry, for example, repeatedly voiced strong criticism of the strict export regulations enforced after the Rabta case, claiming that companies voluntarily renounced lucrative deals because of them all the while knowing that foreign competitors would fill the order. It therefore preferred common regulations in the EC or OECD context and endorsed the CWC as its entry into force would remove many of the trade barriers it faced.[57] Meanwhile, the Federal government is already considering easing export restrictions under pressure of the deep-cutting recession and cost of unification. In Belgium, on the other hand, comprehensive armaments export legislation cannot be fully implemented because of different economic interests between the Flemish and Walloon regions. Whatever the reasons, the more export controls affect items in area 3 the more widespread

opposition to them from economic sectors will become and delegitimize
non-proliferation policies. Third, many a developing country will perceive
broader export restrictions as a new barrier to its legitimate economic and
industrial development erected by the industrialized world. But, because of
the lesser sophistication of the ingredients a proliferator will need, the range
of potential suppliers from which it can obtain them increases significantly.
And as referred to earlier, the number of states participating in anti-
proliferation forums is limited. The proliferator can also spread its
purchases over more countries so that the indications for a chemical
armaments programme will become more difficult to ascertain.

Supply-side non-proliferation policies determine to a large extent the
manner in which second generation CWW proliferation is perceived. The
focus remains on individual countries, purchasing networks, the role of
suppliers, and export controls, and, as such, distracts from the overall
context in which proliferation is believed to be developing. First, all

FIGURE 1

WIDENING CWW EXPORT CONTROLS

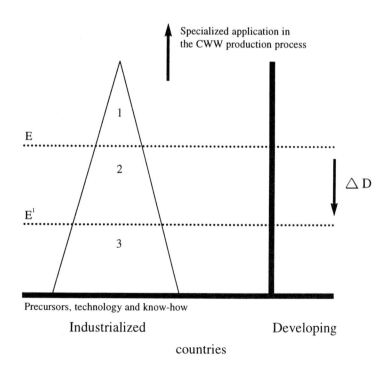

Precursors, technology and know-how

Industrialized   Developing

countries

countries allegedly trying to acquire a CW capability are among the most advanced and richer industrializing nations, an observation that places the description of CWW as the poor man's atomic bomb in perspective. These countries, and many others, have in fact reproduced the industrial and technological preconditions, which, almost eight decades earlier, had allowed the industrial centre to launch CW. In other words, the potential for a CW armament is spreading. However, for those countries in the periphery actually embarking on such a programme, chemical weaponry still represents state-of-the-art military technology requiring a dedicated effort to overcome many obstacles. The importation of technology, expertise, and precursors, which at present accompany such efforts, testifies to this. Thus, the technological barrier may partly explain why so few nations have committed themselves to CW armament. On the other hand, countries which have advanced beyond accomplishments of the second industrial revolution appear far less interested in chemical weaponry. This may explain why most industrialized nations essentially lost interest and why few reports of CWW proliferation in the Asian Pacific rim are available.

Second, the current analytical approach to proliferation ignores the question why in a geopolitical region certain countries move towards a CW capability and others do not. In the Middle East, for instance, why do countries such as Egypt, Iran, Iraq, Israel, Libya and Syria systematically figure on the list of proliferators, whereas others such as Jordan, Kuwait, Qatar, Saudi Arabia and the UAE do not appear to display any interest in CW armament? Each of these countries faces comparable external threats from many directions so that the standard explanation in realist schools of thought is unsatisfactory. At first sight, all countries in the first list, except Israel, experienced revolutions; those in the second are relatively stable conservative monarchies. A regime's need for internal legitimacy through international prestige may therefore be an added incentive to acquire chemical weapons. Another distinguishing characteristic between both groups is the former's fundamental dissatisfaction with the geopolitical status quo, which may be a parameter of a regime's need for either internal or external legitimacy. Further scientific research will have to investigate how such and perhaps other demand-side determinants influence decisions whether to acquire a CW capability.

Second generation proliferation is thus an extremely complex phenomenon, which is still little understood because it is occurring in the present and both the scope and consequences are unclear. Comparison with the first generation, however, reveals some important features. It takes place in the periphery where the industrial base of the centre is being reproduced at a time of increasing trivialization of technology. Within this general context, potential access to a CW capability has broadened and where a regime actually wishes to pursue such military capability, private companies rather than governments act as suppliers. Paradoxically, an offensive CW capability appears to hold the greatest attraction for countries that do not possess the research and development base nor the production capacity, while nations possessing the technology and doing the research seem to have lost interest.[58] This implies that proliferation and deproliferation occur simultaneously.

Defining CWW Proliferation

The notion CWW proliferation may thus refer to different things depending on the time, actors and context. The major question asked today is whether current anti-proliferation measures – mostly national export control legislation – suffice to stem the threat. However, the policy concept defines much of the problem and also suggests a remedy to the exclusion of other insights and options. Export controls consist of restrictions on supply, but do not address demand. Consequently, a whole area of research and insight is being ignored. Yet, most policy-makers and analysts agree that supply-side anti-proliferation measures only buy temporary relief and will ultimately fail. Implicitly, they accept that the lateral spread of CWW is continuous and believe that the Australia Group or a similar body will never be able to found an anti-proliferation regime.

The Chemical Weapons Convention (CWC) is therefore often seen as a panacea. The global disarmament regime commits states to destroy and not to acquire CWW stocks. The new atmosphere of confidence will allow the industrialized world to lift the burdensome export restrictions and industrializing countries will gain virtually unlimited access to chemical compounds and technologies. However, the CWC is not an anti-proliferation treaty and in each of the three generations of CWW proliferation there are certain aspects it does not explicitly address or ignores completely. Without a clear definition of CWW proliferation, both the distinct characteristics of each generation and the manifestation of some elements of past and future mechanisms today could suggest some erroneous conclusions about weaknesses in the convention.

Most of the debate about CWW proliferation conjures up a continuum starting with transfers from industrialized countries to the proliferator, and ending with the latter's acquisition of a CW capability. In some instances, a formal reference is made to a political decision by the proliferating state or the security circumstances in which such a decision has been taken. Without any study in depth of the domestic decision process, the political environment remains static, a condition not normally associated with decision-making. Consequently, no opinion is expressed about the nature of the political environment in which the process evolves. The implication is that once the initial decision has been taken CWW acquisition proceeds along a linear course towards its predetermined end, namely probable – or at least possible – use. Underlying it is an impression of automatism, which, of course, enhances any threat perception already present. Analysis of the US binary weapons programme and the little information available regarding Iraq, however, strongly suggest a far more complex process. The path towards a CWW capability is phased and consequently the outcome of sets of decisions. The question is rather whether these decisions create the political environment or whether they are the result of a reaction to it.

The exclusion of the environment reduces the discussion to fixing the point on the continuum beyond which a state becomes CW capable. Different criteria result in different lists of suspect countries. By projecting proliferation as a continuum, the debate ignores that the recipient country's quest for a CW capability is but an armament dynamic. In the absence of a domestic industrial base, obtaining chemicals, technology and knowledge from abroad is the second best option short of directly buying chemical ammunition. Viewed as such, the importation of these commodities is but one – albeit possibly the fastest – way of structuring the domestic armament dynamic. Proliferation thus deals less with the transfer of these commodities than with the organization of the domestic political and military decision processes and their implementation. We therefore propose the following definition:

CWW proliferation occurs when a political entity decides to acquire a CW capability where such a capability does not yet exist provided this decision is followed by a CWW armament dynamic.

CWW deproliferation occurs as soon as the political commitment to that decision ceases to be renewed or if that political entity explicitly reverses that decision.

The armament dynamic within the proliferating country is the central part of the definition. This opens the way to apply the broad body of theoretical analysis developed over the past decades to the phenomenon. Although the different schools still have to provide a satisfactory overall explanation of the armament process, approaching proliferation in this way has at least two advantages. First, it demystifies the phenomenon as an entirely novel security threat. Although it possesses specific characteristics, it shares many more with armament and decision-making patterns studied in the industrialized world. Second, it breaks with the automatism between the initial decision to acquire a CW capability and the actual deployment or use of such munitions. By introducing deproliferation, it allows for reversals of decisions at any stage in the armament process. Dissenting views and opposing forces always play a role in decision-making. Indeed, insight into the political culture of a nation already goes a long way towards explaining some characteristics central in the current proliferation debate.[59]

Under this definition, the CWC undeniably aims at deproliferation. Accession and ratification constitute an unequivocal decision by a state party possessing or in the process of acquiring chemical weapons to abandon any intent of using, or further developing, producing, and stocking such weapons. Moreover, the fresh international norm the Convention will establish – if successful – may contribute to the deproliferation in non-state parties by weakening political commitments to CW armament programmes. The treaty also prescribes rules of conduct for states parties regarding non-states parties, which, among others, forbid any assistance in a CW armament programme. On the other hand, the CWC wishes to abolish any inequalities inherent in export control systems between member states and to enhance their economic and technological development without any discrimination. It therefore comes as little surprise that the treaty contains numerous references directly or indirectly related to CWW proliferation.

The CWC's confidence in the deproliferation regime is great. By firmly rejecting any hampering of economic and technological development of states parties as well as supporting international co-operation in the field of chemical activities, it stimulates the reproduction of the scientific, technological and industrial preconditions for CW armament programmes. The convention, therefore, does *not* consider the mere presence of the preconditions in a particular country as (part of) a threat to international security. This is the logical outcome of the clear policy decision states parties have made when acceding to the treaty. It is also a prerequisite for treating countries equal with respect to their economic interests under the CWC regime. Such confidence is, of course, the unintended, yet fortunate effect of one of the CWC's balances to overcome developing countries' apprehension that the convention would repeat the NPT's mistakes by enshrining the industrial nations' lead and denying the rest of the world similar development. The convention nonetheless supplements its deproliferation regime with some anti-proliferation measures, for instance, by imposing a strict set of export regulations based on the three schedules of chemicals it defines as part of the verification regime.

Concluding Remarks

CWW proliferation as it is discussed today may in fact refer to different processes and security policies depending on the context. National anti-proliferation measures, whether co-ordinated in an international framework or not, address only that part of the issue that is readily visible to governments in the industrialised countries, namely the transfer of goods, technology, knowledge, and information to regimes in the developing world. However, increased global access to them and the trivialization of technology, as well as competing domestic agendas in the developed world, ensure the failure of such policies.

Self-imposed supply-side restrictions to stem the spread of chemical weaponry are but the outcome of incremental policy-making modelled after the NPT regime. The solution has an important impact on the way the problem is viewed and leads to bean-counting exercises, a prerequisite for legitimizing the export controls in an environment of free trade ideology. The most important consequence is the disregard of motives of certain regimes to acquire chemical weaponry.

The CWC, as a treaty aiming at deproliferation, holds the best promises for reducing chemical threats worldwide by building an environment of confidence and security. Some of the instruments it will employ, apart from verification, are aid and assistance in the area of CW defences and in case of an attack, and equal access to dual-use chemicals and technologies for all states parties. In that sense, the CWC will influence the demand-side with positive incentives.

In the Middle East, the UNSCOM reports on Iraq after its defeat in the Gulf War have conveyed a message of failure of Western export controls rather than one of determination to halt expansionist regimes in their tracks. This has reinforced the belief that self-reliance based on a deterrence doctrine is a better security guarantee than a global disarmament regime. The ambiguity regarding capabilities and intentions inherent in deterrence is a major stumbling block even to achieve a regional security order. A major contribution of the CWC as a deproliferation regime may be breaking this deadlock. Indeed, adherence and ratification by all Middle Eastern states would constitute a great help to global and regional confidence-building, thus paving the way for new security-enhancing initiatives.

NOTES

1. The author wishes to thank Julian Perry Robinson of Sussex University, Nicholas Sims of the London School of Economics and Political Science, and Thomas Stock of the Stockholm International Peace Research Institute (SIPRI) for their constructive comments on an earlier draft of this article
2. The military lexicons of some countries include weapons that work through toxicity as well as items such as smoke and incendiaries under the heading chemical weapons. Chemical warfare weapons refer only to weapons that work through toxicity, thus including the anti-personnel poison-agent weapons, harassing agents (e.g. tear gas) and anti-crop agents (e.g. herbicides). After J.P. Perry Robinson, 'Chemical Weapons Proliferation in the Middle East', in E. Karsh, M.S. Navias and P. Sabin (eds.), *Non-Conventional-Weapons Proliferation in the Middle East: Tackling the Spread of Nuclear, Chemical and Biological Capabilities* (Oxford:

Clarendon Press, 1993), p.69.

3. A.H. Cordesman, 'No End of a Lesson? Iraq and the Issue of Arms Transfer', *RUSI Journal,* Vol.136, No.1 (Spring 1991), p.8.

4. Deployment plans for US binary munition resulted in heated political debates in some European NATO member states, including the Federal Republic of Germany, and almost led to the collapse of the coalition government in Belgium in 1986. J. Badelt, *Chemische Kriegführung - Chemische Abrüstung: Die Bundesrepublik Deutschland und das Pariser Chemiewaffen-übereinkommen* (Berlin: Berlin Verlag, 1994). J.P. Zanders, 'The Debate on Binary Chemical Weapons in Belgium: The Act of 11 April 1962 Revisited', *Vredesonderzoek* 7 (Brussels, Vrije Universiteit Brussel, December 1992). This controversy coincided with other antagonistic US and NATO policies, including the installation of intermediate-range nuclear missiles in Europe, the unilateral adoption of the highly destructive AirLand Battle doctrine by US forces and sustained talk in Washington about winnable limited nuclear war on the European continent.

5. The alarming rate is reflected in the Congressional testimonies of intelligence community officials. During the 1960s seven countries were thought to have an offensive CW capability. The figure doubled in the next decade, increased to over twenty by the end of the 1980s, and was predicted to reach thirty by the end of the century. J.P. Perry Robinson, 'The Supply-Side Control of the Spread of Chemical Weapons', in J.F. Rioux (ed.), *Limiting the Proliferation of Weapons: The Role of Supply-Side Strategies* (Ottawa: Carleton University Press, 1992), pp.57–9. K.C. Bailey, 'Problems with a Chemical Weapons Ban', *Orbis,* Vol.36, No.2 (Spring 1992), p.240 + n.3.

6. Documents as reproduced in Trevor Findlay (ed.), *Chemical Weapons and Missile Proliferation: With Implications for the Asia/Pacific Region* (Boulder, Co.: Lynne Rienner Publishers, 1991), Appendix III.

7. See L.A. Dunn, 'Chemical Weapons Arms Control', *Survival,* Vol.31, No.3 (May/June 1989), p.219, for a late plea on using the expertise of nuclear export controls to stem CWW proliferation.

8. See for instance the Congressional testimonies as reproduced in M.S. Meselson, 'Behind the Nixon Policy for Chemical and Biological Warfare [Senate Committee on Foreign Relations, Hearing of 30th April 1969]', *The Bulletin of the Atomic Scientists,* Vol.24, No.1 (Jan. 1970), pp.27, 32 and 34; in M.S. Meselson, 'Tear Gas in Vietnam and the Return of Poison Gas [Defense Subcommittee, Senate Appropriations Committee, Hearing held in May 1970]', *The Bulletin of the Atomic Scientists,* Vol.27, No.3 (March 1971), at p.19; and in M.S. Meselson, 'Gas Warfare and the Geneva Protocol of 1925 [Senate Committee on Foreign Relations, 26th March 1971]', *The Bulletin of the Atomic Scientists,* Vol.28, No.1 (Feb 1972), pp.3–7. The sequence saw an increased stress on threats emanating from the proliferation of CW readiness. See also M.S. Meselson, 'Chemical and Biological Weapons', in Herbert F. York (ed.), *Arms Control: Readings from Scientific American* (San Francisco: W.H. Freeman and Company, 1973), p.313. The point was also taken up by UK scientist J.P. Perry Robinson at a symposium held on 1 April 1974. Julian P. Perry Robinson, 'Some Implications of Binary Never Gas Weapons', in The Department of Chemistry and Public Affairs (ed.), *Chemical Weapons and US Public Policy* (Washington, DC: American Chemical Society, Nov. 1977), p.12.

9. L. Freedman, 'The Proliferation Problem and the New World Order', in Karsh *et al.,* p.165.

10. Cf. K. Waltz, 'The Spread of Nuclear Weapons: More May Be Better', *Adelphi Papers,* No.171 (London: IISS, Autumn 1981).

11. See, for instance, the contributors in Z.S. Davies and B. Frankel (eds.), 'The Proliferation Puzzle: Why Nuclear Weapons Spread (and What Results)', *Security Studies,* Vol.2, Nos.3/4 (Spring/Summer 1993).

12. D. Feith, 'Three Obstacles to effective Implementation of Chemical-Weapons Control', in K.M. Jensen, D. Wurmser (eds.), *Is It Feasible to Negotiate Chemical and Biological Weapons Control?,* Dialogues from Public Workshops 4 (Washington, DC: United States Institude of Peace, 1990), pp.36–9. Based on the thought that 'no country in history has initiated chemical warfare against an enemy that had, at the time, a retaliatory capability' (p.37), he concluded that,

The most effective way to influence the cost-benefit analysis of initating chemical warfare – which is to say the most effective way available right now to address the chemical-weapons problem – is for potential victims to have the ability to retaliate in kind, and to prepare their forces with defensive gear, medical capabilities, and detection equipment. That, to my mind, is a much more effective means than an arms-control treaty, given the unfortunately primitive state in which international law exists, rendering it, for all practical purposes, impotent to deal with violations...
The military route promises the greatest chance of addressing violations and reducing the danger that they pose to us and to others. Does that mean that proliferation is a good thing or a bad thing? The answer is: It depends on the country. If a country that is fundamentally law abiding, a country on our side – such as Britain – were to obtain a chemical-weapons capability, I believe the danger of initiation of chemical warfare in the world would be reduced. If countries such as Libya, Syria, Iraq, and the Soviet Union were to obtain or increase their chemical-weapons capabilities, that would be a bad thing because the chances of chemical warfare in the world would be increased.' (p.38).

13. Many authors have of course advocated the spread of CW defences because these reduce any military advantage an attacker might hope to gain from CWW use and therefore the overall attractiveness CWW might hold for potential proliferators. Article X of the Chemical Weapons Convention endorses such a view.

14. Cf. J.D. Douglass Jr, N.C. Livingstone, *America the Vulnerable: The Threat of Chemical and Biologlical Warfare* (Lexington, MA: Lexington Books, 1987). H.J. McGeorge II, 'The Deadly Mixture: Bugs, Gas, and Terrorists', *NBC Defence and Technology International,* Vol.1 No.2 (May 1986), pp.56–61. For an early view on how novel binary munitions may thwart terrorist and criminal designs, F.R. Frank, 'Binary Chemical Munitions and the Proliferation of Chemical Warfare Capabilities', in The Department of Chemistry and Public Affairs (ed.), *Binary Weapons and the Problem of Chemical Disarmament* (Washington, DC: American Chemical Society, December 1977), pp.11–12.

15. See note 7.

16. For example, M. Hamm, 'Deterring Chemical War: The Reagan Formula', *Backgrounder,* No.272, (Washington, DC: The Heritage Foundation, 15 June 1983), 21p. M. Hamm, 'Deterrence, Chemical Warfare, and Arms Control', *Orbis* (Spring 1985), pp.119–63. M. Hamm, 'Biochemical Warfare: Deterrence vs Arms Control', *Contemporary Review* (March 1985), pp.127–34. J. Hemsley, *The Soviet Biochemical Threat to NATO: The Neglected Issue,* RUSI Defence Studies Series (Basingstoke: Macmillan, 1987); A.H. Hoeber, *The Chemistry of Defeat: Asymmetries in U.S. and Soviet Chemical Warfare Postures* (Cambridge, MA: Institute for Foreign Policy Analysis, December 1981). A.H. Hoeber, J.D. Douglass Jr., 'The Neglected Threat of Chemical Warfare', *International Security,* Vol.3, No.1 (Summer 1978), pp.55–82.

17. For example, P. Herby, 'Beyond Partial Measures', in J.P. Zanders and E. Remacle (eds.), *Chemical Weapons Proliferation: Policy Issues Pending an International Treaty,* Proceedings of the 2nd Annual Conference on Chemical Warfare (Brussels: Centrum voor Polemologie, Vrije Universiteit Brussel, 1991), pp.93–102. J.P. Perry Robinson, 'Chemical Weapons Proliferation: Security Risks', in Zanders and Remacle (eds.), *Chemical Weapons Proliferation,* pp.69–92.

18. K.C. Bailey, 'Ballistic Missile Proliferation: Can It Be Reversed?', *Orbis,* Vol.35, No.1 (Winter 1991), p.10.

19. M.A. Heller, 'Ballistic Missile Proliferation: Coping with It in the Middle East', *Orbis,* Vol.35, No.1 (Winter 1991).

20. See for instance M. Meselson in C. Moss Helms, M. Meselson and B. Roberts, *Chemical Weapons and Security in the Middle East,* Proceedings from a Congressional Briefing, (Washington, DC: American Association for the Advancement of Science, 11 Sept. 1990), p.16.

21. S. Fetter, 'Ballistic Missiles and Weapons of Mass Destruction', *International Security,* Vol.16, No.1 (Summer 1991), p.41.

22. K.C. Bailey, 'Problems with a Chemical Weapons Ban', p.240.

23. G.S. Pearson, 'Biological Weapons: Their Nature and Arms Control', in Karsh *et al., Non-*

Conventional-Weapons Proliferation, pp.99–134. J.E. Stern, 'Will Terrorists Turn to Poison?, *Orbis,* Vol.37, No.3 (Summer 1993), pp.393–412.

24. Chlorine at the end of the eighteenth century: phosgene in 1812. The blistering action of mustard gas had already been described around 1880.

25. L.F. Haber, *The Poisonous Cloud: Chemical Warfare in the First World War* (Oxford: Clarendon Press, 1986), pp.15–16.

26. Ibid., p.15; D. Richter, *Chemical Soldiers; British Gas Warfare in World War 1* (Lawrence: University Press of Kansas, 1992), pp.15–16.

27. The Declaration of St. Petersburg of 1868 to the Effect of Prohibiting the Use of Certain Projectiles in Wartime; The International Declaration concerning the Laws and Customs of War (Brussels Conference, 1874); the Annex to the Hague Conventions of 1899 and 1907.

28. Regarding fact and fiction, as well as reported research proposals in Great Britain, France, and Germany, see L.F. Haber, *The Poisonous Cloud,* pp.19–21.

29. Under *generation* is understood a certain set of proliferation characteristics which occurred for the first time at a certain stage in the history of CW, but which may be reproduced later at different locations without necessarily following the historical order.

30. Throughout his book *The Poisonous Cloud,* L.F. Haber, details many of the examples in this paragraph.

31. Until 1945 Germany remained the exception. However, regarding proliferation both the military and governmental agencies remained the key actors.

32. J.P. Zanders, 'The Destruction of Old Chemical Munition in Belgium', paper delivered to the conference The Challenge of Old Chemical Scrap-Munition and Toxic Armament Wastes held at the *Wehrwissenschaftliche Dienststelle der Bundeswehr für ABC-Schutz,* Munster (FRG), organized by the Stockholm International Peace Research Institute, 18–21 October 1993.

33. R. Kunz and R.D. Müller, *Giftgas gegen Abd el Krim. Deutschland, Spanien und der Gaskrieg in Spanisch-Marokko 1922–1927,* Einzelschriften zur Militärgeschichte 34 (Freiburg: Verlag Rombach, 1990), chapter iv.

34. Peacetime daily production was to be 1 ton of mustard gas, 1.5 tons of phosgene, and 1.25 tons of Dick (ethyldichloroarsine). The plant included the corresponding filling facilities for shells, bombs and grenades (ibid., p.68).

35. Ibid., p.69. Great Britain in particular wished to retain control over the Straits of Gibraltar and supported Spain's colonial war because in case of defeat France would dominate over the whole of Morocco.

36. J.P. Perry Robinson, 'Origins of the Chemical Weapons Convention', in B. Morel and K. Olson (eds.), *Shadows and Substance: The Chemical Weapons Convention* (Boulder, CO: Westview Press, 1993), p.39.

37. Kunz and Müller, *Giftgas gegen,* pp.23, 59.

38. M. van Zelm, 'Verification of the Destruction of CW Agents: The Obong Operation', in H. G. Brauch (ed.), *Verification and Arms Control: Implications for European Security,* The Results of the Sixth AFES-PRESS Conference, Part 1: Abstracts and Discussion. AFES-PRESS Report 35 (Mosbach, FRG, 1990). The Netherlands destroyed the remainder of the stock between 1978 and 1979 at the request of the Indonesian government.

39. Other theories on the origin of Egyptian CWW exist, but strong doubts about their validity persist. See SIPRI, *Chemical and Biological Warfare, Volume 1: The Rise of CB Weapons,* (Stockholm: Amqvist & Wiksell, 1971), p.161; SIPRI, *Chemical and Biological Warfare, Volume V: The Prevention of CBW* (Stockholm: Almqvist & Wiksell, 1971), p.227.

40. R.Harris and J. Paxman, *A Higher Form of Killing: The Secret Story of Gas and Germ Warfare* (UK: Triad/Granada, 1983), pp.173–83. Hansaard (Commons), Vol. 202, no.43, col. 16, Written Answers, 20 Jan. 1992 (as quoted in the *Chemical Weapons Convention Bulletin* 15 (March 1992), p.14, lemma 20 Jan. 1992).

41. United States General Accounting Ofice, *Israel: Use of US-Manufactured Tear Gas in the Occupied Territories,* GAO/NSIAD-89-128 (Washington, DC: GAO April 1989).

42. For detailed analysis, see J.P. Zanders, 'Mechanisms behind the Imhausen-Rabta Affair', in Zanders and Remacle, *Chemical Weapons Proliferation,* pp.3–40.

43. A.H. Cordesman, *After the Storm. The Changing Military Balance in the Middle East*

(Boulder, CO: Westview Press, 1993), p.152.

44. A. Darwish, 'Libya Building Poison-Gas Plant', *The Independent*, 16 Feb. 1993 p.9. D. Jehl, 'Libya Building a Poison Gas Factory, US Intelligence Says', *International Herald Tribune* 19 Feb. 1993, p.7, –, 'Thais Prepare for US Attack on Libyan Plants', *International Herald Tribune*, 5 Oct. 1993, p.6. –, 'Thais Won't Be Expelled, Libyan Says', *International Herald Tribune*, 24 Nov. 1993, p.5.

45. A. Wellmann, *Weiterverbreitung chemischer Waffen: Zum Beispiel Irak, Beschaffung und Einsatz chemischer Waffen durch den Irak 1980–1990*, Arbeitspapiere der Berghofstiftung für Konfliktforschung 44 (Berlin: Berghof-Stiftung für Konfliktforschung, 1991), pp.16–29.

46. –, Bonn stoppt Giftgas-Frachter. *Frankfurter Rundschau*, 10 Aug. 1992. –, Bonn läßt Frachter mit Giftas-Chemikalien Stoppen. *Frankfurter Allgemeine Zeitung*, 10 Aug. 1992, p.2. –, Poison Gas for Syria Is Intercepted. *International Herald Tribune*, 10 Aug. 1992, p.2. *Arms Control Reporter*, 1992, p.704. E-2.66.

47. K.C. Bailey, *Doomsday Weapons in the Hands of Many: The Arms Control Challenge of the 1990s* (Urbana and Chicago: University of Illinois Press, 1991), pp.61–2.

48. *Arms Control Reporter*, 1993, p.704. E–2.94; M. Richardson 'US Asks Asians to Help Curb Weapons', *International Herald Tribune*, 27 July 1993, pp.1,4.

49. If China and Iran – presently signatories – become state parties to the CWC, it is doubtful whether the USA would be able to trigger a challenge inspection simply on the basis of the transaction. Schedule 2 chemicals can according to Part VII, §31 of the Verification Annex be transferred to or received by other states parties. Contrary to the provisions relating to Schedule 1 chemicals (Part VI), no quantitative limits or reporting requirements for such transactions are included. Installations producing or processing such compounds above specified quantities must be declared and are subject to verification and inspection routines. Schedule 3 chemicals may even be transferred to states not party to the CWC provided the recipient country certifies that these will not be used for purposes prohibited by the convention following the requirements in Part VII, §26.

50. N. Kristof, 'China Accuses US of Halting Ship, Denies It Carries War Chemicals', *International Herald Tribune*, 9 Aug. 1993, p.2. –, 'China Assails US on Suspect Ship', *International Herald Tribune*, 12 Aug. 1993, p.2. Editorial, 'Poison Gas on the Way?', *International Herald Tribune*, 12 Aug. 1993, p.4. L. Weymouth, 'Link China's Trade Status to Arms Sales, Not Rights', *International Herald Tribune*, 13 Aug. 1993, p.6. –, 'US Says Suspect Ship Is near Iran', *International Herald Tribune*, 17 Aug. 1993, p.2. –, 'Saudis Await Arms' Ship', *The Independent*, 26 Aug. 1993, p.15. J. Mann, 'US Dispute with China Deepening to Hostility', *International Herald Tribune*, 27 Aug. 1993, pp.1, 4. P. Reeves, 'US and China Set to Clash after Sanctions', *The Independent*, 27 Aug. 1993, p.9. *Arms Control Reporter*, 1993, pp.704. E–2. 101–103.

51. J.P. Perry Robinson, 'Origins of the Chemical Weapons Convention', Table 4.3.

52. A realist school of thought will most likely influence such a government's security policies, accentuating the prominence of external security threats in the discourse.

53. M. Brzoska, 'Behind the German Export Scandals', *The Bulletin of the Atomic Scientists*, Vol.45, No.6 (July 1989), p.33.

54. From a press-release by Foreign Minister Genscher, 19 Jan. 1987, as quoted in *Stichworte zur Sicherheitspolitik, Presse- und Informationsdienst der Bundersregierung* (Bonn, February 1987), p.48.

55. Unterrichtung durch die Bundesregierung, *Bericht der Bundesregierung an den deutschen Bundestag über eine mögliche Beteiligung deutscher Firmen an einer C-Waffen-Produktion in Libyen*. 11. Wahlperiode, Drucksache 11/3995 (Bonn: Deutscher Bundestag, 15 February 1989), p.15.

56. Such active governmental involvement certainly blurs the distinction between first and second generation proliferation, which, in any case, should be considered ideal types. Acquiescence in private companies' involvement in the Libyan Rabta project explains to a large extent the German government's reluctance to take action after the initial American complaints. Some of these firms had already been linked to Iraq's CW programme. Such duplicity is also illustrated by the prosecution of the UK-based company Matrix-Churchill for delivering tools and machinery to Iraq despite governmental knowledge that executives

were informants for the British intelligence services. The fuzziness between the three ideal types underscores our basic argument that the traditional approach to the proliferation issue misses many of the actors, their role and motives.

57. D. Männig, 'At the Conclusion of the Chemical Weapons Convention: Some Recent Issues Concerning the Chemical Industry', pp.134–5. The author also points to similar costs from strict environmental legislation which exceed limits imposed in neighbouring countries.

58. J.P. Perry Robinson, 'Chemical Weapons Proliferation in the Middle East', p.47.

59. The definition will be difficult to make operational from a policy analyst's point of view. It cannot answer a question like 'who has taken the decision when'. However, it is meant as an instrument to gain deeper understanding of a process and not as one for bean-counting countries in the developing world. Nevertheless, future research applying the results of theoretical analysis of armament dynamics may allow for greater differentiation.

Ballistic Missiles in the Middle East:
Realities, Omens and Arms Control Options

AARON KARP

Introduction

What ever happened to ballistic missile proliferation in the Middle East? At the time of Desert Storm it was one of the most pressing issues in international security, leading to major proposals from many quarters, some calling for bold arms control initiatives, some for redesign of the international non-proliferation system, others for redirection of defensive planning. In the intervening years the issues involved hardly changed at all, but their place on the international agenda sank to near invisibility.

Perhaps much of the frenetic debate over missile proliferation in the late-1980s and early 1990s was overblown; no one in the Middle East is in a position to rain ICBMs down around the world. But the problem is serious and gradually deteriorating. Responses currently in place have done much to slow the process of proliferation. Export controls in particular have been more successful than many previously thought possible. Today's dangers come not from the most ambitious ballistic programmes, but from more modest missiles based on more manageable technologies. Although the risks of missile proliferation have receded slightly, there is a growing need for more aggressive political measures to ensure that the dangers cease growing altogether.

The Curious Disappearance of Missile Proliferation

Perhaps the most important transformation in ballistic missile proliferation in recent years is such a change in the feeling of urgency. When rediscovered in the 1980s missile proliferation – combined with its siblings, nuclear and CBW proliferation – seemed to pose an immediate, immense and entirely novel risk to international peace and security. Yet only a few years later the spread of missiles has been accepted as part of the military landscape. The danger it poses, once blindingly obvious to every schoolboy, has lost much of its immediacy. With its immediacy has gone much of the impetus to deal with the problem. Yet the missiles and their dangers remain much as before.

Starting with the numerous revelations in 1987–88 showing how many countries in the region were trying to acquire long-range ballistic missiles, the issue shocked an international community previously unaware of the scope of the problem. In reality virtually all of the programmes that caught media attention in the late-1980s could trace their roots back for years. Some stretched back for decades. But a series of highly publicized first launches, the use of missiles in the Iran–Iraq War, and missile purchases by Saudi Arabia and others pushed the issue to the top of the global policy agenda.

One reaction was a flurry of activity in political capitals around the world. Export controls were strengthened everywhere, pledges not to transfer were negotiated with most potential suppliers, investments in missile defences were reoriented from intercontinental to regional threats. These initiatives culminated in the well-publicized initiatives from President Bush and President Mitterrand for Middle Eastern arms control and disarmament, proposals focusing largely on the ballistic missile problem.

Within a period of months, though, the fuss over Middle Eastern missiles had all but vanished. The irony is hard to avoid; perceptions of the threat declined but the threat itself remains much the same. Most of the missiles of greatest concern remain in the region. While some programmes have been stopped, others have taken their place. Today the issue is lively at the working level where policy-makers and public officials deal with continuing efforts to control the spread of missile technology. But except for those ministerial backwaters, the issue is barely visible.

Why the loss of interest? General forces were part of the cause. To some extent, the rise and fall of Middle Eastern missile proliferation followed the inevitable parabolic curve of human attention. Without periodic crises to arouse interest, policy issues tend to drift and disappear. The unique dynamic of the end of the Cold War also played an important role. Missile proliferation first gained attention at a particular moment when the decline of superpower antagonism left the world sensitive to new threats to international security. The issue lost salience just as ethnic conflict was emerging as the most immediate danger of the post-Cold War world.

More specific factors also made it easy to overlook the continuing importance of ballistic missile proliferation in the Middle East. The most dramatic was the defeat of Saddam Hussein. Although Iraq was one of the last countries in the region to display a serious interest in acquiring long-range missiles, Saddam's excesses made him the personification of Middle Eastern missile proliferation. Saddam's frenzied procurement efforts, his Scud attacks against Iran, his bombastic rhetoric and final attacks on Israel and Saudi Arabia made it easy to overlook the missile programme of neighbouring countries. After his defeat, with his remaining long-range missiles and production facilities destroyed and other relevant capabilities subject to permanent UN safeguards, it was easy to forget other Middle Eastern missile threats.

A second specific factor was the rising salience of North Korea as the Iraq of the 1990s. The significance of North Korea's armament programmes became apparent just as the Iraqi threat disappeared. With an advanced nuclear weapons programme, chemical and biological weapons capabilities, and a ballistic missile programme remarkably similar to Iraq's before 1991, North Korea inevitably would overshadow other proliferation concerns.

What is more surprising perhaps is the degree to which North Korea eclipsed virtually all other aspects of the proliferation agenda. This dominance partially stems from the serious risks of a second Korean war, but also from the tendency of the Clinton administration to focus on a single issue at a time. Indeed, it is not just Middle Eastern missile proliferation that is being overlooked by Washington, but Middle Eastern security altogether.

The most important factor for the declining interest in missile proliferation, however, is the maturation of the issue itself. A mature policy is characterized by a narrowing of the discussion on policy options, reflecting a consensus over the nature of the problem and the range of permissible policy responses.[1] With agreement on basic principles, debates become less frequent and tend to focus on increasingly particular issues. Disputes still can occur, but the solidification of positions makes debates increasingly formal and predictable.

When it comes to Middle Eastern missile proliferation, the basic framework is in place to guide international policy-making for many years to come. While officially declaring that missile proliferation is unacceptable, at a practical level the international community has made essential adjustments to cope with the reality of missile proliferation. It has undertaken the easiest and least costly steps to minimize the severity of the challenge. These include changes in export law and policy, establishment of the multi-lateral Missile Technology Control Regime, a routine process of diplomatic consultation among potential exporters, and initiation of a number of defensive programmes. While these steps do nothing to reverse the course the proliferation, they make the existing environment less overtly threatening. If they cannot make the situation genuinely acceptable, they can make the inherent ambiguities of proliferation less extreme and more tolerable.

Strategic and Domestic Stasis

Middle Eastern governments have made more subtle but comparable adjustments of their own. Their own ballistic missiles are fully integrated into their strategic postures. In many cases these weapons also have become important bulwarks of national legitimacy as well. The argument here is not that the dangers of missile proliferation have been eliminated or even significantly reduced. Rather, the dangers have been made sufficiently acceptable for the issue to drop from the daily political agenda.

Certainly the countries of the region have had enough time to get used to the contemporary facts of life. Israeli leaders first had to confront the missile issue in the early 1960s, in a period of grave insecurity which provoked Israel's decision to develop both nuclear weapons and ballistic missiles. Additional moments of serious debate over the missile threat came after the Scud and Frog attacks in the 1973 war and again in the mid-1980s as the dimensions of regional proliferation and the synergism with chemical and biological weapons became evident. Although it was widely thought at the time to harken an era of unprecedented instability, the Iran–Iraq War of the Cities in 1988 ironically augured an era of complacency that continues to this day.

The actual experience of Saddam's missile attacks in 1991 was extremely traumatic for the Israeli people.[2] For elite decision-makers, by contrast, the effects were more ephemeral. The Israel military, the Allied coalition and the Saudi leadership all took the attacks in their stride. For the first time the use of missiles did not lead to a wide-ranging debate in Israel or elsewhere in the Middle East over how to cope. The consensus was that Israel – with its own deterrent forces, American assistance in the form of Patriot defences, and its own Arrow programme (as well as the indirect assistance of the entire Allied coalition) – had done as well as it could hope to. Israel acknowledged the maturity of its own missile proliferation policy by sticking to the status quo.

Arab governments also appear to be dedicated to nothing so much as the strategic status quo.[3] It is an environment in which missiles will play an increasingly important role, but not so important as to trigger a mad rush to acquire anything that burns rocket fuel. Arab and Iranian rocket ambitions can be appreciated only from the perspective of overall regional force developments. For most Middle Eastern countries, the strategic quandary of the 1990s is how to preserve their military capabilities. Only the most wealthy are undertaking significant modernization. Outside of the tiny Gulf sheikhdoms, none is expanding its military forces. Large arms purchases continue, but few observers suggest that the region is in the midst of anything resembling the explicit arms race of the 1950s to 1970s.

After Desert Storm, Saudi Arabia led Western-oriented Arab governments in a rearmament binge unlike any the region has seen since mid-1970s. A few countries led by Egypt, Israel and Turkey received large quantities of second-hand equipment as it was decommissioned from European and American inventories under the terms of the CFE treaty and cascaded to regional friends and allies.

For all this activity, no major actor in the Middle East is expanding its overall forces. Rather, defence spending is going almost exclusively into preservation of extant forces. Most countries are engaged in no more than modernization, intended not to increase their absolute capabilities but to preserve the utility of their existing force structures. Countries like Iran, Libya and Syria face an extremely difficult strategic situation, forced to rely on Soviet-style conventional forces in which they can have no confidence after the defeats of 1982 and 1991. They lack the finances to modernize those forces fully, even with the latest Russian or Chinese equipment. Moreover, they have little hope of matching the informational capabilities, the intelligence gathering abilities and command and control skills which stood at the foundations of Israel's victory in the Beka'a Valley and the allied defeat of Iraq.[4]

For countries lumbered with increasingly dubious conventional forces, ballistic missiles offer a partial exception to the seeming immutability of the strategic status quo. For Arab governments and Iran, ballistic missiles continue to be viewed as an alternative to conventional forces, one of the few paths left to acquiring useful military power. Although the goal of defeating Israel never has been more elusive, through ballistic missiles they can aspire to retain some measure of direct influence over Israel's ability to use its own forces. The lesson of Iraq's missile attacks on Tehran in 1988 and against Israel in January-February 1991 have not been lost. Ballistic missiles may not be sufficient for victory, but they may be enough to prevent utter defeat. Under the right circumstances they can compel governments to take actions they would not seriously consider otherwise.

In addition to their unique strategic role, ballistic missiles play a special role in Middle Eastern domestic politics. The importance, some argue the outright dominance of domestic political needs, has won increasing appreciation in recent efforts to understand the evolution of national armed forces.[5] The role of domestic factors in ballistic missile acquisition is especially salient. In addition to their orthodox role deterring foreign adversaries in war-time, missiles contribute directly to domestic political power in peace-time.

For countries with meagre technological resources, a missile programme can be a vital symbol of the nation's technological competence. Where ballistic missiles are essentially strategic, as in Israel, they tend to be treated as state secrets. Where the role of missiles is largely symbolic they are more easily acknowledged and sometimes even publicized. They are displayed at parades, and presidents attend historic launches and commissioning ceremonies. As symbols of state power and the legitimacy of authority, ballistic missiles have an importance largely independent of their strategic and tactical utility. For many Middle Eastern states, their possession has become an end in itself, comparable to the royal stables, palaces and ceremonial guards of another era.[6]

The importance of domestic motives gives ballistic missile programmes a permanence they could not have in a purely strategic environment. They become part of the fabric of the regime and cease to be weapons in any practical sense. Instead they evolve into something more valuable to the state itself, evidence of national worth, testimony to national ambition. Whether a country's rockets are deployed by the hundreds or limp alone in stagnant development programmes, they are a source of great pride among nations otherwise convinced of their powerlessness and incompetence.

Threats for the Coming Century

What happened in the early 1990s, then, was not the disappearance of Middle Eastern ballistic missile proliferation but its normalization. As the rate of technological progress slowed and other regions became more dynamic, the Middle East became a strategic backwater, less interesting to outside observers because of its resistance to change.

A brief review of the key actors in the region, however, reveals that interest in long-range rocketry is virtually unchanged from the days of more intense scrutiny. No Middle Eastern country is on the verge of dramatic technological breakthroughs in the 1990s. But none has ceased trying to make progress, and several continue gradually accumulating capabilities. It is this gradual development of long-range rocketry in the Middle East that outside policy-making must prepare to confront.

Egypt

Egypt's rocketry research is the oldest in the region, dating from Nasser's visionary programme of the mid-1950s. By the mid-1960s that programme had come to an end, due in part to Israeli political pressure and attacks on the German scientists leading the enterprise, and to Egypt's own mismanagement.[7] Twenty years later Egypt became involved with Argentina, Iraq and a complicated European consortium trying to develop the 1,000 km Condor missile, but this too fell victim to political opposition from the United States and internal ambivalence.[8] Indeed, the strongest force restraining Egyptian ambitions today is its own strategic ambivalence, a growing comfort in the status quo that first led to abandonment of nuclear ambitions and now long-range rocketry as well.[9]

With the most advanced industrial base in the Arab world and considerable rocketry experience, Egypt could be a regional leader if it were so inclined. Nevertheless, by the early 1990s all Egyptian rocketry projects appeared to be dormant. A replacement for the Frog missile, the Sakr-80, was fully developed but apparently never entered series production. Egypt is widely believed to have supplied the Scud missiles that North Korea reverse engineered to establish its own ballistic missile programme. But unlike Iran and Syria, Egypt has not been reported as a buyer for North Korean Scud versions. Instead, reports focus on continuing technical co-operation with Pyongyang and the possibility that Egypt may have a Scud factory of its own. There is no evidence, however, that Egypt is actively involved in missile production.[10]

Iran

Iran may have the most ambitious rocketry programme in the Middle East after Israel, but its ability to make tangible progress is increasingly dubious. The effects of Iraqi missile attacks are still debated, but one result was to redouble Iran's own efforts.[11] Iranian leaders emerged from the Iran–Iraq War convinced that 'missiles are the most important weapons today'.[12] After revealing roughly a dozen artillery rocket and ballistic missile projects in 1987–88, Iran's programme appears to be frustrated by its lack of financial resources, its inability to attract technical assistance, and its own managerial incompetence. Of the numerous projects started during the war, only artillery rockets like the 40 km Oghab reached series production, The status of the ambitious Mushak artillery rockets with ranges up to 160 km are more obscure. They may have entered series production during the war but were dropped soon after as their inadequacies became apparent.[13]

Despite its indigenous ballistic missile programme, Iran is almost completely dependent upon North Korea and China for missiles and technical aid. There is a growing consensus that Iran cannot 'overcome non-technical constraints on weapons development', especially political uncertainty and bureaucratic incompetence.[14] Sharam Chuban emphasizes the simple lack of financial resources to undertake a serious rocketry programme.[15]

From North Korea, Iran has purchased a current inventory of some 200 to 300 slightly improved Scud-B missiles and 150 longer-range Scud-Cs. From China came artillery rockets with ranges of up to 90 km. The level of acquisition points to the seriousness of Iranian intentions and the weight of financial limitations. If national economics permitted, acquisition of North Korean missiles undoubtedly would be on an enormous scale. Iran appears to be investing in domestic assembly as a substitute for indigenous development.[16]

Iraq

Iraq's missile infrastructure was largely destroyed under the terms of UN Security Council resolution 687, which permits the country no missiles or development technology for missiles over 150 km range. Long-term monitoring by UNSCOM under resolution 715 will ensure that Iraq cannot develop larger systems without attracting international notice.[17] Of equal importance, erstwhile suppliers like France and Germany have reoriented their policies and now will have nothing to do with Saddam Hussein.

Despite the lingering burden of its defeat in 1991, there is no evidence that Iraq has abandoned any of its military ambitions. It retains some of its infrastructure and engineers. A new rocketry programme would take many years to restore the country's 1991 capability – at which time it still had not manufactured a single ballistic missile. Yet it seems likely that some such work has already begun.

Iraq may hope to shift work to friendly countries, just as Hans von Seeckt moved German R&D to Russia in the 1920s.[18] In the late 1980s there were reports of efforts to move some development to sympathetic countries like Mauritania and Sudan. But new sources of technology would still have to be found. Today only North Korea is a serious possibility, but Saddam Hussein has shown immense determination and undoubtedly will try to cultivate other sources.

Israel

Israel remains the unchallenged leader in Middle East rocketry, having deployed the Jericho-1 since the early 1970s and the Jericho-2 since the late 1980s. It is the only country in the region with an active space launch programme, based on the Shavit booster, a derivative of the Jericho-2. With heavy financial support from Washington it is developing the Arrow ATBM interceptor. It also is the only Middle Eastern country with nuclear weapons, some of which certainly must arm its long-range missiles.

While the outlines of the Israeli programme are widely acknowledged, few if any details are confirmed. The exact numbers and capabilities of its missiles, the operating service, their launch sites and armament all remain obscure.[19] Missions and doctrine, as Avner Cohen has argued regarding the entire nuclear establishment, probably are deliberately ambiguous.[20] It would appear that Israel has strong reasons to be satisfied with its current overall deterrent force and has little reason to develop new ballistic missiles so long as existing ones can be kept in service, but it faces no external constraints, only internal ones.

Libya

Libya first brought widespread attention to missile proliferation through its co-operative programme with the German firm Otrag in the early 1980s. The Otrag programme was technically misconceived, doomed from the start and possibly intended as nothing more than an investment scheme. Yet occasional reports indicate that Libya has not lost the ambition of developing missiles of its own. In mid-1993, for example, a shipment of solid rocket fuel was intercepted while in transit from Russia.[21]

In practice Libya relies entirely on Scud-B missiles acquired in the 1970s and 1980s from the Soviet Union. Its inventory is very large, with 80 launchers. It could have anywhere from 240 to 800 or even more Scud missiles.[22] Considering the country's large chemical weapons programme, its missiles have to be taken seriously in any case. Current financial problems and declining military goals have weakened Libya's desire for further missile purchases, but there is no evidence that this is anything other than a temporary lull.

Saudi Arabia

Saudi Arabia may be the region's most contented missile power. In 1987–88 it acquired a large force of Chinese DF-3 IRBMs; variously estimated at 30 to 120 of the 2,850 km missiles. Acquired partly out of fear of Iran and partially due to annoyance with America's refusal to furnish anything similar, the missiles are evidence of a mood, not a programme. A reasonable bet is that the missiles will be withdrawn in the next few years.

Syria

Syria is in many respects the most mysterious of the region's missile powers. Over the years it has assembled a large Scud force from the Soviet Union and North Korea. It also has smaller quantities of old short-range Frog missiles and more accurate SS-21s. It undoubtedly would like more of the latter, which Russia still is trying to sell, but seems to be inhibited by their high cost. It is widely believed that Syria has developed chemical warheads for its missiles, although their effectiveness is impossible to determine.

Despite its commitment to missile forces, Syria is unusually passive about the development of its missile force. Syria almost seems to be content to bide its time and buy whenever the deal is good. Over the years Syria has shown little interest in developing its own manufacturing ability. There are reports of interest in a Scud assembly facility and shipments of components have been intercepted.[23] However, the facility and the parts are more likely for the maintenance and overhaul of the country's sizeable inventory, which probably includes several hundred missiles.

Most Middle East missile programmes have been in place for decades now, gradually accumulating Scuds and mastering Scud technology. What is most impressive is not their technical accomplishments but their persistence. Few countries abandon long-range rocket development because of its impracticality or excessive cost. The elegant logic of Rand-style cost-benefit analysis is not a useful guide here. Although progress may be slow and occasionally comical, its path is ineluctable. The outcome may not be certain, but the dangers remain as real as ever.

The most serious dangers of missile proliferation in the Middle East derive from the Scud-type technology. These are ideally suited to the semi-industrial capabilities of most countries in the region.[24] With sufficient outside help, Scud technology can be stretched from a normal range of 280 km to ranges of 1,000 km. These range limits define a technological plateau, a realm of minimal challenges in which countries like Egypt, Iran, Iraq and Syria can continue to make progress. It is within this technological plateau that the most serious export control problems will be found, and where the need for arms control limitations are most pressing.[25]

The Scud threat should be taken very seriously. Not only can Scuds carry CBW or nuclear warheads, but their conventional effects have had significant effects in several wars.[26] The number of missiles in the region is unknown, but it could be much larger than commonly assumed. Since the missiles themselves are easily concealed, counting estimates traditionally have been based on numbers of launchers. With a total of roughly 127 Scud launchers currently in Arab and Iranian hands, the usual counting rules of three missiles per launcher would allow for 371 Scud missiles in the Middle East today.[27] It is time to drop this rule of thumb, which was based on Soviet field deployment patterns, not actually stockpiling.

All evidence shows that Middle Eastern countries routinely stockpile much larger quantities, 10 to 20 or more Scuds per launcher. Iraq, with some 32 mobile and 14 fixed launchers before the 1991 Gulf War, would have had 136 Scuds using the conventional formula. In fact on the morning of 17 January 1991 it had over 700 on hand, almost 20 for each launcher. Similarly, Iran and Syria have purchased a total of 350 to 550 North Korean Scuds (both B and C models) since 1988, but apparently no additional launchers. As a result it is safe to conclude that Middle Eastern arsenals include roughly 1,200 to 2,400 Scud missiles, and possibly more. The evasiveness of Scud forces contribute further to their place as the region's primary missile proliferation problem.

More advanced rockets, requiring multiple staging or clustered designs, advanced fuels, fully inertial guidance and aerodynamically refined warheads are beyond their capabilities. Although some countries will acquire relevant bits and pieces of technology for such rockets, they cannot create the complete infrastructure, nor can they manage an undertaking of such scale and delicacy by themselves. Certainly they cannot do so in secret; the technical demands of such a programme inevitably will lead a visible trail, while the missiles themselves will be readily identified.

While the Gaddafis of the world may dream of 2,000 km missiles or even ICBMs to hit New York, their only hope is to find a country willing to sell them some. At this level, beyond the limits of the easily mastered technology of Scud-type weapons, export controls have immense potential and the role of arms control is less urgent.

The Riddle of Control

While few would question its desirability, the feasibility of controlling Middle Eastern missile forces is a question usually dismissed with reflexive pessimism. Despite this common assumption, there are grounds for cautious optimism that the spread of ballistic missiles can be contained.

Approaches to restraining Middle Eastern ballistic missile forces fall into four general categories: unilateral initiatives of force reduction; arms control agreements focusing on ballistic missiles specifically; general arms control initiatives in which ballistic missiles are but one component; and export controls. All of these approaches are potentially valuable and deserve aggressive prosecution. But only the last named approach, export controls, can be readily implemented. While other approaches must be pursued, export controls will remain the bulwark of international restraint on Middle Eastern missile proliferation for many years to come.

Unilateral Initiatives

Unilateral initiatives have a bad reputation, being associated with starry-eyed idealism and the glorification of weakness. This caricature obscures the fact that countries routinely abandon major military programmes, including ballistic missiles, when they believe they are unnecessary or no longer in the national interest. Britain long ago gave up its land-based ballistic missile programme and France is in the process of doing the same today. Since the end of the Cold War the United States and Russia have cut many strategic programmes, some in response to purely domestic initiatives, but others due to the multilateral INF and START treaties.

Having seen how mutual acceptance of the status quo and economic pressures made it possible for European governments to reduce their military outlays and forces significantly, some analysts have argued that similar forces could have the same effect in the Middle East.[28] The region is not immune to this logic. Egypt gave up on its German-designed missiles of the 1960s; Algeria retired its small Frog missile force in the 1980s; and Kuwait has shown no interest in replacing the Frog missiles it lost in the 1990 invasion.[29]

While similar decisions seem likely in the foreseeable future, they will be too irregular and too easily offset by other missile acquisitions to be of much effect. Economic forces already are inhibiting acquisition of additional ballistic missiles in many countries, slowing North Korean Scud sales and hampering Russian efforts to sell the SS-21.[30] But these forces seem insufficient to persuade many governments to drop weapons already in service or abandon long-range procurement goals.

At present the mostly likely candidate for unilateral restraint is Saudi Arabia. As noted previously, it is unlikely to keep its Chinese-supplied DF-3 IRBMs in service in the long run. The missiles are very costly to maintain and their deterrent value is very questionable. The Saudi regime, moreover, gains little if any domestic legitimacy from possessing them and can point to its recent across-the-board military modernization as a more important symbol for domestic audiences. No other regional missiles come to mind as easily as a ripe candidate for unilateral reduction.

Negotiated Control of Ballistic Missiles

Negotiated control of ballistic missiles has greater potential. The analogy to arms control experiences in Europe and between the superpowers stands as a vivid demonstration of what can be accomplished. In both those cases, ballistic missiles were the primary target for control efforts; it was progress restricting missiles that led to wider agreements like the CFE treaty.

There are a large number of proposals for restraining Middle Eastern ballistic missile proliferation. These range from a regional INF treaty to a global ballistic missile test ban or an outright comprehensive missile ban. This was the basic approach behind the Bush and Mitterrand plans for Middle East arms control advanced in the wake of Desert Storm.[31] All of these proposals have great merit and deserve serious attention. While their individual strengths and weaknesses can be debated, however, they all suffer from the basic flaws undermining any effort to restrict a specific strategic technology in the Middle East.

Despite the dangers of destablization and uncontrollable conflict, few if any governments in the region act as if there is a genuine ballistic missile problem. A technology is ripe for prohibition only when all sides agree that the disadvantages of its possession outweigh any advantage. Clearly this is not the case in the Middle East, where Israel relies on missiles as an essential element of existential deterrence, where Arab governments prize them as their only instrument of direct influence over Israel, and many governments use them as a symbol of national legitimacy.

Viewed from the presidential palace, the advantages of missile possession are clear, while the disadvantages are obscure by comparison. Few governments seem to regard missiles as inherently destabilizing; rather they view only the other side's missiles that way. Like American opponents of gun control, Middle Eastern governments appear to see the technology has something essentially desirable, tainted only by the irresponsibility of a few outlaws. From this perspective, most regional leaders appear to view any agreement to control or banish Middle Eastern ballistic missiles as something that would cost more than it is worth.

As has been argued elsewhere regarding the US-Soviet experience, arms control sometimes puts the technological cart before the political horse.[32] Any regime to control ballistic missiles in the Middle East presupposes a degree of mutual acceptance still rare in the region. Only the détente between Egypt and Israel comes close, and this is offset by the antagonisms of others. One is left with the conclusion that negotiated restrictions on ballistic missiles will be feasible only after a general framework for Middle Eastern peace has been established, undermining the military role of ballistic missiles, and developed to the extent that ballistic missiles gradually lose their other appeals as well. Missile control would emerge not as a special case for regional arms control, but as one aspect of a comprehensive settlement.

General Middle East Peace Settlement

A peace settlement would be the most effective basis for regional control over ballistic missiles. Unfortunately there is not much outside powers can do in this regard except offer encouragement. The key to such arrangements, as demonstrated by the experiences of the superpowers in Europe and Argentina-Brazil, appears to lay in the resolution of regional political disputes. As often happens in post-Cold War discussions of specific regional peace and security issues, this leads to the conclusion that the key to regional solutions lies not in the specifics of controlling ballistic missiles, but in the generalities of regional conflict resolution.

The most valuable European precedent for Middle East arms control is to demonstrate the overwhelming importance of political consensus. Once Cold War antagonisms evaporated, arms control became risibly easy. The completion of the INF agreement in 1987 showed that ballistic missiles, which previously stood out as the most spectacular manifestation of antagonism, could all but disappear as an issue. As a strategic document, the treaty was forgotten almost before the ink was dry. Even the appearance of unexpected complications could not disturb the new harmony, so strong were its political foundations. One of the little secrets of INF was the discovery a few months after its completion of previously unacknowledged

SS-23 missiles in East Germany, Czechoslovakia and Bulgaria. At the height of the Cold War, such a disclosure would have brought negotiations screeching to a halt. But in 1988 these revelations barely warranted recognition. Indeed, Bulgaria and the Czech Republic and Slovakia still have their SS-23 missiles, and no one really cares.[33]

A general regional peace settlement undoubtedly is the best way to redress the dangers of Middle Eastern missile proliferation.[34] That said, the current Arab–Israeli dialogue offers little more than a basis for hope. Israeli and Arab positions are deadlocked in much the same way the Soviet Union and the US were in the early years of the Cold War in the 1940s and 1950s. In an atmosphere of grave suspicion, each side approaches the issue of a general arms settlement from opposite ends, with minimal expectations and negligible results.

Israel seeks a political dialogue and intermediate measures like CSBMs with the promise of arms restraint to follow. Arab states led by Egypt want Israel to surrender its strategic weapons first and promise political accommodation later. The deadlock has not been alleviated by the arms control working group of the Madrid peace process.[35] In the long run this process may yield a durable accommodation in which the dangers of Middle Eastern missile proliferation can dissipate. But in the short run there is no choice but to rely on other tools.

Export Controls and the Missile Technology Control Regime (MTCR)

Export controls continue to have the most immediate utility of any approach to restrain missile proliferation. Although export controls have little effect on missiles already in the region, they can be highly effective in preventing the introduction of additional and more advanced systems. Despite region-wide interest in domestic missile production and decades of effort, only Israel has a significant indigenous missile industry today. Every other ballistic missile in the region was either imported from abroad or developed by foreign engineers relying on imported equipment. This dependence gives outside suppliers considerable leverage if they are willing to exert it.

From its birth in 1985–87, the MTCR has evolved into an increasingly popular and effective body co-ordinating export controls. At its meeting on 14 December 1993 in the Swiss town of Interlaken, formal MTCR membership grew to 25 with the addition of Argentina and Hungary.[36] Virtually every other potential supplier except for North Korea and Arab governments unilaterally adheres to MTCR standards. These standards themselves have become much more severe since 1991, when technical thresholds were lowered to cover all missiles capable of carrying relatively small CBW warheads. In practice the threshold for permissible missile exports has been lowered to make it difficult to sell missiles with maximum ranges over 150 km. An exception in the original document permitting technical support for civilian space launch programmes, still in the formal MTCR guidelines, informally has been narrowed to prohibit such transfers to countries that also have ballistic missile programmes.

In the Middle East the results of all this diplomatic activity are easily seen. The United States long ago stopped selling ballistic missiles. Russia no longer sells Scud-B missiles despite great economic temptations. China too has not supplied its 300 km M-11 or other tactical missiles despite a large potential market. Possibilities for missile sales remain; at the 1993 Abu Dhabi Air Show, Moscow displayed its 120 km SS-21 and the Pentagon is debating the possibility of exporting the 130 km ATACMS. China also continues to help Iran develop artillery rockets, some with ranges of over 100 km. Transfers of missile technologies have also virtually evaporated as European governments drafted new laws and policies and began to enforce them aggressively. While there is a continual need to tighten restrictions and promote enforcement, the nature of the missile market is fundamentally different from a decade ago.

Export restrictions are especially effective in stopping the spread of long-range ballistic missiles, systems capable of ranges of over 1,000 km. At this level, beyond the plateau of easily mastered technology, the technical demands surpass what any would-be missile power can accomplish alone. Even with such help, Saddam was unable to deploy such a system, although he might have had more success given time. Without massive assistance, the task is not something that Iran or any Arab state can manage itself. The only risk is that they will acquire such weapons from a foreign supplier, North Korea or conceivably China.

The export control approach is more ambivalent against Scud technology. Old and relatively simple, this lies well within the technological plateau, permitting determined but less technically advanced states to reverse engineer Scuds for local production or stretch it to create missiles like Iraq's 900 km al Abbas and North Korea's 1,000 km No-Dong-1. Egypt may be able to produce Scuds today. Iran, Libya and Syria probably would like to be able to do so as well. As they pursue this goal, foreign technical assistance will be very helpful, but probably not essential. Export controls can slow their Scud programmes considerably, perhaps by as much as two or three decades. But they cannot halt the slow mastery of such technology altogether.

In the next decade, export controls will remain the key barrier to greater missile proliferation in the Middle East. The critical problem is enforcement, especially regarding renegade suppliers like North Korea. For this there is no satisfying answer; dealing with actors who refuse to accept the prevailing norms of international society is the greatest challenge of efforts to create a peaceful world order, as mysterious and pervasive as it is essential.

The Normative Basis for Control

The greatest problem confronting export controls as the key instrument restraining missile proliferation is not their effectiveness but their inability to create an image of fairness. Although export control is a regime in the legal sense, its basis in adversarial delineations makes it more like an alliance politically. From the perspective of key regional spokesmen, of which India is the most vocal, the whole approach discriminates against the sovereign rights of regional governments to arm themselves as they see fit, to acquire a weapon accepted among other countries. The critique is important because it casts doubt on the legitimacy of North–South export controls in general.

This challenge ultimately is a question of world order. Will future international security affairs be dominated by the pursuit of distinct national interests organized only through us-against-them alliances, or will it give a greater role to collective security organizations based on universal principles? Most missile suppliers are divided on such issues, willing to sacrifice some self-interest, but not if it means providing potential adversaries with weapons like long-range ballistic missiles.

The normative issue in this instance focuses largely on regional space launch projects. India and Israel have reached important milestones in the creation of reliable domestic space launch capabilities. Other countries including Brazil and some East Asian countries are interested in doing the same. Although such projects make little sense commercially, they are of great importance as prestige symbols. Given the dual-use nature of long range rocket technology, however, their direct military applications cannot be overlooked. The MTCR originally endorsed such endeavours, but official opinion has clearly grown less tolerant over time.

The revelation in April 1992 that Russia had previously agreed to provide engine technology for Indian space launchers showed that this question is not an abstraction. This deal, worth an estimated $100–250 million, was harshly criticized in Europe and North America. Although intended to serve civilian objectives, it also would have given India new military potential. The MTCR is not very helpful on this issue, since it permits members (Russia is not a member) to transfer such technology with proper assurances. The dispute points to the need to resolve the larger issue of aid to civil space launch projects if the MTCR is to be fully consistent. The Russian government finally succumbed to aggressive American diplomacy and financial inducements and modified the Indian deal to minimize technology transfer.[37]

This victory was of great importance for the credibility of the regime, but it left normative objections to the regime unresolved. The impact of regional criticism of the discriminatory nature of the MTCR has not been great otherwise. Western leaders may feel some regret, but not enough to reconsider their policies. Contrary to the statements of regional spokesmen, there is no evidence of any country accelerating its rocket projects simply to spite the outside powers trying to slow them down; large rockets are too costly to pursue so frivolously.

Indeed erstwhile adversaries in Latin American and East Asia increasingly support the regime. Even in India there is growing awareness of the advantages of joining.[38] In the Middle East, Israel is a unilateral subscriber, while Egyptian officials indicate that Cairo is not opposed to the MTCR, but would prefer that its work was opened to permit wider consultation and easier access to civilian technology.[39]

Beyond Export Control

Although the international community has no choice but to rely on export controls, the approach will never be technically sufficient or politically satisfying. Especially within the domain of the technological plateau, its weaknesses will gradually become more and more apparent over the years. Even with the best export controls, countries throughout the Middle East gradually will master Scud technology to establish large forces of missiles within the 300 to 1,000 km spectrum.

The real job of export controls is, like other non-proliferation regimes, not to stop totally and reverse the spread of ballistic missiles, but to promote stability and reduce the dangers of rapid change, to slow the overall pace of proliferation and buy time for political settlements. The lessons of recent experience in Argentina-Brazil, South Africa and Taiwan show that buying time can be extremely valuable in and of itself. The differences between those situations and the Middle East are too great to overlook, but they are not so great as to preclude hope of progress. Export controls will contribute to progress toward a political settlement by promoting stability and making military developments more predictable.

But what if a Middle East peace settlement remains as elusive as ever? The most practical solution to the missile race in the Middle East may not be to try to stop it altogether, but to aim more modestly. In the near term most missile acquisition can be discouraged through aggressive promotion of the MTCR. In the long term broader efforts can build toward the political accommodation required to render remaining missile forces irrelevant.[40] For Middle Eastern ballistic missile proliferation, irrelevance may be a more practical goal than disarmament. While it is extremely difficult to envisage Israel and Syria dismantling their strategic forces, for example, one can readily conceive of a political environment in which strategic forces simply cease to matter.

NOTES

 1. The concept of maturity is developed at greater length in Aaron Karp, 'The Maturation of Ballistic Missile Proliferation', in William C. Potter and Harlan W. Jencks, (eds.), *The International Missile Bazaar* (Boulder: Westview, 1994), Ch.1.
 2. Martin Navias, *Saddam's Scud War and Ballistic Missile Proliferation,* London Defence Studies no.6 (London: Brassey's for the Centre for Defence Studies, 1991).
 3. Keith Krause, 'Middle Eastern States in the Global Military Order', *Annals of the American Academy of Political Science* (Sept. 1994).
 4. I am grateful to Geoffrey Kemp for making this point clear to me.
 5. Michael N. Barnett, *Confronting the Costs of War: Military Power, State, and Society in Egypt and Israel* (Princeton: Princeton University Press, 1992); and Etel Solingen, 'The Domestic Sources of Regional Regimes: The Evolution of Nuclear Ambiguity in the Middle East', *International Studies Quarterly* (June 1994).
 6. This assessment is heavily influenced by Clifford Geertz' classic *Negara: The Theatre State in Nineteenth Century Bali* (Princeton: Princeton University Press, 1980) pp.13, 123–5.
 7. Joseph S. Bermudez, Jr., 'Egypt's missile development', in *The International Missile Bazaar,* pp.25–7. According to Avishi Margalit, the first successful letter bombs were invented by the Israeli Mossad as part of Operation 'Damocles' to intimidate German rocket engineers in Egypt. Margalit, 'The Violent life of Yitzhak Shamir', *New York Review of Books,* 14 May 1992, p.22
 8. Herbert Krosney, *Deadly Business: Legal Deals and Outlaw Weapons* (New York: Four Walls Eight Windows, 1993), pp.133–68.
 9. A unique treatment of Egypt's apparent lack of interest in nuclear weapons is Shyam Bhatia, *Nuclear Rivals in the Middle East* (New York: Routledge, 1988) pp.47–63.
10. Bermudez, 'Egypt's Missile Development', pp.32–4.
11. More recent assessments tend to allow Iraqi missile attacks a more decisive role than earlier studies. For example, Shahram Chubin, *Iran's National Security Policy: Capabilities, Intentions and Impact* (Washington: Carnegie Endowment for International Peace, 1994), pp. 21–2; and Stephen C. Pelletiere, *The Iran–Iraq War: Chaos in a Vacuum* (Westport: Praeger, 1992) p.136.
12. Ali Akbar Hashemi Rafsanjani quoted from April 1988 in Chubin, *Iran's National Security Policy,* p. 22.
13. Joseph S. Bermudez, 'Iran's Missile Development', in *The International Missile Bazaar,* pp. 60–1. Bermudez reports of ongoing work on a 200 km version of the Mushak, p.62.
14. W. Seth Carus, 'Proliferation and Security in Southwest Asia', paper presented at the 1993 US Central Command Southwest Asia Symposium, 21 May 1993, p.8.
15. Chubin, *Iran's National Security Policy,* pp. 34–8.
16. *The Washington Times,* 16 June 1994; Bermudez, 'Iran's Missile Development', pp. 64.
17. Paul Lewis, 'Bowing to U.N., Iraq will Permit Arms Monitors', *New York Times,* 27 Nov. 1993', p.1; and Tim Trevan, 'UNSCOM: activities in 1993', *SIPRI Yearbook 1994* (Oxford: Oxford University Press, 1994), Ch. 19.
18. Carus, 'Proliferation and Security in Southwest Asia', p.4.
19. Detailed accounts exist, like Jack Gee, *Mirage: Warplane for the World* (London: MacDonald, 1971), pp. 196–7; and Seymour M. Hersh, *The Sampson Option: Israel, America and the Bomb* (London: Faber and Faber, 1991). These either repeat old, uncon- firmed tales or fill in the gaps with assertions paraded as fact.
20. Avner Cohen, 'Patterns of Nuclear Opacity in the Middle East', in Tariq Rauf (ed.), *Regional*

Approaches to Curbing Nuclear Proliferation in the Middle East and South Asia (Ottawa: Canadian Center for Global Security, 1992) pp.14–41.

21. Michael R. Gordon, 'U.S.Tries to Stop Russian–Libya Deal', *International Herald Tribune*, 24 June 1993.
22. The number of launchers is from *The Military Balance 1993–1994* (London, International Institute for Strategic Studies, 1993), p.122.
23. *The Nonproliferation Review*, Vol. 1, No. 1, p. 142–3; and ibid.,Vol. 1, No. 2 (Winter 1994), p.192.
24. Yezid Sayigh, *Arab Military Industry: Capability, Performance and Impact* (London: Brassey's 1992), pp.234, 239.
25. The concept of the technological plateau is developed more fully in Aaron Karp, *Ballistic Missile Proliferation: the Politics and Technics* (Oxford University Press, 1995), Ch.8.
26. The most cogent efforts to dismiss their significance stress the fact 39 Iraqi missiles caused only two direct fatalities in Israel. Anyone personally involved in the experience surely would disregard this argument as pedantic at best. George N. Lewis, Steve Fetter and Lisbeth Grunlund, *Casualties and Damage from Scud Attacks in the 1991 Gulf War* (Cambridge, Massachusetts: MIT, Defense and Arms Control Studies Program, 1993).
27. Launcher figure compiled from *The Military Balance* 1993-1994.
28. Yahya M. Sadowski, *Scuds or Butter? the Political Economy of Arms Control in the Middle East* (Washington, DC: Brookings, 1993).
29. Aaron Karp, 'Ballistic Missile Proliferation', *SIPRI Yearbook 1989* (Oxford: Oxford University Press, 1989), pp.291, 302.
30. Steven Zaloga, 'The Tochka Tactical Ballistic Missile System', *Jane's Intelligence Review*, Jan. 1994, pp.6–10.
31. Gerald M. Steinberg, 'The Middle East', *Encyclopedia of Arms Control*, Vol. 1 (New York: Charles Scribner & Sons, 1993, pp. 183–4. For an example of a detailed proposal, Kathleen C. Bailey, 'Arms Control for the Middle East', *International Defence Review*, No. 4 (April 1991), pp. 311–14.
32. Colin S. Grey, *House of Cards* (Ithaca: Cornell University Press, 1992).
33. *The Military Balance 1993–1994* (London: IISS, October 1993), p.75.
34. Mark A. Heller, 'Coping with Missile Proliferation in the Middle East', *Orbis* (Winter 1991), pp.24–7.
35. Gerald M. Steinberg, 'Middle East Arms Control and Regional Security', *Survival* (Spring 1994), pp.126–40.
36. 'Missile Technology Control Regime meets in Switzerland', press release, US Arms Control and Disarmament Agency, 14 Dec. 1993.
37. Edmund F. Scherr, 'US, Russia Agree on Missile Technology Control Guidelines', *USIA Wireless File*, 16 July 1993.
38. Gautam Adhikari, 'Requiem for non-alignment', *Times of India* (New Delhi), 26 May 1992; Dilip Mukerjee, 'The Nuclear Option: Ambiguity Difficult to Maintain', ibid., 9 June 1992.
39. Discussions with Mahmoud Karem, Director of Disarmament Affairs, Egyptian Ministry of Foreign Affairs, and Mounir Zahran, Egyptian Ambassador to the United Nations, in Geneva, 14–15 Feb. 1994.
40. A similar suggestion is developed more fully by Efraim Karsh and Yezid Sayigh, 'A Co-operative Approach to Arab-Israeli Security', *Survival* (Spring 1994), pp.114 25.

The Regional Context

Domestic Aspects of Strategic Postures: The Past and Future in a Middle East Nuclear Regime

ETEL SOLINGEN

This paper examines domestic aspects of the debate over the establishment of a regional nuclear regime in the Middle East. It does so in order to offset the marginal attention paid to the impact of domestic processes and institutions in the definition of strategic outcomes.[1]

The call for incorporating domestic politics into the study of international regimes is not new but, with few exceptions, has been rarely followed by actual applications.[2] That failure has not been the subject of great controversy in the analysis of nuclear options in the Middle East, because neorealist assumptions about the primacy of state survival considerations have gained unparalleled analytical supremacy. The potential for physical annihilation compelled a neorealist point of departure, even when neorealist assumptions led to no particular saddlepoint, or solution (in logical terms, the search for survival could have led to a range of means and outcomes).

That different domestic actors are likely to define strategic options with different considerations in mind seems self-evident. Domestic groups weigh different international outcomes according to the latter's potential effect on their own political and institutional pay-offs. The pay-offs associated with different outcomes can be affected by different mixes of side-payments. For instance, no military establishment entrusted with maintaining conventional deterrence would endanger its access to conventional weapons, the means with which it maintains its mission.

In general terms, domestic actors rank their preferences according to the rate at which they discount the future, their degree of receptivity to transparency, their sensitivity coefficients to gaps in gains, and/or their definition of a 'balanced exchange'. These four, of course, are influenced by the extent to which actors are concerned with short-term political/electoral gains or with longer-term institutional and bureaucratic survival. Thus, the conventional military establishment may be open to absolute (mutual) gains and transparency at the nuclear level while resisting anything other than relative gains in conventional weaponry. A certain political party may be reluctant to ratify an agreement that does not make its own positional gains clear. Strategic postures are nested in a multidimentional space where foreign aid and investment, technological change, electoral cycles (or their equivalent), and conventional military balances intersect in often unpredictable ways.

If one construes the past evolution of Middle East nuclear postures with these considerations in mind, where does one look in trying to understand the emergence of nuclear opaqueness on the one hand, and a stillborn regional regime on the other?[3] Were these outcomes compatible with the ability of relevant domestic groups to pursue their own political agendas? Were they perhaps even optimal in terms of increasing their internal political latitude? A positive answer to these questions might render domestic considerations a powerful contender in the arena where alternative ways of conceptualizing strategic behaviour claim relative superiority.

This study begins with an overview of the historical evolution of nuclear postures in the region, and ends with an assessment of changes in recent years that may affect present and future postures.

The Past

During the last three decades the Middle East has been considered in the non-proliferation literature to host elements of a nuclear deterrence model, albeit falling short of the overt version of that model that has characterized, for instance, the United States – former Soviet Union strategic balance. Instead of a full-blown open race, we have had an overall ambiguous pattern, with no open acknowledgement of existing nuclear military capabilities or of intentions to acquire nuclear weapons. This ambiguity (nuclear 'opaqueness') has been present both among states, such as Iraq and Iran, that had commited themselves to multilateral full-scope safeguards (through Non-proliferation Treaty membership), as well as in Israel, which had not made such commitments.

Several explanations have been put forth for the emergence of opaqueness; they include, *inter alia*, the presence of both superpowers as barriers to a full-blown overt nuclear race, and the evolving strength of the non-proliferation regime.[4] Presumably, both forces acted to restrain all regional actors through potentially punitive sanctions, forcing them to veil their postures and to submerge their capabilities. The sources of opaqueness, however, can also be traced to domestic considerations, which at the very least reinforced external constraints, and possible presented an equally compelling reason for maintaining opaqueness. Internal considerations not only shed light on the sources of opaqueness; they also rendered the establishment of a regional regime implausible, given the respective domestic win-sets within each of the Middle Eastern potential partners to a regime.[5]

Opaqueness in Israel: Overdetermined?

A survey of Israel's nuclear postures reveals weak domestic support for an open deterrent. Opaqueness, instead, increased the latitude of powerful political coalitions and institutions to pursue their respective agendas. On the one hand, there was Ben-Gurion and his followers, among whom support for a nuclear deterrent was strongest. Moshe Dayan even came close to declaring the existence of such a deterrent.[6] On the other hand, there were the nuclear sceptics, including some mainstream opponents of Ben-Gurion within the ruling party Mapai, as well as leftist coalition partners (particularly the pro-Soviet Mapam and Ahdut Haavoda).

In light of this opposition, Ben-Gurion avoided discussing nuclear policy in full cabinet meetings, while nurturing the nascent programme from his own political resources.[7] The Dimona nuclear complex was started through private fund-raising in 1957, without the knowledge of the Knesset's Foreign Affairs and Security Committee or the approval of its Finance Committee.[8] Clearly, Ben-Gurion's faction could find ample political ammunition to fuel the country's nuclear programme in Arab calls for the obliteration of Israel, and in active Arab procurement of non-conventional capabilities by the 1950s, including missile and chemical weapons technology. In December 1960 Ben-Gurion addressed the Israeli Knesset on this topic, in response to an inquiry from US Secretary of State Christian Herter.[9] The timing of the disclosure, and its venue, revealed the interplay of domestic and external considerations.

Opaqueness was instrumental to the maintenance of Israel's Labor coalition. The fragile nature of ruling coalitions stemmed from the inability of any single party to command a clear majority of votes, which granted small parties the power to impose their view on the basis of their coalitional 'value'. Mapam's and Ahdut Haavoda's influence within Israel's politically powerful General Federation of Labor (*Histadrut*), for instance, enabled these parties to extract concessions from their coalition partners.[10] The leadership of these two parties, including the influential Yigal Allon, rejected an overt deterrent that could unleash a destructive regional race, as well as inflame the anti-nuclear feelings of pro-Soviet constituencies within their parties and exacerbate Soviet sensitivity to Israeli nuclear activities.[11] They consequently opposed then Deputy Defence Minister Shimon Peres' efforts to seek French and West German technical and defence co-operation.[12] Popular opposition to closer relations (particularly military co-operation!) with West Germany was not confined to Mapam and Ahdut Haavoda, and had the potential of igniting a Cabinet crisis, as it did in 1957 and 1959.[13] Eventually, Ben-Gurion's German policy accelerated his political exit.

Coalition and party politics thus played a role in propelling opaqueness as a solution in the early years; different parties had different associations with external actors and different receptivities to transparency. This is far from arguing that policy preferences could be completely reduced to pure political calculi. Ben-Gurion led Israel into statehood out of the ashes of concentration camps, and regarded the survival of the state as his life's historical mission. Such was the goal of other Israeli leaders as well, however, many of whom were not persuaded that a nuclearized Middle East would either guarantee Israel's existence or command extensive domestic support.[14]

As argued, opponents of a nuclear deterrent in the 1950s and 1960s included not only leaders of Ahdut Haavoda (Yigal Allon, Israel Gallili) and Mapam (Yaacov Hazan, Yair Zaban), but also leading members of Mapai (such as Prime Ministers Levy Eshkol and Golda Meir, Defence Minister and later *Histadrut* secretary-general Pinhas Lavon, Finance Minister Pinhas Sapir, and Foreign Minister Abba Eban).[15] Eshkol (formerly a Finance Minister as well) and Sapir were the architects of an incipient policy of economic liberalization, adjustment and privatization, conceived in the early 1960s, aimed at attracting foreign investment and promoting exports. Moving away from a statist, mercantilist strategy and toward economic solvency implied greater reliance on international markets and new political alliances. Eshkol thus opposed nuclear expenditures and was willing to effect some changes in the nuclear programme, which also made him appear more responsive to US concerns.[16] The US commitment to supply Israel with conventional weapons is often interpreted as a trade-off accepted by Eshkol (in exchange for nuclear restraint), but can also be regarded as useful ammunition for Eshkol – in domestic terms – to pursue a policy he favoured anyway.

Another prominent Knesset member from Mapai, Eliezer Livne, founded the Committee for Denuclearization of the Middle East in 1961 – including prestigious Israeli scientists – which enjoyed wide access to high-level Labor figures.[17] Ben-Gurion's tensions with his own Mapai party can be traced to the bitter Lavon Affair of 1955, arguably Israel's foremost political scandal to this day. This affair, involving accountability for a botched espionage operation in Egypt, ultimately led to Ben-Gurion's departure from Mapai, and the creation, before the 1965 elections, of a new party, Rafi, known to a few as 'the atomic party'.[18] Ben-Gurion's political foe Pinhas Lavon (close to the Ahdut Haavoda and Mapam leadership), ridiculed the group around Ben-Gurion as the self-appointed 'defence avant-garde', while Allon accused the same group of 'defence demagoguery'.[19] In effect, important sections of Rafi's constituency valued their leaders' image of reliability and technological sophistication regarding matters of national survival. .

With Ben-Gurion's resignation in 1963 (in the midst of debates over relations with West Germany), his own influence over nuclear policy declined (his Rafi followers merged into the Labor Alignment in 1969). Opaqueness continued to provide an equilibrium solution, particularly when Dayan became Defence Minister in 1967 under Prime Minister Eshkol, in a cabinet where Ahdut Haavoda's Allon had been most influential on defence matters. The policy found its institutionalization in the formula articulated by Eshkol, that has since become the country's only declared – and highly ambiguous – policy on the nuclear issue, namely that Israel would 'not be the first to introduce nuclear weapons to the Middle East'. Dayan's occasional references – as Defence Minister – to the advantages of an open deterrent did not prevail within the cabinet headed by Golda Meir in the early 1970s either.

It is hardly surprising, given our discussion so far, that Israel's endorsement of a nuclear-weapon-free zone (NWFZ) in 1975 was formally submitted to the UN General Assembly by no other than Foreign Minister Allon, with considerable support from most political leaders and the Israeli public.[20] By that time, supporters of an open deterrent were becoming marginalized (but far from irrelevant, given the impact of an intractable Arab position on Israeli public opinion). Former Chief of Staff Yitzhak Rabin declared in 1974, in response to former Defence Minister Moshe Dayan's call for nuclear weapons: 'Attempts to rely on mystical weapons are negative trends'.[21] Moshe Dayan eventually joined Labor's main competitor, Likud, and served as its foreign minister.

A Likud-led coalition defeated Labor in 1977, backed by forces opposed to an Israeli withdrawal from the West Bank and Golan Heights. Likud's rejection of a territorial compromise on the basis of the security requirement for strategic depth could have weakened the party's ability to claim the additional need for a nuclear deterrent.[22] The continuation of opaqueness also prevented any further deterioration in Likud's troubled relationship with the United States. The policy was upheld in spite of apparent shifts among some prominent Likud leaders. Defence Minister Ariel Sharon, traditionally associated with the 'conventional' school of thought, declared that 'Israel cannot cope with the conventional arms race with the Arabs who have superiority in manpower and capital'.[23] This statement echoed earlier statements by Dayan.[24]

The two classical coalitions in Israeli politics have responded differently to mixes of outside pressures and inducements. Labor-centred coalitions have used external carrots and sticks (political and economic) to build domestic consensus favouring territorial compromise and a comprehensive political settlement. They have been more receptive than Likud-centred coalitions to use effective international tools (United Nations peacekeeping forces, US diplomacy) to induce trust in regional agreements and compromises among its constituents.[25] A recent statement by Deputy Foreign Minister Yossi Beilin summarizes the aims of Labor diplomacy: 'to use the new situation in order to become a more welcome member of the international club'.[26] Likud-led coalitions have generally used external pressures to coalesce forces opposed to a territorial settlement on the West Bank or to a withdrawal from the Golan Heights.

These differences between the two coalitions do not necessarily imply a different receptivity to intrusive (external) verification measures and to international inducements for denuclearization of the region, which everybody opposes. However, such differences may presage a gap between the two coalitions, regarding their respective visions of the 'the day after' a comprehensive Middle East peace is reached. Influential former Likud ministers like Ariel Sharon, Yuval Neeman and Rafel Eitan are known to oppose a NWFZ.[27] Moreover, Likud refused to rely on the International Atomic Energy Agency to neutralize Iraq's pursuit of nuclear weapons; in 1981 the Begin government launched an attack on Iraq's Osirak reactor (three weeks before general elections and with Likud lagging in the polls) enunciating the Begin Doctrine, while Labor opposed the strike.[28] Such cleavages, however, did not always easily carry over into a clear-cut party-based partisanship favouring or opposing overt deterrence.

Opaqueness accommodated more than coalitional considerations; it prevented bitter encounters among the conventional and nuclear establishments, a divided scientific community, competing economic agencies, and parties to a potentially explosive public debate.

On the one hand, the influential Israeli military establishment (and its associated military-industrial complex) fundamentally resisted reliance on a nuclear deterrent.[29] This position is not at all unusual among conventional military establishments in countries with an ambiguous nuclear programme. Maintaining conventional superiority had been a long-standing objective of the Israeli Defence Forces.[30] Supporters of an open, full-fledged nuclear deterrent often invoked its value as a means to reduce the need for conventional forces.[31] Such claims represented a potential institutional threat to the conventional military establishment, exacerbating competition for dwindling budgetary resources. Moreover, an overt deterrent could have threatened the external network of procurement of conventional weaponry (high performance combat aircraft in particular) and of sourcing for locally-produced equipment.[33] The military establishment was particularly sensitive to the fact that about 50 per cent of the defence budget was covered by US military aid. Finally, Israel's Defence Forces would have been required to maintain their conventional deterrent and fighting missions even in light of diminished capabilities, at potentially much higher human costs.

On the other hand, there was the prestigious Israel Atomic Energy Commission (IAEC) and Israel's nuclear industrial infrastructure, estimated to be relatively small, particularly compared to the extensive network of conventional arms producers.[34] The IAEC's autonomy diminished with Ben-Gurion's departure, and the agency was transferred from the Ministry of Defence to the Prime Minister's office, under Levy Eshkol. The composition of the IAEC was then broadened to include representatives of civilian sectors, including energy, medical, and agricultural research, as well as the Ministry of Finance.[35] This diversification was more than compatible with opaqueness, allowing nucleocrats with divergent agendas (civilian versus military uses of nuclear energy) to cohabit the IAEC. In the end, an opaque programme was the perfect means to sidestep budgetary transparency, to weaken oversight by financial agencies, to avoid bureaucratic hurdles, and to ward off potential challenges from the scientific community.

Prominent scientists had opposed the nuclear programme and six out of seven members of IAEC resigned by 1957, allegedly on the basis of their rejection of nuclear weapons and of the opportunity costs of a nuclear programme for the advancement of basic research.[36] Only Professor Ernst David Bergman – a prominent member of Rafi, founder of the science corps within the Israeli military, and principal adviser to Ben-Gurion on nuclear matters – remained, until Eshkol replaced him in 1966, arguably as part of an effort to freeze the development of the Dimona facilities.[37] The incident with the IAEC and its scientists had more of a symbolic than a practical impact (the programme required technology more than science). In light of the social valuation of scientists in Israeli society, too much attention on the incident had the potential for weakening popular support. From the point of view of the general argument advanced in this paper, it is interesting to highlight the role that maximizing institutional support for basic science played in shaping the position of this prestigious group of scientists.

The benefits of opaqueness also reached sectors that were not directly involved in nuclear policy, but feared potentially detrimental consequences from an unrestrained nuclear posture. In particular, the Israeli economy was highly dependent on Western financial flows, that supported a vast network of state agencies and powerful General Federation of Labor (*Histadrut*) enterprises, as well as a growing private sector. Mapai, Mapam, and Ahdut Haavoda enjoyed great support within *Histadrut*, unlike Ben-Gurion's followers. Political constraints precluded ruling coalitions from reducing external dependence by shifting the burden of financing economic development, welfare, and defence, to Israeli society.[38] Important and increasingly concentrated financial and economic institutions subsidized by the state resisted any prospects of upsetting their lifeline dependence on foreign (mostly US) capital, investment and technology.

If there was one single item that had the highest potential of concatenating an economic severance from external sources of economic support, the open embrace of a nuclear deterrent was it. Western powers had developed a regime with formal and informal injunctions, designed to persuade would-be newcomers to the nuclear club that such intentions would involve costly consequences in the economic arena, among others.[39] No Israeli ruling coalition could have survived the domestic political fallout of economic sanctions. Democratic leaders facing electoral approval are far more constrained in distributing the punishing costs of sanctions than has been the case with, for instance, the Iraqi leadership. Finally, the financial agencies of the state (Treasury in particular) have had a long-standing, at times very bitter, dispute with defence agencies over the military budget. Although the size of Israeli nuclear investments is not publicly known, and is often assumed to have been relatively small, the added defence burden of a large-scale programme had the potential of exacerbating such tensions. In a relatively small economy, the opportunity costs of such a programme could not have been kept entirely invisible.

Opaqueness in the Arab World: Regime Survival

Just as opaqueness reflected an equilibrium among Israeli political forces, it was more expedient for successive coalitions in the Middle East to maintain domestic consensus over opaqueness than to embrace overt deterrence. In particular, ambiguity about Israel's – and other Arab states' or Iran's – capabilities helped stem popular challenges to unstable regimes and allayed the concerns of both the conventional military establishment and of economic groups (state agencies as well as private actors). First, any formal recognition that Israel had nuclear weapons would have forced leaders to counter that capability, in response to popular dissatisfaction with the idea of an Israeli nuclear monopoly.[40] What Jabber labels the imperative of 'deterrent emulation' is evident from statements like 'It must be made clear that we cannot possibly stand idly by if Israel introduces atomic weapons into the area' (President Sadat) and 'We in Syria have a counterplan, in the event that Israel gets nuclear weapons' (President Asad).[41]

Those who were most forceful in declaring that Israel in fact *had* such weapons without a shred of doubt – Iraq and Libya – also embarked in the most extensive efforts in the Arab world to acquire nuclear weapons.[42] The more Arab leaders pointed to a clear-cut Israeli capability, the more compelled they became to forge a coherent response to it. Opaqueness, instead, offered at least a partial fig leaf for resisting domestic pressures; it made it possible for Sadat and other Egyptian officials to argue that, although they believed Israel was capable of manufacturing a nuclear bomb, it [Israel] 'does not have nuclear weapons'.[43] President Asad and King Faisal pronounced similar statements imputing to Israel a potential, rather than an actual weapon. Opaqueness thus mitigated the immediate political pressure to match Israeli capabilities and, at least in some instances, helped buy time off for efforts to achieve nuclear parity.[44]

The following statement by Mohamed Hasanayn Heikal strengthens the argument that the drive to measure-up with Israeli nuclear endowments was less of a response to strategic interaction considerations and had primarily a domestic basis: 'Israel has nuclear weapons but will not use them unless she finds herself being strangled'.[45] This recognition that Israeli nuclear capabilities – whatever they may be – have been designed as defensive, rather than offensive tools, is particularly astounding coming from the foremost advocate of nuclear weapons in Egypt. Israel's survival motive, however, has been widely acknowledged, despite attempts by radicals to invest an Israeli weapon with offensive objectives. As King Hussein of Jordan declared, the Israelis would not use a nuclear device 'unless they were in mortal danger'.[46] Strategic interaction, in other words, might have arguably played a greater role – in strengthening support for *national* (*qaumyia*) nuclear deterrents – in the context of inter-Arab or Arab-Iranian relations than of the Arab–Israeli conflict.[47]

In addition to this more or less common constraint shared by most Arab regimes, opaqueness was reinforced by the international-domestic links of competing politics of industrialization. Throughout most of the Cold War era two basic types of coalition – both leaning on the military – ruled over Middle Eastern countries. On the one hand, there were inward-looking nationalist-populist groups which conquered the state to implant pan-Arab versions of Soviet-style regimes (Syria, Iraq, Libya and Egypt in the 1950s and 1960s). This group was the most active in pursuing nuclear weapons.[48] Yet their project was constrained by the fact that Soviet economic support was critical to their ability to maintain domestic legitimacy for their comprehensive revolutionary objectives.

Transgressing the boundaries of the superpower consensus to stem the proliferation of nuclear weapons throughout the world endangered those objectives. These constraints (which transcend the foreign–domestic boundary) precluded a policy of overt deterrence *but not one of opaqueness,* and they may well explain these countries' eventual decision to sign the

NPT. Signing it was not altogether equivalent to abiding by its spirit, as was often suspected and more recently confirmed in the case of Iraq.[49] *De facto*, therefore, these coalitions implemented a policy of opaqueness that had the double advantage of not compromising the foreign benefactors of their domestic power base while nurturing important political segments in that base.

On the other hand, there were coalitions relying on the political, military and/or economic support of the United States and Western Europe, primarily in Saudi Arabia and the Gulf states, Jordan, Lebanon and Egypt (1970s and 1980s). For these coalitions, nuclear 'restraint' was also a requirement to maintain the external support on which the interests of important domestic segments relied. Lack of restraint (a pursuit of weapons capabilities) implied bilateral and mutilateral economic sanctions, likely to damage the concentrated interests of rising industrial, contracting and commercial sectors in expanding trade and investments.[50] Restraint (ideally in the form of a NWFZ) was in line with embracing regional policies that would not threaten the domestic beneficiaries of international economic, financial and political exchanges. These benefits included debt-forgiveness, export markets, technology transfer, food imports, aid, and investments. The beneficiaries were generally among these regimes' most economically powerful constituencies, such as the oil-exporting industries in the Gulf and the tourist-based and *munfatihun* ('openers') economies of Egypt and Jordan.[51] Leading exemplars of such coalitions – Iran and Egypt under the Shah and Sadat respectively – played an entrepreneurial role in advancing the idea of a NWFZ, for the first time in 1974.

The impact of the political-economic nature of ruling coalitions on nuclear postures can be traced quite clearly in the case of Egypt, in its evolution from a Nasserite strategy of redistribution and import-substitution industrialization to Sadat's post-1973 accumulation-and-growth blueprint.[52] Nasser was reported to have pursued nuclear weapons from the Soviet Union at the height of their strategic alliance, and nuclear technology more generally from other suppliers.[53] M. Hasanayn Heikal, an adviser to Nasser and the editor of Egypt's influential *Al-Ahram*, was himself an ardent supporter of an Arab nuclear deterrent.[54] It was the requirements of transforming the domestic political economy through *infitah* (economic liberalization) – the 'economic crossing' – that compelled Sadat to negotiate an unprecedented peace treaty with Israel.[55] That *infitah* was launched in 1974, the same year Egypt advanced, for the first time, the idea of a NWFZ, is quite suggestive. Sadat understood the prerequisites of his domestic economic programme, that precluded a nuclear arms race with a formidable opponent.[56]

Abandoning nuclear ambiguity would also deal a blow to Sadat's domestic political foes, particularly Nasserist, pro-Soviet groups which he regarded as a constant threat to his rule, and which included prominent nuclear advocates. Transcending nuclear ambiguity had the additional advantage of suiting the external requirements of Sadat's strategy for Egypt's transformation, namely, improving relations with the West. President Nixon visited Egypt that year, as a symbol of solidifying US–Egyptian relations. By 1979, Sadat was requesting a foreign aid package of $18 billion from the G-7 group. Egypt's ruling coalition had tied its grand strategy of industrialization to 'internationalist' instruments. The attempt to secure the political survival of its domestic coalition may also explain Egypt's regional entrepreneurship in brokering between regional parties to a regime, pointing to overlapping interests, and designing innovative arrangements, such as a Security Council role in establishing a NWFZ.[57]

Key to regime survival in most Arab Middle Eastern countries was the support of the military as an institution. An overt nuclear posture posed similar – and in some cases magnified – challenges to the expansion of conventional military establishments and their industrial complexes in the Arab world and Iran, as they did in Israel.[58] The military has been arguably the most powerful political institution in these countries, unconstrained by concerns with subordination to civilian authorities or democratic challenges. Yet the protracted economic crisis in each of these states imposed some limits on the ability of Arab regimes to extract resources from civil society.[59] Structural adjustment programmes often had adverse effects on arms imports and on the special privileges of military officers.[60] Economic reform also strengthened the hands of civilian technocrats, politicians and economic institutions in charge of adjustment programmes. Under conditions of contracting resources, the pursuit of a nuclear deterrent would have exacerbated the need for trade-offs in military budgets, while leaving intact the conventional mission of 'freeing Arab lands'.[61]

Opaqueness, instead, enabled military establishments highly dependent on the flow of weapons, technology and military aid to maintain their power basis. Opaqueness also ensured and extended the institutional half-life of Atomic Energy Commissions, mostly through hidden budgetary allocations and the absence of oversight. The relative strength of nuclear establishments in the Arab world is not easy to assess, but there is evidence that only Iraq's Ba'th regime managed to coalesce a strong infrastructure of interests (technical communities and state agencies) employing 20,000 people with an investment of $10 bn.[62] Iraq promised to become the first Arab state to obtain a military nuclear capability,[63] and the oil bonanza provided the means to back this commitment. Most other nuclear establishments had more severe budgetary and industrial-technological constraints and were likely to forgo advocating overt competition with a highly reputable Israeli, or with fellow Arab or Iranian counterparts.

Summing up, this historical review of the domestic sources of nuclear postures suggests that opaqueness prevailed in the region for many years because it served the parochial political and institutional concerns of most relevant actors well.

The Present and a Future Regime: Which Way the Middle East?

The revolutionary changes in global politics and economics at the end of the Cold War – including the results of the Gulf War – have precipitated regional and domestic changes in the Middle East. These changes led to the Madrid peace process, to the momentous agreements between Israel and the Palestine Liberation Organization (PLO) in September 1993, to the peace Treaty with Jordan, and to a new set of relations between Israel and the Arab world.[64]

The latent conditions for this turnabout can be found in the broader process of political and economic change affecting the region in recent years, and in a new modality of coalitional politics in the Middle East. On the one hand, liberalizing domestic coalitions aiming at greater integration with the world economy have become more widely entrenched than ever before. Their strategies of industrialization – and the need to secure economic benefits to its supporting constituencies – required the kind of security arrangements that would gain the blessing of the international community.[65] The Gulf War epitomized the willingness of these coalitions to embrace a more 'internationalist' – rather than a narrow regional – approach. This process culminated in their decision to enter into unprecedented bilateral and multilateral negotiations with Israel, a process started in Madrid in 1991.

On the other hand, an alternative alliance of political and economic forces has begun challenging liberalizing coalitions throughout the region. The common denominator in this nationalist-populist grouping is the rejection of 'Western' regimes on the basis of threatened material or ideal-confessional interests. On the material side, economic liberalization and orthodox stabilization plans, particularly as imposed by the International Monetary Fund (IMF) and other financial institutions, endanger import-competing firms with close ties to the state and domestic markets, unskilled, blue-collar workers, white-collar and other state employees, small firms, politicians who oppose the dismantling of state enterprises (a rich source of political patronage), and the underemployed intelligentsia.[66]

Radical Islamic groups are perhaps the most significant ideological force in the region espousing an alternative political economy of development.[67] Its tenets include a repudiation of ties to the international economy and its perceived associated scourges: inequalities, corruption, unemployment and enslaving indebtedness. In the words of Hasan al-Turabi, leader of Sudan's National Islamic Front, Islam seeks justice and will 'challenge those who enjoy an advantage under the present world order, in economic relations between north and south, in the UN structure, in the monopoly of information, technology or armaments'.[68]

Islamic coalitions often include 'bourgeois fractions, some rural agrarian capitalists, notables and estate-owners, and the virtually proletarianized members of the state-employed petite-bourgeoisie, the underemployed intelligentsia, and the large student population'.[69] The common thread in this logrolled alliance is the advancement of a new socio-political order in which the idea of a peace settlement with non-Muslims seems a contradiction in terms, confounding the clear Islamic dichotomy of *dar-al-Islam* (Islamic realm) and *dar-al harb* (realm of warfare). The domestic political appeal of radical (also labelled fundamentalist) movements stems from their call to redress global inequities and frozen hierarchies, and from their willingness to advance 'extreme', final, redeeming solutions to social and political problems.[70] Islamic movements were the most active opponents to the Camp David Peace accords and, more recently, to any negotiations with Israel, including the Madrid peace process.[71]

These two contending coalitions – liberalizing and nationalist-populist-confessional – face a new common strategic regional context, and within it, the newest regional nuclear dilemma. The dilemma stems from a growing inability to question the existence of Israel's alleged nuclear arsenal, a position that had become untenable since the mid-1980s, partly as a consequence of Mordechai Vanunu's declarations to the London *Times*.[72] Regardless of the latter's reliability, it is far harder today to uphold what growing sections of public opinion throughout the Middle East now consider a fiction: that Israel is not yet a nuclear power. Thus, the instrumentality of an ambiguous posture – as a response to an ambiguous threat – to maintaining a balance of domestic interests has withered away. The two coalitions have thus been forced to define contrasting solutions to this dilemma.

Liberalizing coalitions, including Israel, the PLO, Jordan and Egypt, are now negotiating an arms control regime in the context of the multilateral peace process.[73] In the past, Israeli proposals for a NWFZ through direct negotiations were rejected, with Arab states pushing for immediate universal accession to the NPT, without negotiations.[74] The Madrid process offers a new context, where a nuclear regime is to be negotiated through direct negotiations among the partners. There are profound disagreements over the appropriate sequence in tackling conventional and non-conventional aspects of an arms control regime, with Egypt maintaining a firmer demand for Israel's acceptance of NPT status than a decade ago.[75] Yet, the balance of these ongoing negotiations is a huge step forward towards a future regime that could have never been conceived of in the past.

Radical nationalist and/or Islamic coalitions have not, thus far, shown a willingness to negotiate any regimes. In fact, Iran discontinued its formerly active role in promoting a NWFZ at the United Nations in 1979, in the aftermath of the Islamic revolution.[76] Iran has become the foremost representative of a coalition basing its political power on contempt for Western political and economic principles. Reformist, 'economy first', or 'pragmatic' currents (including Rafsanjani) favouring *economic liberalization* (*Baz-Sazi*, rebuilding) have not yet prevailed in Iran.[77] Radical Islamic organizations in control of bloated state industries and charity foundations have little incentive to transfer their power to private entrepreneurs, or to discontinue challenging 'Western' regimes and institutions.[78] The continued struggle between these two factions explains the tension in Iran's foreign policy in general, and nuclear postures in particular. On the one hand, President Rafsanjani has forcefully denied any nuclear weapon designs by Iran, an NPT signatory.[79] On the other hand, Vice-president Sayed Ayatollah Mohajerani argued in 1992 that, 'We, the Muslims, must co-operate to produce an atomic bomb, regardless of UN efforts to prevent proliferation'.[80]

The advocacy of an 'Islamic bomb' is not new; it was conceived less in the context of a coherent military strategy and more as an instrument to offset psychological injuries and arguably to restore pride and prestige. In the words of Pakistani physicist Hoodbhoy, 'the concept behind the term [Islamic bomb] is of Muslim origin. The idea of a nuclear weapon for collective defence of the entire Muslim *ummah* was, after all, articulated and advocated by Muslim leaders who recognized its popularity and determined to benefit from it'.[81] However, fundamentalist movements are not an ideological monolith, and an 'Islamic nuclear club' seems little more than a myth, as Hoodbhoy himself argues, particularly considering the past record of success of integrative frameworks (pan-Arab, pan-Islamic) in the Middle East.[82] Whatever nuclear capabilities Iran may be interested in seeking, they are now a problem of the international community, and not merely of its neighbours, and may thus require the kind of international intervention engineered for Iraq, through a UN Special Commission.[83]

The coalitional cleavages just described – between liberalizing and militant regimes – shape Israel's own dilemma; this is a rather different dilemma to that Israel has confronted for most of its existence as a state. On the one hand, changes in the Arab world toward liberalization and the end of armed struggle have strengthened segments of the Israeli electorate and leadership calling for a negotiated territorial compromise. The *intifada* had earlier sensitized the Israeli public to the need for political, rather than techno-military solutions to Israel's security predicament. On the other hand, most of the major actors in the region are assumed to have chemical weapons and strenuously to pursue biological, ballistic missile, and in some cases, nuclear capabilities (Iran and Iraq, in particular).[84] Most major Arab states have not signed the 1992 Chemical Weapons Convention. Syria, Lebanon, Iraq and Iran are not party to the multilateral regional peace talks. Moreover, the unprovoked Scud attacks by Iraq during the Gulf War – and their threatened chemical payload – transformed public perceptions of the country's vulnerability.[85]

There has been no popular debate in Israel over the merits of alternative nuclear futures. However, in 1986 almost 66 per cent of the public explicitly rejected basing Israel's security on nuclear weapons or their use, under any circumstances.[86] Following Saddam Hussein's threats to 'incinerate half of Israel' with chemical weapons, in 1991, 88 per cent of Israelis responded that the use of nuclear weapons could be 'justified in principle'.[87] That percentage fell to 66 per cent only two years later. In 1993, 72 per cent of the sample also supported the idea of abandoning all non-conventional weapons if the other countries in the region did so as well. These responses not only render themselves to ambiguous interpretations but, as with other surveys in other countries, reveal some volatility (and perhaps flexibility) on popular attitudes regarding nuclear issues.

Labour's electoral comeback in 1992 has already helped transform Israel's place in the region. An arms control regime is under discussion in the context of multilateral peace talks, and could take one of two forms:[88] first, a *limited* regime, ensuring compliance with non-deployment, an agreement not to attack each others' nuclear facilities, perhaps a comprehensive test ban, and other confidence-building measures; and second, a *NWFZ*, imposing a complete ban on the production, purchase, test, use, or presence of nuclear weapons (as with the South Pacific's Rarotonga and Latin America's Tlatelolco Treaty).

An *effectively-verified* regime to free the region from all weapons of mass destruction may now, more than ever before, be part of Israel's domestic win-set.[89] Yet, before Israel relinquishes any of its alleged advanced nuclear weapons, such a regime will have to be:

1. Far more robust than what current NPT procedures can guarantee, and regionally-based. Israeli concerns with compliance have been vindicated by the widespread Iraqi violations of NPT rules.[90]
2. Far more comprehensive than narrowly nuclear. It will require a ban on all weapons of mass destruction.
3. Far more inclusive than the countries currently represented in the multi-

lateral arms control negotiations.[91]

4) Far more rooted in a comprehensive political settlement than the ongoing official discussions are. There are signs of growing Arab recognition that the alleged Israeli nuclear deterrent will not whither away prior to such settlement.[92] Yezid Sayigh, co-ordinator of the Palestinian team to the Multilateral Working Group on Arms Control, suggested that 'nuclear disarmament and the establishment of a nuclear-weapons-free zone could be delayed until the conventional threat was removed'; such concessions would, of course, need to be reciprocated in other areas.[93]

All this implies that we are only at the beginning of a long road, and internal developments within each country will largely define its course.

NOTES

1. The first such attempt, on which this article is based, was entitled 'The Domestic Sources of International Regimes: The Evolution of Nuclear Ambiguity in the Middle East', and appeared in *International Studies Quarterly*, Vol. 38, No.4 (June 1994). pp.305–38. The original version included an extended discussion of neorealist, neoliberal institutionalist and reflective-interpretive dimensions of the problem, which are excluded here.

2. On the inattention to domestic politics, see Charles Lipson, 'International Co-operation in Economic and Security Affairs', *World Politics*, Vol. 37, No. 1 (Oct. 1984), pp.1–23; Robert Axelrod and Robert O. Keohane, 'Achieving Co-operation under Anarchy: Strategies and Institutions', in Kenneth A. Oye (ed.), *Co-operation under Anarchy* (Princeton: Princeton University Press, 1986); Stephan Haggard and Beth A. Simmons, 'Theories of International Regimes', *International Organization*, Vol. 41, No. 3 (Summer 1987), pp.491–517; and Helen Milner, 'International Theories of Co-operation among Nations: Strengths and Weaknesses', *World Politics*, Vol. 44 (April 1992), pp.466–96. For a pioneering effort see Robert Jervis, 'From Balance to Concert: A Study of International Security Co-operation', in Kenneth A. Oye (ed.), *Co-operation under Anarchy*.

3. For alternative conceptualizations of opaqueness see, *inter alia*, Yair Evron, 'Israel and the Atom: The Uses and Misuses of Ambiguity, 1957–1967', *Orbis*, Vol. 17 (1974), pp. 1326–43; Robert E. Harkavy, *Spectre of a Middle Eastern Holocaust: The Strategic and Diplomatic Implications of the Israeli Nuclear Weapons Program* (University of Denver: Monograph Series in World Affairs, Vol. 14, No.4, 1977); Ben Frankel, *Opaque Nuclear Proliferation* (London: Frank Cass, 1991); and Shlomo Aronson, *The Politics and Strategy of Nuclear Weapons in the Middle East* (Albany: State University of New York Press, 1992).

4. These explanations are explored more fully in Etel Solingen, 'The Domestic Sources of International Regimes: The Evolution of Nuclear Ambiguity in the Middle East', *International Studies Quarterly*, Vol. 38, No.4 (June 1994), pp.305–38, and 'The Political Economy of Nuclear Restraint', *International Security* Vol. 19, No. 2 (Fall 1994), pp. 126–69. See also Alan Dowty, 'Nuclear Proliferation: The Israeli Case', *International Studies Quarterly*, Vol. 22 (1978), pp.70–120; Shai Feldman, *Israeli Nuclear Deterrence* (NY: Columbia University Press, 1982); Louis R. Beres, *Security or Armaggedon* (Lexington: Lexington Books, 1986); Avner Yaniv, *Deterrence without the Bomb* (Lexington: Lexington Books, 1987); Michael Mandelbaum, *The Fate of Nations – The Search for National Security in the Nineteenth and Twentieth Centuries* (Cambridge University Press, 1988); Yair Evron, 'Israel', in Regina C. Karp (ed.), *Security with Nuclear Weapons?* (Oxford University Press, 1991); and Geoffrey Kemp, *The Control of the Middle East Arms Race* (Carnegie Endowment for International Peace, 1991). On norms embodied in the NPT see Joseph S. Nye Jr., 'Maintaining a Non–proliferation Regime', *International*

Organization, Vol. 35, No.1 (Winter 1981), pp. 15–38; Lawrence Scheinman, 'Does the NPT Matter?', in Joseph F. Pilat and R. E. Pendley (eds.), *Beyond 1995: The Future of the NPT Regime* (New York: Plenum, 1990); and George H. Quester, 'Conceptions of Nuclear Threshold Status, in Regina C. Karp (ed.), *Security with Nuclear Weapons?.*

5. Win-sets are all possible international agreements acceptable to domestic constituencies. See Robert D. Putnam, 'Diplomacy and Domestic Politics', *International Organization,* Vol. 42, No. 3 (Summer 1988), pp. 427–59.

6. Yaniv, *Deterrence*; Lewis A. Dunn, *Controlling the Bomb – Nuclear Proliferation in the 1980s* (Yale University Press, 1982).

7. On the low enthusiasm for Ben-Gurion's nuclear project among his cabinet ministers and their concerns with cost considerations, see Dan Raviv and Yossi Melman, *Every Spy a Prince* (Boston: Houghton Mifflin, 1990), p.69. On the central role played by Ben-Gurion's enmity to Mapam in his political choices, and on his recognition of Mapam's electoral strength, see Uri Bialer, 'Facts and Pacts: Ben-Gurion and Israel's International Orientation, 1948–1956', in R. W. Zweig (ed.), *David Ben-Gurion – Politics and Leadership in Israel* (London: Frank Cass, 1991).

8. Uri Bar-Joseph, 'The Hidden Debate: The Formation of Nuclear Doctrines in the Middle East', *The Journal of Strategic Studies,* Vol.5 (1982), p. 211; Aronson, *The Politics,* p.67. The nuclear programme was even placed exclusively under a new intelligence agency created for that purpose (Lakam), apparently behind the back of the official intelligence community (Raviv and Melman, *Every Spy,* p.69).

9. Simha Flapan, 'Nuclear Power in the Middle East', *New Outlook* (July 1974), pp.46–54.

10. Michael Shalev, *Labor and the Political Economy in Israel* (Oxford University Press, 1992). Ben-Gurion often attacked the *Histadrut* as a 'state within a state' and advocated a more statist alternative (*Mamlachtiut*).

11. 'If our hypothetical choice would be between a symmetrical ownership of nuclear weapons and a symmetrical absence of such weapons, *our choice should be a conventional balance over a nuclear one*', Yigal Allon, Betachbulot milhama (Tel Aviv: Hakibutz Hameuchad, 1990). On debates within Allon's party on the nuclear question, see Ha'aretz (14 March, 1962). See also Yair Evron, *Israel's Nuclear Dilemma* (Ithaca, NY: Cornell University Press, 1994), p.6.

12. Flapan, 'Nuclear Power'; Tom Segev, *The Seventh Million: The Israelis and the Holocaust* (New York: Hill and Wang, 1993). On the French–Israeli nuclear agreement of 1957, see Evron, *Israel's Nuclear Dilemma,* pp.3–4.

13. On the sharp 1963 debates in connection with German scientists' presumed participation in Egyptian development of chemical, missiles and bacteriological weapons, see Segev, ibid., pp.374–6.

14. On the possibility that domestic opposition to an open deterrent might be strong, see Stephen J. Rosen, 'Nuclearization and Stability in the Middle East', *Jerusalem Journal of International Relations,* Vol.1 (1976).

15. Peter Pry, *Israel's Nuclear Arsenal* (Boulder: Westview, 1984); Yaniv, *Deterrence*; Evron, Israel's *Nuclear Dilemma.*

16. Efraim Inbar, 'Israel and Nuclear Weapons since October 1973', in Beres, *Security,* p.62; Evron, ibid., p.6; Gerald M. Steinberg, 'The Political Economy of Science and Technology in Israel: Mutual Interests and Common Perspectives', in Etel Solingen (ed.), *Scientists and the State: Domestic Structures and the International Context* (Ann Arbor: University of Michigan Press, 1994), p.250.

17. Avner Cohen, 'Nuclear Weapons, Opacity, and Israeli Democracy', in Avner Yaniv (ed.), *National Security and Democracy in Israel* (Boulder: L. Rienner, 1993). Mapam adopted the committee's programme – invoking international guarantees – in its official platform. .

18. Aronson, *The Politics.*

19. Allon, *Betachbulot.*

20. Mahmoud Karem, *A Nuclear-Weapon-Free Zone in the Middle East – Problems and Prospects* (New York: Greenwood Press, 1988), p.95; Frank Barnaby, *The Invisible Bomb – The Nuclear Arms Race in the Middle East* (London: I. B. Tauris, 1989), p.158.

21. Inbar, 'Israel and Nuclear Weapons', p.64.

22. On such security requirements, see statement by Binyamin Natanyahu in *Yediot Ahronot* (15 July, 1988).
23. Quoted in Hewedy (1989:21). Sharon's statement seems to reflect a shift here, by suggesting that Israel can be defeated in a conventional arms race. Other sources aver that Sharon opposes an open deterrent *as well as* a NWFZ. See Yoram Nimrod, 'Arms Control or Arms Race?' *New Outlook* (Sept./Oct. 1991), p. 16. For the evolution of Sharon's thinking on nuclear deterrence in the region see also Bar-Joseph, 'The Hidden Debate', p.222; and Inbar, 'Israel and Nuclear Weapons', p.65.
24. Yaniv, *Deterrence*, p.195.
25. In his memoirs, Allon went as far as favoring a coercive prevention of nuclear proliferation by nuclear powers (Allon, *Betachbulot*, p.191).
26. Eric Silver, *Financial Times* (7 Dec. 1992).
27. Nimrod, 'Arms Control'.
28. Efraim Inbar, *War and Peace in Israeli Politics – Labor Party Positions on National Security* (Boulder: L. Rienner, 1991), p.105; Amos Perlmutter, Michael Handel and Uri Bar-Joseph, *Two Minutes Over Baghdad* (London: Vallentine Mitchell, 1982). On Likud's forerunner Gahal's support for a nuclear option, see Flapan, 'Nuclear Power', p.52. On Menachem Begin's own doubts about an explicit nuclear deterrent, see Evron, *Israel's Nuclear Dilemma*, p.10.
29. Inbar, 'Israel and Nuclear Weapons', p.66; David Horowitz, 'The Israeli Concept of National Security', in Yaniv, *National Security*, p.45. Some military hardliners resisted reliance on nuclear weapons, including Chiefs of Staff Yigal Yadin and Yitzhak Rabin (Rosen, 'Nuclearization', p.8; Inbar, 'Israel and Nuclear Weapons'. On the military-industrial complex, see Alex Mintz, 'The Military–Industrial Complex: American Concepts and Israeli Realities', in Bruce Russett, Harvey Starr, and Richard Stoll (eds.), *Choices in World Politics: Sovereignty and Interdependence* (NY: W.H. Freeman, 1989); and Michael N. Barnett, *Confronting the Costs of War – Military Power, State and Society in Egypt and Israel* (Princeton University Press, 1992).
30. On the domestic context of Israeli conventional strategy, see Mandelbaum, *The Fate of Nations;* and Barnett, *Confronting.*
31. Yaniv, *Deterrence*; Evron, 'Israel'.
32. The military budget was about 20 per cent of Israel's GNP by the late 1980s (Yaniv, *Deterrence*).
33. On the expressed link between an Israeli promise not to develop nuclear weapons and the US commitment to supply conventional weapons in the early 1960s, see Evron, 'Israel and the Atom', p.1338; and McGeorge Bundy, *Danger and Survival* (Vintage, 1988).
34. Gerald M. Steinberg, 'Israel: An Unlikely Nuclear Supplier', in William C. Potter (ed.), *International Nuclear Trade and Non-proliferation* (Lexington: Lexington Books, 1990).
35. Flapan, 'Nuclear Power', p.52; Dowty, 'Nuclear Proliferation', p.110.
36. Aronson, *The Politics*, p.62; Steinberg (1994:250).
37. Dowty, 'Nuclear Proliferation'.
38. Barnett, *Confronting.*
39. By 1976 the US Congress had passed the Symington Amendment, mandating a cut-off of military or economic aid to a country importing a reprocessing plant. See Lawrence Scheinman, *The International Atomic Energy Agency and World Nuclear Order* (Washington: Resources for the Future, 1987); and Nye, 'Maintaining'. By 1979 the US Non-proliferation Act formally precluded the US government from providing economic assistance to a country acquiring nuclear weapons. Whether or not the United States would have actually applied such sanctions on Israel may be debatable, but the risk was quite concrete in the eyes of Israeli leaders.
40. Paul Jabber, 'A Nuclear Middle East Infrastructure, Likely Military Postures and Prospects for Strategic Stability', *ACIS Working Paper No.6* (Los Angeles: UCLA/CISA, 1977); Karem, *A Nuclear-Weapon-Free Zone.*
41. Both quotes from Feldman, *Israeli Nuclear Deterrence*, p.11.
42. Jabber, 'A Nuclear Middle East'; Dunn, *Controlling the Bomb.*
43. For this and other public denials, see Feldman, *Israeli Nuclear Deterrence*. Even Nasser, who

had warned against Israel's development of a nuclear weapon, declared that Dimona was not yet being used for that purpose (London *Observer*, 5 July 1964).

44. On Egypt's efforts see Paul Jabber, *Not By War Alone - Security and Arms Control in the Middle East* (Berkeley: University of California Press, 1981). On Syria's efforts, see *Newsweek*, 3 April 1978 and *Mednews* 5, 21 (3 Aug. 1992), p. 1. On Saddam Hussein's see Dunn, *Controlling the Bomb*; and Beres, *Security*.

45. Feldman, *Israeli Nuclear Deterrence*, p.87.

46. Ibid.

47. See efforts by Saudi Arabia, Egypt and others to preclude an Iraqi or Libyan nuclear weapon, and statements by Egypt's former Foreign Minister Ismail Fahmy against signing the NPT, to preclude strategic advantages by Libya and Iraq, as well as by Israel (quotes from the opposition paper *A-Sha'ab* in Bar-Joseph, 'The Hidden Debate', p.208. On Arab countries' concern with Iranian nuclear designs, see Yezid Sayigh, 'Middle Eastern Stability and the Proliferation of Weapons of Mass Destruction', in E. Karsh, M. S. Navias and P. Sabin (eds.), *Non-Conventional Weapons Proliferation in the Middle East* (Oxford: Clarendon Press, 1993).

48. R. F. Pajak, *Nuclear Proliferation in the Middle East* (Washington DC: National Defence University Press, 1982); Dunn, *Controlling the Bomb*.

49. Saddam Hussein was reported to have asked his senior nuclear adviser: 'Dr. Jaffar, if we stay in the NPT, will it in any way hinder the clandestine nuclear programme?' Jaffar reported his own answer to have been an immediate and unequivocal no (David Kay, 'Iraqi Inspections: Lessons Learned', *Eye on Supply*, Vol. 8 (1993), p. 88.

50. On these sectors see Leonard Binder, *Islamic Liberalism: A Critique of Development Ideologies* (Chicago: University of Chicago Press, 1988); and A. Richards and J. Waterbury, *A Political Economy of the Middle East - State, Class, and Economic Development* (Westview, 1990).

51. On the *munfatihun*, who facilitate exchanges with a global market, see J. Waterbury, *The Egypt of Nasser and Sadat - The Political Economy of Two Regimes* (Princeton: Princeton University Press, 1983).

52. Waterbury, ibid.

53. Jabber, *Not By War Alone*, p.34.

54. Article in *Al-Ahram*, 23 Nov. 1973 reported on *Foreign Broadcast Information Service* (Non-proliferation) 26 Nov. 1973:G1,G2. Sadat fired Heikal as editor of *Al-Ahram* in early 1974. Other pro-Soviet proponents of such weapons reportedly included Ali Sabri, General Sadek, Science Minister Salah Hedayat, and arguably Foreign Minister Ismail Fahmy, who resigned to protest Sadat's peace initiative (Jabber, 'A Nuclear Middle East;' Bar-Joseph, 'The Hidden Debate'; Nimrod, 'Arms Control'.

55. Mandelbaum, *The Fate of Nations*; Janice G. Stein, 'Deterrence and Reassurance', in P. E. Tetlock, J. L. Husbands, R. Jervis, P. C. Stern, and C. Tilly, *Behavior, Society, and Nuclear War* (Oxford University Press, 1991), Vol. 2, pp.8–72; Ibrahim A. Karawan, 'Sadat and the Egyptian–Israeli Peace Revisited', *The International Journal of Middle East Studies* 26 (1994); and, dissenting, Shibley Telhami, *Power and Leadership in International Bargaining – The Path to the Camp David Accords* (NY: Columbia University Press, 1990).

56. Nimrod, 'Arms Control'.

57. Karem, *A Nuclear-Weapon-Free Zone*.

58. On military budgets and roles, see R. Springborg, *Mubarak's Egypt: Fragmentation of the Political Order* (Boulder: Westview, 1989); Yezid Sayigh, *Arab Military Industry: Capability, Performance and Impact* (London: Brassey's, 1992); and R. Owen, *State, Power, and Politics in the Making of the Modern Middle East* (Routledge, 1992).

59. H. Beblawi and G. Luciani, *Nation, State and Integration in the Arab World.Vol II: The Rentier State* (Croom Helm, 1987); Sayigh, *Arab Military Industry*; Barnett, *Confronting*.

60. Springborg, *Mubarak's Egypt*; Yahia Sadowski, *Scuds or Butter? The Political Economy of Arms Control in the Middle East* (Washington DC: Brookings, 1993), pp.32–5.

61. On state revenues and expenditures in the Arab world see Beblawi and Luciani, *Nation, State and Integration*.

62. Sayigh, *Arab Military Industry*; Kay, 'Iraqi Inspections;' *Joint Publications Research*

Service (16 April 1993:24).

63. Feldman, *Israeli Nuclear Deterrence*, p.73.

64. On changes in Arab positions leading to the recognition of Israel by the PLO in the late 1980s, see Yehoshafat Harkabi, *Israel's Fateful Hour* (Harper and Row, 1988), and M. Muslih, 'The Shift in Palestinian Thinking', *Current History* (Jan. 1992), pp.22–8.

65. On Syria's, Lebanon's and Jordan's business class interest in international competitiveness and peace with Israel, see W. E. Schmidt, *New York Times*, 27 June 1993:1.

66. Robert R. Kaufman, 'Domestic Determinants of Stabilization and Adjustment Choices', in Russet *et al.* (eds.), *Choices in World Politics*; Miles Kahler, 'International Financial Institutions and the Politics of Adjustment', in V. Kallab and R. E. Feinberg (eds.), *Fragile Coalitions: The Politics of Economic Adjustment* (New Brunswick: Transaction, 1989).

67. On the principles of an Islamic political economy, see Emile Sahlieh, *Religious Resurgence and Politics in the Contemporary World* (NY:State University of New York Press, 1990); J. L. Esposito, *Islam and Politics* (Syracuse University Press, 1991); Hasan al-Turabi, 'Islam, Democracy, the State, and the West', *Middle East Policy*, Vol. 1 (1992), pp.49–61; and Timur Kuran, 'Fundamentalisms and the Economy', in M. E. Marty and R. S. Appleby (eds.), *Fundamentalisms and the State - Remaking Polities, Economies, and Militance* (Chicago: University of Chicago Press, 1993).

68. Turabi, ibid., p.53. In practice, however, both the Islamic regime in Sudan and Iran *do* strive to follow IMF-conditionality arrangements.

69. Binder, *Islamic Liberalism*.

70. On militant Islam 's readiness to use violence, and its 'politics of redemption', see M. J. Deeb, 'Militant Islam and the Politics of Redemption', *Annals* AAPSS Vol. 524 (1992), pp. 52–65.

71. On extremist Egyptian Islamic groups' opposition to Camp David, see A. A. Ramadan, 'Fundamentalist Influence in Egypt', in Marty and Appleby (eds.), p.168. On radical Islam calls to keep Saudi Arabia 'out of non-Islamic pacts and treaties (including the Peace process) and to build up its armed forces, see S. Haeri, 'Saudi-Arabia: A warning to the King', *Middle East International* (24 June 1991). On Hamas' calls for the elimination of Israel through Jihad and opposition to negotiations, see Muslih, 'The Shift', and T. D. Sisk, *Islam and Democracy* (Washington DC: United States Institute of Peace, 1992).

72. On Vanunu's declarations, see London *Sunday Times* (5 Oct. 1986).

73. R. Jeffry Smith, 'State Department Meeting on Mideast Arms Control Opens Without Rancor', *Washington Post* 12 May 1992:A12. Syria announced its willingness to sign an IAEA safeguards agreement but refuses to participate in the Multilateral Working Group on Arms Control (*The Washington Post* 11 Feb. 1992:A16).

74. Arab states had specifically qualified their NPT obligations to exclude the recognition of Israel. Therefore, the mere extension of NPT procedures to Israeli facilities – the essence of Arab and Iranian proposals at the UN – was unacceptable to Israel. See George H. Quester, *The Politics of Nuclear Proliferation* (Johns Hopkins University Press, 1973); and Karem, *A Nuclear-Weapon-Free Zone*, pp.95–100.

75. Etel Solingen, 'Multilateral Arms Control in the Middle East: The Issue of Sequences', *Peace and Change*, Vol. 20, No.2 (June 1995 forthcoming).

76. Karem, *A Nuclear-Weapon-Free Zone*, p.103.

77. On these currents, see Ibrahim A. Karawan, 'Monarchs, Mullas, and Marshals: Islamic Regimes?' Annals AAPSS, Vol. 524 (1992), pp.103–19; Nicky R. Keddie and F. Monian, 'Militancy and Religion in Contemporary Iran', in M. Marty and S. Appleby (eds.), *Fundamentalisms and the State - Remaking Polities, Economies, and Militance* (Chicago: University of Chicago Press, 1993); and Sadowski, *Scuds or Butter?* p.63.

78. Chris Hedges, *New York Times* (11 June 1993:A3 and 14 June 1993:A6).

79. *PPNN Newsbrief* (Winter 1992), p15.

80. Pervez Hoodbhoy, 'Myth-Building: the "Islamic Bomb"', *The Bulletin of the Atomic Scientists* (June 1993), p.43. See also Ayatollah Mohajerani's interview distributed by the official Iranian news agency, quoted in R. Jeffry Smith, 'Officials Say Iran is Seeking Nuclear Weapons Capability', *Washington Post*, 30 Oct. 1991:A1. According to Spector and Smith, Ayatollah Mohammed Beheshti, a close adviser to Khomeini, urged an Iranian

scientist: 'It is your duty to build the atomic bomb for the Islamic Republican Party'. See Leonard S. Spector with Jacqueline R. Smith, *Nuclear Ambitions - The Spread of Nuclear Weapons 1989–1990* (Boulder: Westview, 1990), p.208. On Iran's alleged efforts to acquire nuclear capabilities, see also Sayigh, 'Middle Eastern Stability;' *Eye on Supply,* 8 (Winter 1993), pp.9–16; Frontline (PBS 13 April 1993).

81. On Pakistan's Islamic bomb, see Brahma Chellaney, 'South Asia's Passage to Nuclear Power', *International Security,* Vol. 16 (1991), p.59. On Saudi and Libyan support for an Islamic deterrent see Barnaby, *The Invisible Bomb.* On an Islamic and a black African bomb see Ali A. Mazrui, 'The Political Culture of War and Nuclear Proliferation: A Third World Perpspective', in Hugh Dyer and L. Mangasarian (eds.), *The Study of International Relations* (London: Macmillan, 1989).

82. On the failure of pan-Arabism to create cohesive regional alliances, see Stephen S. Walt, *The Origins of Alliances* (NY:Cornell University Press, 1987). On the demise of pan-Arabism see Fouad Ajami, *The Arab Predicament* (Cambridge University Press, 1981). On the competition between Libya and Pakistan for the primacy of an Islamic bomb see Barnaby, *The Invisible Bomb.* On the myth of Monolithic Islam see Esposito, *Islam and Politics*; and Karawan, 'Monarchs, Mullas'. For the contrary view that the Islamic movement is fundamentally uniform see Sudanese leader Hasan al-Turabi's statement in Martin Kramer, 'Islam vs. Democracy', *Commentary* (Jan. 1993), pp.35–42.

83. Yehoshafat Harkabi, 'Haseder Haolami Ve-dilemot Hagirun shel Haezor' (The World Order and Dilemmas of Regional Nuclearization), Paper delivered at a Conference on Nuclearization of the Middle East at Tel-Aviv University, 15 May1993.

84. Alan Platt, 'Arms Control in the Middle East', in Stephen L. Spiegel (ed.), *The Arab–Israeli Search for Peace* (Boulder: L. Rienner, 1992).

85. On the impact of the *intifada* on strategic thinking, see Asher Arian, Politics in Israel (Chatham House, 1989), p.218. On responses to Scud attacks see James Leonard, 'Steps Toward a Middle East Free of Nuclear Weapons', *Arms Control Today* (April 1991), pp.10–4.

86. Asher Arian, A. I. Talmud and Tamar Herman, *National Security and Public Opinion in Israel* (Boulder: Westview, 1988); Evron, 'Israel', p.281.

87. Asher Arian, *Israel and the Peace Process: Security and Political Attitudes in 1993* (Jaffee Center for Strategic Studies, Tel Aviv University, Memorandum No. 39, 1993).

88. A regime implies mutual policy adjustments by each participating state, geared to improve the position of all sides, through a joint policy process of co-ordination and collaboration, generally underpinned by an institutional foundation of principles, rules, and decision-making procedures. See Stephen Krasner, *International Regimes* (NY:Cornell University Press, 1983); and Robert O. Keohane, *After Hegemony – Co-operation and Discord in the World Political Economy* (Princeton: Princeton U. Press, 1984).

89. See Foreign Minister Peres's statement at the chemical weapons Conference (*PPNN Newsbrief* No. 21, First quarter 1993:2) and his statement in Bonn, in response to Chancellor Kohl's question on Israel's willingness to join the NPT. On the receptivity of parts of the Israeli establishment to gradual denuclearization of the Middle East, see also Evron, *Israel's Nuclear Dilemma,* pp.269–70.

90. On Israel's longstanding preference for a regional arrangement, and one that includes all states in the region and adjacent to it see Ran Marom, 'Israel's Position on Non-proliferation', *The Jerusalem Journal of International Relations,* Vol. 8, No. 4 (1986), pp. 118–23. On a common Arab–Israeli proposal for a regional framework, see Efraim Karsh and Yezid Sayigh, 'A Cooperative Approach to Arab–Israeli Security', *Survival* Vol. 36, No. 1 (Spring 1994), p.122.

91. Incidentally, most potential partners to such a regime are not yet democratic, a fact that often raises questions of credibility of commitment. However, the applicability of 'liberal-democratic co-operation' arguments to specifying a Middle East regime may be limited, both on logical and empirical grounds. See Michael W. Doyle, 'Liberalism and World Politics', *American Political Science Review,* Vol. 80 (1986), pp.1151–70. For an application to nuclear regimes see Solingen, 'The Political Economy'.

92. To consolidate a regime in weapons of mass destruction, 'the Arab members will have to

renounce any alliances directed against Israel once it [Israel] has fully complied with the achieved settlement'. See M. Z. Diab, 'An Arms Control Regime for an Arab–Israeli Settlement', in Stephen L. Spiegel (ed.), *Practical Peacemaking in the Middle East* (New York: Garland, 1995 forthcoming), p.111.
93. Sayigh, 'Middle Eastern Stability', p.200.

Confidence- and Security-Building Measures in the Arab–Israeli Context

YAIR EVRON

Although the concept of CSBM[1] was first used in the European context, the substance of it can be identified in many arrangements that have obtained in the Arab–Israeli region throughout the Arab–Israeli conflict. The present paper focuses first on the historical evolvement and application of CSBM in the Middle East,[2] and the distinction between them and CSBM in Europe; second, on future CSBM that might be introduced as part of the expected peace agreements.

In Europe, the main concern of the Western powers was initially the possibility of a surprise attack. Consequently, the main emphasis in the CSBM agreed upon at the Conference on Security and Co-operation in Europe (CSCE) meeting in Helsinki (1975) and the Conference on Disarmament in Europe (CDE) in Stockholm (1986) has been on measures for limiting the potential for surprise.[3] A secondary and related objective that gradually emerged was to increase overall stability in the military relationship between East and West. These objectives were accomplished through increased transparency; exchange of communications about future military exercises above a certain manpower ceiling; allowing the opponent military coalition to observe in place military exercises; and later on, controls on the escalation of crisis through pre-arranged procedures. Indeed, the process of CSBM continued even after the end of the Cold War (the Vienna documents of 1990 and 1992) with the emphasis on overall stability enhancement on the European continent.

Several definitions of CSBM have been used. Since transparency was central in the European context, initial definitions focused on it. Transparency is aimed at diminishing the uncertainties of both sides regarding their military situation, thus increasing their confidence. In order to include additional dimensions of the effects of CSBM, however, a more comprehensive and structured definition is required. The following, while limited to the strategic-military dimension, covers all these aspects: CSBM are measures taken in the strategic-military area that regulate the military behaviour of states in conflict, leading to the reduction of uncertainty on both sides in regard to:

- general military escalation
- crisis escalation
- surprise attacks
- low-level violence.

Once this is secured, each party will feel more confident that its costs resulting from offensive violence of the opponent would be smaller than before the CSBM had been applied. The corollary of this effect is that, following the application of CSBM, each party should feel less confident if it plans offensive military action.[4]

CSBM fall into several categories. First, there are those measures relating to communications between opponents; some of the CSBM in the European context, such as advance notification about military exercises, belong to this category. Second are 'physical' measures, that is, measures affecting actual military hardware and deployments; the most common among these is the creation of demilitarized zones, or areas of limited military deployment. Third are measures affecting military behaviour; for example, 'rules of engagement' between air forces or navies.

CSBM, Arms Control and Security Regimes

Whereas CSBM focus on the regulation of military forces, rules of engagement and other measures designed to enhance confidence and stability, arms control deals in a more restricted way with quantitative limitations or reductions of various weapon systems. Because both aim at enhanced strategic stability, there is some overlapping between CSBM and arms control, and arms control also has a confidence-building orientation. However, as noted, the instruments are different.

When CSBM are elaborate, persist over time and are combined with stable mutual deterrence (or stable deterrence by the party committed to the defence of the status quo), the potential for the emergence of a security regime may develop. A security regime between conflicting parties is based on shared interests in the preservation of the status quo. It comprises sets of mutual expectations that the parties would adhere to the 'rules' of the regime, and also various established procedures for dealing with different aspects of the regime. One approach suggest that in some developed security regimes, 'norms' of behaviour emerge, are internalized by the parties, and dictate policy outputs. Another approach regards regimes as intervening variables that, in addition to interests, serve as an input into the decision-making process.[5]

Some sets of CSBM in the Arab–Israeli region have indeed developed into limited security regimes.

CSBM in the Arab–Israeli Zone

Since the end of the 1948 War, Israel and its four Arab neighbours have at different times applied various sets of CSBM. These have included both formal and informal arrangements. The formal arrangements include the four armistice agreements of 1949 between Israel and Egypt, Israel and Jordan, Israel and Syria, and Israel and Lebanon; and also the 1974 Israeli–Syrian agreement concerning the military situation on the Golan, the 1974 and 1975 Israeli–Egyptian agreements (Sinai I and Sinai II), and the military components of the Israeli–Egyptian peace agreement of 1979.

Among the informal 'packages' of CSBM have been the continuing Israeli–Jordanian military understandings and sometimes co-ordination extending (with some breakdowns) from the 1950s to the 1990s; the *de facto* demilitarization of the Sinai from 1957 to 1967; and the Israeli–Syrian system of 'red lines' obtaining in Lebanon from 1976 to the present (with the intermission of the war and its aftermath during 1982–85).

The 1949 Armistice System

The system of the armistice agreements created in 1949 developed into what could be termed as a limited security regime[6] that was an important factor in whatever strategic stability[7] obtained from 1949 to the mid-1950s.

The armistice agreements were initially regarded as an intermediate measure serving as an introduction to peace. Although this was certainly the Israeli hope, the Arab attitude toward them soon changed, and the agreements were increasingly perceived as only fulfiling a military function. Indeed, the agreements soon became an alternative to political settlements.

The agreements formalized the end of hostilities and demarcated the lines between combatants. They also created formal institutionalized mechanisms whose objective was to settle outstanding disputes stemming from the agreements. These were the Mixed Armistice Committees, in which the parties to the agreements participated and whose chairmen were United Nations representatives. Thus a system was created that enabled the exchange of direct communications between the parties, which in turn facilitated the settlement of disputes. Usually these disputes were about the military situation along the borders. Increasingly, in the Israeli–Egyptian and Israeli–Jordanian committees, the main focus of contention was the armed infiltration into Israel and Israeli military retaliation. In addition to the activity of the committees, the UN organ, UNTSO (United Nations Truce Supervision Organisation), which had been created during the 1948 War and had a body of international observers at its disposal, served as a further component of the security regime that evolved around the armistice agreements. Although both sides – Israelis and Arabs – were occasionally unhappy about UNTSO's activities, these nevertheless provided a machinery that contributed to stability in the area.[8] Finally, through UNTSO or directly, the parties were allowed to appeal to the Security Council when disputes could not otherwise be settled.

The armistice agreements were necessary in order to formalized the end of hostilities. But the evolvement of a security regime based on these agreements, comprising the various formal elements detailed above, depended on three sets of factors. Most important among them was the common desire of all the parties to avoid further military friction. Accordingly, the parties used the mechanisms of the regime to resolve many of the disputes that occasionally erupted between them. The parties had a shared interest in the successful maintenance of the regime so long as they wished to avoid escalation to another round of hostilities. Israel had no interest in another war; the Arab parties had other political preoccupations and also were cognizant of Israel's superior military power. In the absence of peace, the agreements and the various mechanisms of the regime enabled the parties to maintain strategic stability along the borders. Indeed, eventually the regime appeared to be a convenient alternative to peace.

Another set of factors that helped maintain the regime, though eventually contributing to its collapse, was regional. Israel and Jordan had overlapping or coincidental regional political interests that drew them together. The two of them were the main benefactors of the war, and they shared an interest in stabilizing the status quo created by the war. Egypt and Syria were involved in their internal domestic affairs; in the case of Egypt this included the struggle against the British colonial presence there. Both, therefore, were interested in stability along the border with Israel.

The third set of factors was the international situation, which was initially also conducive to the uninterrupted operation of the regime. Until the mid-1950s, the Cold War did not penetrate the Middle East and the Western powers enjoyed considerable influence over interstate developments in the region. Overall they supported the armistice regime as an important component of the region's stabilization.[9]

By 1954–55, however, both the regional and international environments began to change. Tensions within the Arab world combined with the penetration of the Cold War into the Middle East to undermine strategic stability in Israeli–Arab relations.[10] But the main reasons for the collapse of the regimes were the escalating violence along the borders and the gradual loss of political interest by the parties in the regime's usefulness.

The Israeli–Lebanese agreement held until the late 1960s, when the Palestinian organization Fatah began its operations from Lebanon. The

Israeli–Egyptian agreement served as a stabilizing factor until about 1955, when the combination of armed infiltration from the Gaza Strip and escalating Israeli military retaliation led to the breakdown of the system.[11] Similarly, the Israeli–Syrian armistice system held sway until the mid-1950s, though significant escalation along the border began only in 1964. The Israeli–Jordanian armistice came under great pressure during the mid-1950s, again because of armed infiltration and escalating Israeli reprisals. Israel and Jordan, however, in the latter half of the 1950s and especially during the 1960s (the 1967 war briefly disrupted this relationship) and thereafter, succeeded in reestablishing some military co-ordination on an informal basis.[12]

Partial *De Facto* Demilitarization of Sinai, 1957–67

A significant CSBM was the *de facto* demilitarization of the Sinai during 1957–67.[13] Following the Israeli withdrawal from the Sinai in 1957 in the aftermath of the Sinai Campaign of 1956, Egypt deployed in this area only in small units, with the majority of the Egyptian army based near the Suez Canal. This strategy was not imposed on Egypt in any formal way; rather, it reflected Egypt's assessment that a large concentration of its forces in the Sinai and especially near the international border with Israel would force the latter to launch a pre-emptive strike. The Egyptian government was well aware of the Israeli conditions of *casus belli,* one of which was precisely a large concentration of Egyptian forces near the Israeli border.

The *de facto* demilitarization of Sinai served as a major CSBM, and it was the most important factor promoting strategic stability between Israel and Egypt for a decade. In the first place it eliminated the risk of direct military friction between the two armies; moreover, the wide buffer zone minimized the risk of a surprise attack by Egyptian forces on Israel. Indeed, when in May 1967 Egypt remilitarized the Sinai, this precipitated a major crisis that culminated in the Israeli military strike that June.[14]

The Israeli–Syrian 'Red Lines' System in Lebanon

Another example of an informal CSBM is the creation of the system of 'red lines' between Israel and Syria in Lebanon.[15] The system emerged as a result of indirect contacts (through Washington) between Jerusalem and Damascus in early 1976. At the time, Syria was concerned about the deteriorating situation in Lebanon and reached the conclusion that only its own military intervention could halt the civil war and the process of disintegration there. However, cognizant of the Israeli security interests in Lebanon, Damascus approached Washington and invited American mediation between it and Jerusalem. After a while, Israel responded favourably through Washington to the idea of Syrian intervention, conditioned on limitations on Syrian freedom of military behaviour. Damascus accepted these Israeli limitations in general terms, though modifying them, and indeed from that point until 1982 regulated its military behaviour within Lebanon in accordance with them. The red lines consisted, first, geographical limitations on the area in which the Syrian army could operate. Initially, Syrian forces were not to move south of an imaginary line running 10 km south of the Beirut–Damascus highway. Eventually the Syrian forces, with tacit Israeli acceptance, moved south beyond that line, but not south of the Zaharani river. A second limitation concerned the size of forces: Israel insisted that Syria would deploy no more than one brigade without tanks. In response, Damascus asserted that it would use those forces that were necessary for the successful implementation of its intervention. Indeed, eventually a whole division including armour was used. Another important condition was the non-deployment of surface-to-air missiles within Lebanon. The Syrians adhered to this limitation, though partly violating it during the Zahle crisis of 1981 in response to what they regarded as an Israeli violation of the tacit understandings between the two states. Finally, Syria accepted limitations on its air and naval activity in Lebanese air space and territorial waters respectively. With the outbreak of the 1982 Lebanon War, the system collapsed; it was renewed, however, albeit with modifications, following the Israeli withdrawal in 1985.

The system of red lines served as a major CSBM. Although allowing for Syrian military intervention, it regulated it in ways that protected vital Israeli security interests. Thus, both sides implemented their strategies in Lebanon while reducing their uncertainties about what they perceived as security threats.

The 1974 Golan Agreement[16]

In contrast to the Sinai *de facto* demilitarization and the red lines understandings in Lebanon, which were informal (and to some degree even tacit) arrangements, the Israeli–Syrian 1974 agreement concerning the Golan was formal, explicit and detailed. It was important for several reasons: first, it terminated the phase of the 1973 War; second, it delineated demilitarized zones and zones of limited military deployment, thus considerably reducing the danger of escalation from unintended, direct confrontational contacts between the opponents; it also provided for the introduction of third parties as observers and as a conduit for the positions and complaints of both sides. Altogether then, this agreement played an important role in stabilizing the military situation on the ground. Syria had a political interest in changing the status quo on the Golan. But Israeli military superiority, demonstrated yet again in 1973, was sufficient to deter Damascus from initiating military action by itself. Because the two parties were convinced that the agreement promoted their respective strategic interests, they implemented it rigorously. Whether Syria would have participated in another war as part of a military coalition with Egypt or with Iraq is an open question. In the event, with the conclusion of the Israeli–Egyptian peace treaty, Syria probably assessed that it was incapable of winning by itself, even in a limited campaign.

Sinai I and Sinai II[17]

In 1974 Egypt and Israel agreed to formalize the cease-fire that had followed the 1973 War, with an agreement that served as an important security measure until it was replaced by the Sinai II agreement in September 1975. Both agreements included detailed arrangements for the creation of areas of limited military deployment that served as buffer zones. This facilitated the process of Israeli withdrawal from areas it had conquered in the war. The agreements also contained detailed arrangements for verification and control, thus diminishing the parties' uncertainty about possible defection.

Another important aspect was the significant American involvement in the execution of the agreements, which served as a further guarantee against violations. Moreover, the 1975 agreement provided for American compensation to the aggrieved party in case of defection by the opponent.

Although the agreements did not explicitly serve as an introduction to formal peace, in retrospect it is clear that they were instrumental in paving the way to the Israeli–Egyptian peace treaty.

The Peace Treaty[18]

With the signing of the peace treaty in 1979, Israeli–Egyptian strategic and military relations underwent a major transformation. For the first time, the military clauses that formed part of the treaty were backed by a new political relationship characterized by accommodation rather than conflict. Thus, the basic motivations and intentions of the parties were of a different nature from those serving as background to the former CSBM. This new political context contributed to the smooth functioning of the military part of the agreement.

The security regime created by the treaty consisted of several elements: demilitarization of a large part of Sinai; limitations on the deployment of ground forces in other parts of Sinai; arrangements limiting air and naval movements; the creation of binational military committees for overseeing the operation of the agreement and discussing issues in dispute; the creation of a multilateral force (MFO), including American forces, to verify the agreement. All these elements constitute a perfect body of CSBM.

The record of the regime created by these CSBM has been very good. Moreover, the military commissions have demonstrated their ability to resolve most of the small-scale disputes arising from time to time; few of these had to be referred to the respective governments and resolved on that level.

The Israeli–Egyptian agreement and its experience could serve as an excellent model for future CSBM between Israel and other neighbouring Arab countries. The details may vary, however, depending on local conditions such as geographical and topographical factors. The Israeli–Egyptian case demonstrates the ability of parties to resolve military disputes in the context of political and security agreements. The successful application of the military agreement is an additional aspect of the overall success of the peace treaty.

CSBM in the Middle East and in Europe: Some Comparative Comments

The inventory of CSBM in the Middle East has been richer than in Europe. On the face of it, it seems paradoxical that precisely in a high-intensity conflict such as the Arab–Israeli one, the CSBM were introduced at an early stage. There are several possible explanations:

• In the absence of formal peace, war termination necessitates arrangements organizing the transition from warfighting to the no-war phase. These usually regulate military behaviour and thus fall into the category of CSBM. Thus, it was precisely the frequency of wars in the Middle East and the absence of formal peace agreements that led to the introduction of various CSBM. The situation in Europe has been, of course, very different.

• Precisely the persistent concern about the outbreak of war in the Arab–Israeli region, including the possibility that small-scale violence along the borders might escalate into large-scale war, obliged the parties (so long as they wished to avoid such war) to establish mechanisms and procedures for regulating their military forces and behaviour. The objective has been to prevent both small-scale military friction and large-scale escalation.

• Whereas Europe, during the Cold War, was basically a bipolar system, the Middle East has always been a multipolar one. Moreover, in the Middle East there have always been several simultaneous interstate conflicts on various levels. The possibility of spillover from one conflict to another was always present, as has been the possibility of catalytic activity, i.e. attempts by one regional actor to trigger a war between two other ones. States desiring to avoid unintended escalations had, therefore, to apply measures regulating their and their opponent's military behaviour.

● Even during the worst periods of the Cold War, West and East maintained open diplomatic contacts through which communications could be sent. In the absence of such contacts in the Arab–Israeli region, various CSBM had to be designed for controlling escalation and undesired military friction.

The CSBM in the European context differed in emphasis from those obtaining in the Middle East. In Europe, at least until the mid-to-late 1980s, CSBM focused primarily on enhanced transparency of military behaviour in order to reduce the threat of surprise attacks.[19] More recently, CSBM in Europe were designed also to increase overall stability. In the Middle East, the range and objectives of CSBM have been much wider.

Finally, in the European context, various formal arms control agreements have been ratified (Intermediate Nuclear Forces [INF] Conventional Armed Forces in Europe [CFE] and the withdrawal of battlefield nuclear weapons). These covered both nuclear and conventional armaments, and had considerable confidence-building effect. In the Middle East, apart from several tacit or informal understandings among suppliers regarding controls on the arms race, there have been no arms control agreements.

Future CSBM in the Arab–Israeli Region

The previous discussion was descriptive and analytical; we turn now to a prescriptive/analytical discussion.

The Egyptian–Israeli peace treaty of 1979 opened a new era in Arab–Israeli relations. The political and ideological thawing in overall Arab attitudes toward Israel, which was detectable already in the late 1960s and the 1970s, has accelerated and many sections in Arab political and decision-making elites have increasingly adopted a more nuanced and moderated position regarding Israel. The notion of Israel's political legitimacy has both spread and deepened.

Although, as has been suggested in this essay, Arab states had been ready over periods of time – even during fierce conflict – to maintain and fortify strategic stability with Israel, and have largely done so through various elaborate CSBM, the new political atmosphere between Arab states and Israel has certainly created a more conducive context for maintaining strategic stability. Moreover, whereas in the past some of the CSBM were perceived as an alternative to peace and as an instrument to enable the parties to avoid war even during the no-peace periods, in the new political context CSBM would be an element in formal peace settlements, contributing to their success and, by the same token, increasing the costs of their violation.

The other side of the coin is that it will be impossible to agree upon and maintain a future formal peace settlement without extensive security arrangements consisting of both arms control and CSBM. This is because of the many factors operating against stability in the region and the consequent centrality of security considerations for all the parties. Moreover, since Israel is called upon to relinquish territories, it expects that security arrangements will be agreed upon to compensate it for the strategic losses. Finally, the elements of confidence building in the CSBM system would presumably reduce anxieties and some might socialize military elites in the advantages of co-operation. Indeed, throughout the negotiations held in the Madrid process and outside it, ideas for CSBM and arms control have already been continually raised. At present many of them are being discussed in the context of the multilateral talks on Arms Control and Regional Security (ACRS); they have been a topic of the Oslo negotiations and will surely become a central issue of the Israeli–Syrian negotiations.

The rich inventory of CSBM obtaining over the years in the Middle East could provide insights for future bilateral CSBM. The conditions for their success, as well as their failure where indeed they have failed, are significant for the future. The Israeli–Egyptian CSBM incorporated in the peace treaty could serve as a partial model for future bilateral CSBM.

First, the formal and explicit nature of future CSBM could reduce the uncertainties that attended past informal CSBM and thus diminish fears about defections and violations. Second, the political process currently evolving promises, as mentioned, a more conducive context for the achievement and persistence of CSBM. However, by the same token, a major breakdown in the peace negotiations would destabilize existing CSBM, primarily the 1974 Golan agreement, and, less certainly and depending on political conditions, also the Israeli–Jordanian relationship and the Israeli–Egyptian overall relationship. Third, extra regional parties played an important role in some of the historical CSBM. It is likely that their role in the future, especially in the Syrian–Israeli context, will continue to be important. On the other hand, in cases where two parties have accumulated extensive co-operation experience over the years, as between Israel and Jordan, there is no need for direct involvement of third parties in a system of CSBM. Fourth, formal peace coupled with extensive CSBM could provide the conditions for the creation of a comprehensive co-operative security regime.

It is beyond the scope of this article to discuss in detail issues that are currently under diplomatic negotiations or might become so very soon. Instead, only the possible general features of future CSBM will be considered here.

Future CSBM will fall into four categories:

1. 'Physical' arrangements, such as demilitarization of zones, areas of limited deployment of forces, and limitations on the deployment of specific weapon systems.
2. Regulation of military behaviour, which could consist of 'rules of engagement' of military units, primarily in the air, and other measures for regulating areas in which the armed forces of parties confront each other.
3. Increased communications between the parties, comprising two distinct categories: first, the creation of various mechanisms for settling disputes in the military area as well as for advance notification about military exercises or other threatening aspects of military operations; second, mutual learning about the strategic doctrines and intentions of the parties.
4. Crisis prevention and crisis management mechanisms.

Israeli Security Concerns

The discussion of possible future CSBM must take into consideration the security realities in the region and the security concerns of the parties. From the Israeli point of view, a withdrawal from the West Bank and the Golan Heights poses several grave security risks. Extensive CSBM of various types are needed in order to balance these risks. In addition, Israel has to weigh the risks involved in the basic asymmetry between itself and its neighbours: the Israeli standing army is much smaller even than that of Syria, let alone a combination of several Arab armies. Therefore, a surprise attack before Israel's reserve forces can be mobilized constitutes a grave threat. Finally, Israel must always beware of the danger of a political change that might result in the formation of a wide Arab military coalition. Therefore, the Israeli strategic posture has to take into account different threatening scenarios.

Israeli–Palestinian CSBM

The Palestinian position is relatively simple; their main concern is not strategic but political. They desire to create an independent entity, and are cognizant of their basic and permanent total military inferiority *vis-à-vis* Israel. For them, therefore, the main objective is Israeli withdrawal, and they are most probably ready to accept limitations on military deployments in their future territory. It is likely, however, that there would be disagreements with Israel concerning the size and composition of whatever military forces they ultimately wish to establish.[20] Against the background of Israeli security concerns and the Palestinian position, it is likely that the Israeli–Palestinian CSBM would relate primarily to problems of terrorism and the ways in which all the territories in the West Bank and Gaza from which Israeli forces withdrew would become demilitarized, except for police and gendarmerie forces equipped with light arms for internal security tasks.[21] Israel will probably insist on its continued military presence in some important security zones.

Israeli–Jordanian CSBM

The Jordanians are also aware of their basic military inferiority *vis-à-vis* Israel and apparently are not aiming to increase their military capability relative to Israel. Moreover, their commitments to general Arab causes are more than balanced by their shared political interests with Israel, among them their concern about the possibility of other Arab forces being deployed in their own territory. Following the Washington Declaration, the Jordanians have moved to formal peace with Israel and to various CSBM.

Because of Israel's concern about the possibility of penetration of hostile Arab forces into Jordan, it would be logical for Israel to search for wider defence arrangements with Jordan that could make such penetration unlikely. Thus, Israeli–Jordanian security relations should combine measures to pre-empt terrorism as well as long-range understandings regarding the possibility of joint defence arrangements on the high strategic level. Indeed, the current Jordanian–Israeli strategic negotiations in the context of the peace treaty are focusing already, among other things, on ideas such as a defence treaty.[22] In addition, Israel would probably share with Jordan an effort to involve Jordan politically and strategically in the West Bank.[23]

Israeli–Syrian CSBM

The Syrians seek primarily to regain political sovereignty over the Golan and simultaneously to remove the threatening Israeli forces deployed there so close to Damascus. As a quid pro quo, they are apparently ready to enter into peaceful relations with Israel. They are conscious of Israel's overall military superiority, though part of the Syrian elite, which possibly has not yet accommodated itself to Israel's existence, may entertain the hope that a new political configuration in the Middle East and globally will provide Damascus an opportunity to launch an attack on Israel. In view of this, extensive security arrangements are required. The CSBM that would form part of a peace treaty would probably involve extensive measures for demilitarization of parts (or the whole) of the Golan Heights from which Israeli forces would withdraw (probably in a very gradual way) coupled with demilitarization of areas beyond the Golan. The latter may also include areas in which only limited forces are deployed, and limitations on the deployment of specific weapon systems. In addition, the CSBM there will have to include extensive mechanisms for communications between the parties and for the creation of organs to monitor, verify and control the different security arrangements. Syria's regaining of political and civilian control on the Golan would certainly diminish considerably its motivation for war with Israel. However, withdrawal from the Golan, which topographically dominates the north of Israel, would be a net strategic loss for Israel. The CSBM there would have to compensate Israel for this.

In view of the asymmetry in the size of the *standing* armies and a potential for Syrian surprise attack resulting from the withdrawal from the Golan, it is likely that Israel will search for additional measures to diminish its uncertainty. At present the order of battle of the standing Syrian ground forces consists of seven armoured, three mechanized and one special forces/infantry divisions. This formidable force, equipped with more than 4,000 tanks of which 1,500 are of top quality, gives the Syrian high command a continuous offensive option against Israel should they choose to launch a surprise attack. Distances in the Israeli–Syrian region are such that Syrian units could theoretically move quickly into the Golan and capture it. Israeli withdrawal from the Golan or most of it enhances this option. One possible way to diminish this potential is to change the structure of the Syrian army so that it would rely more heavily on reservists; the mobilization of the latter would then provide for warning time. Another possibility is to limit weapon systems that are clearly offensive. Syria, however, would probably oppose such ideas. They have other security concerns apart from Israel: their latent conflicts with Iraq and Turkey and their involvement in Lebanon. Yet in view of Israel's strategic loss resulting from the withdrawal, these are reasonable demands.

American Involvement

Another major issue concerns the possibility of greater American involvement in the maintenance of the security regime that might evolve following peace and withdrawal.[24] A formal and explicit American undertaking to react by military means against a party violating the security arrangements on the Golan will be, as argued below, highly credible, and serve as a powerful deterrent. The deployment of an American unit on the Golan by itself, or more likely as part of a multinational force (the MFO in Sinai could provide a useful model), would probably even further enhance the credibility of the American commitment. This credibility stems in the first place from the strong American interest in the success of the agreement and in stability in the Middle East. It should be stressed here that the main question is not whether the United States is likely actually to intervene (though for the reasons cited above it is probable that it would) but what would be the Syrian assessment of this likelihood. It is difficult to believe that Syria – especially with its diminished motivation for war – would risk war against both militarily superior Israel and the United States.

Finally, American intervention need not involve the use of ground forces. It could involve air and missile strikes in co-ordination with Israeli military activities. The 1991 Gulf War demonstrated the effectiveness of such strikes. This mode of operation would also considerably diminish the expected number of American casualties, which in turn would lessen the likelihood of opposition by the American public. These calculations would again enhance the deterrent credibility of a formal American commitment.

To sum up, CSBM related to an Israeli–Syrian peace agreement should be designed so as to diminish the threat of any military friction; of a major unintended escalation; or of a surprise attack by Syria with the objective of remilitarizing the Golan, or of using the Golan, after its remilitarization, as a base for further attacks on Israel proper. Prevention of friction could be achieved through the creation of buffer zones on the ground and the codification of various aerial 'rules of engagement'. Demilitarization of zones, coupled with limitations on the offensive capabilities of the Syrian army, the overall Israeli deterrence posture, and formal American guarantees of the agreement, would make a Syrian surprise attack a low-probability contingency. The establishment of direct communications between the sides could contribute to all these objectives.

There are important differences between the roles CSBM would play in the Israeli–Jordanian contexts, on the one hand, and the Israel–Syrian context on the other. First, there is a strong element of intercommunal relations in the Israel–Palestinian context, which would continue even if a Palestinian state or Palestinian–Jordanian federation were created. Consequently, security problems resulting from intercommunal strife would be the focus of concern. Second, the shared political interests of Israel and Jordan and the long tradition of *de facto* security co-operation between the two states make it easier to establish trust between them. Moreover, the shared political and strategic interests provide a basis on which strategic co-operation could emerge. Finally, neither the Palestinians nor the Jordanians desire to compete militarily with Israel, since the gap in military capabilities is in any case very substantial.

The Israel–Syrian context is very different. For one thing, there has been a long tradition of fierce conflict and lack of direct communication. For another, Syria's military power, though inferior to Israel's, is still very significant and its ability to inflict damage on Israel quite substantial. Consequently, the need for CSBM is much more pronounced than in other contexts; yet an accommodation between the two states would require much time as well as careful attention to the interactions between the political and strategic dimensions.

The focus of CSBM, then, would be different in the three contexts. Although in formal terms, the demilitarization of zones would be an essential element on all fronts, the main issue in the Israeli–Palestinian context would be prevention of terrorism and intercommunal strife. Israeli–Jordanian strategic co-operation on different levels would be the main domain of CSBM. In both these contexts, therefore, there is no need for American presence and involvement.

In the Israeli–Syrian context, the main concern would be prevention of major escalations and measures related to the general balance of military power, as set forth above.

Multilateral Regional CSBM

Although all the historical cases of CSBM in the Arab–Israeli region have been bilateral, the peace process has opened the way to multilateral arrangements. Some of these are already being discussed in the multilateral talks in the arms control committee operating in the second 'track' of the Madrid talks. These include:
(a) the establishment of a regional centre for crisis prevention and crisis management;
(b) rules regarding naval activities;
(c) mechanisms for learning about strategic intentions and doctrines; and
(d) measures to control weapons of mass destruction.
We shall now consider some of the features of (a) and (d).

A Regional Crisis Management Centre

There may be two alternatives with respect to the role of this centre. As an *interstate communications centre,* its function would be primarily to transmit signals and information between the parties regarding an evolving crisis. Ideally, it should identify a crisis in its initial (pre-crisis) phase and provide the decision-makers with reliable information that would help them manage the conflict. As a *crisis management centre,* its function would be to pre-plan strategies designed to pre-empt or halt processes leading to crisis. This would involve long-term strategic planning aimed at identifying political, social and military developments that might result in instability and crisis. The centre could also develop contingency plans for the managements of crisis once they erupted.

The two types could contribute to strategic stability in a variety of ways:

(a) early identification of flash points and the development of an inventory of contingency plans for crisis preemption or management;

(b) mutual learning and socialization of the parties about their respective strategic intentions as well as potential areas of co-operation;

(c) the creation of a body of planners and researchers that would devote its time to crisis learning and management;

(d) the creation of a multinational organization with a common body of vested interests in crisis prevention; this group could also serve as a lobby in its members' respective states; and

(e) the existence of ready and efficient channels of communications at the disposal of the parties

Weapons of Mass Destruction

The proliferation in the Middle East of weapons of mass destruction and of different types of surface-to-surface missiles (SSM) poses grave threats to the regional states. These threats, however, are perceived differently by the states. On the Arab side, the Israeli nuclear capability is perceived as a grave threat. However, so long as they regard this capability purely as a deterrent against existential threats to Israel, their concern will probably be limited. By the same token, Syria and Iraq (until its capability was destroyed in the Gulf War) have perceived their chemical weapons capability as a partial deterrent against Israel's nuclear monopoly. Similarly, Syria regards its SSM as a deterrent and counter to Israel's profound conventional air superiority.[25]

Israel regards its own image as a nuclear state as an element in its overall strategic doctrine (though it continues to rely primarily on its conventional capability for both deterrence and warfighting). At the same time, most Israeli leaders perceive the possible proliferation of nuclear weapons to other regional states as the most dangerous existential threat facing Israel, and regard the regional proliferation of chemical weapons and of SSM as gravely threatening.[26]

Because of these opposing preceptions of security threats, formulating an agenda for arms control of weapons of mass destruction is a difficult task. In any event, it is not the purpose of this article to make detailed suggestions for such an agenda. Moreover, arms control measures in the narrow sense, that is, elimination of categories of weapons or of their quantitative limitations, are not among my concerns here. I shall, however, briefly consider some CSBM regarding one category of weapons of mass destruction, namely nuclear weapons.

From the Israeli point of view, the preferable situation is that of continued nuclear monopoly coupled with limitations on other types of weapons of mass destruction and on SSM. It appears unlikely, however, that this will materialize. In the first place, Arab states will not give up their chemical weapons capability since they would link doing so to Israeli denuclearization. Furthermore, and this indeed is the graver threat, it is possible that gradually other regional powers will seek a nuclear weapons capability. From the Egyptian point of view, not only does the Israeli capability affect Egypt's power position but it might provoke other regional powers into eventually seeking a similar capability, thus undermining Egypt's overall position in the region.

It is possible that Arab, especially Egyptian, concern about the Israeli capability would diminish if it became absolutely clear that this capability has only two purposes: deterrence against an existential threat to Israel, for example, the possibility of a major defeat for Israel during a war launched by a grand Arab war coalition; and deterrence against a hostile regional power that had equipped itself with nuclear weapons. One can envisage the development and application of CSBM that would strongly constrain Israel accordingly. This could be done through clear-cut Israeli undertakings to the United States to lower even further the saliency of the nuclear component in Israel's strategic approach, to use nuclear weapons only for 'last resort' deterrence, and not to apply a doctrine of battlefield uses. The United States, for its part, could underwrite these pledges and guarantee to other regional powers the Israeli self-imposed limitations.[27]

Israeli acceptance of the Bush and Clinton initiatives concerning a halt in the production of fissionable materials regionally and globally could also serve this confidence-building objective. At present both Israel and the Arab states have reservations about this initiative – Israel because it would mean a halt to a continuing operation (namely a 'cap' on Dimona), the Arab states because it would freeze a situation in which Israel continues to have a nuclear capability whereas the Arab states must permanently accept nuclear inferiority.

It is possible, however, that a combination of the CSBM mentioned earlier and acceptance of the American initiative would reduce Arab concerns as well as the pressures of the pronuclear lobbies in Egypt (weak as these pressures are there) and in other Arab countries.

Summary

Arab–Israeli relations since 1949 and until recently, were characterized by fierce conflict, with many crises and acts of violence, including five major wars. Yet the dyadic relations between Israel and each of its various neighbours differed, each having special features. Divergent political priorities of Arab states coupled with assessments of the high costs attendant on hostilities against Israel convinced Egypt, Syria and Jordan to accept systems of CSBM with Israel. These CSBM were designed primarily to prevent unintended escalations leading to general war and to lower the overall level of military friction between the parties. During the first half of the 1950s, these CSBM were formal (with some related informal understandings); later they became primarily informal; then reverted to a system of formal agreements: the Golan arrangement in 1974, Sinai I and II, and the Egyptian–Israeli peace treaty. Two informal sets of CSBM, in Lebanon and between Israel and Jordan, persisted until the present.

These CSBM contributed to stability for periods of time, but broke down in the mid-1950s, again in 1967, and in 1982 in Lebanon. (From 1967 to 1973 there were no CSBM in the Israeli–Egyptian and Israeli–Syrian contexts.) CSBM failures were caused by political and military factors: uncontrolled small-scale violence along the borders (coupled with regional and global political developments), as was the case in the 1950s; the spillover of inter-Arab-state conflicts into the Arab–Israeli relationship, as was (with other contributing factors) the case in 1967; change of definition of the national security interests by Israel, as was the case in 1982 in Lebanon.

CSBM by themselves are not, therefore, necessarily a guarantor of peace and stability. Their formalization, though a significant factor, is also not an insurmountable barrier against failure. Finally, extra-regional actors' involvement in CSBM, while important, is not a sufficient stabilizing condition.

Nevertheless, CSBM are necessary for maintaining stability. If introduced within overall normal peaceful relations, they will likely persist for longer periods. The formalization together with American involvement in them would certainly enhance their durability. Finally, over time they could contribute to the evolvement of genuine security regimes, which could, in turn, contribute to redefinition of national security interests. The benefits of co-operative security relationships would gradually convince decision makers that the very maintenance of the security regime is a more important national interest than other competing interests.

NOTES

1. For initial definitions of CBM, see Jonathan Alford, 'Confidence-Building Measures in Europe: The Military Aspects', in *Adelphi Paper*, No. 149 (1979); John Holsti, 'Confidence

Building Measures: A Conceptual Framework', *Survival,* 25 (Jan.–Feb. 1983). For a more elaborate definition see Volker Rittberger, Manfred Efirger and Martin Mendler, 'Toward an East-West Security Regime: the Case of Confidence and Security Building Measures', *Journal of Peace Research,* Vol. 27, No.1 (1990), pp.55–74.

2. For some references to CSBM in the Middle East see, *inter alia,* David Dewitt, 'Confidence and Security Building Measures in the Third World', *International Organisation* (Summer 1987); Yair Evron, 'Arms Control in the Middle East: Some Proposals and their Confidence-Building Roles', *Adelphi Paper,* No.149 (1979); Yair Evron, 'Confidence Building in the Middle East', in Dore Gold (ed.), *Arms Control in the Middle East* (Boulder CO: Westview, 1990); Gerald M. Steinberg, 'Middle East Arms Control and Regional Security', *Survival,* Vol.36, No.1 (Spring 1994). For accounts of the actual application of CSBM in the Arab–Israeli region without conceptualizing them as such, see: Itamar Rabinovich, *The Road Not-Taken* (New York: Oxford University Press, 1991); Arieh Shalev, *The Israeli–Syrian Armistice Regime 1949–1955* (Boulder, CO: Westview Press, 1993).

3. On CSBM in Europe see, *inter alia,* Michael Holms, 'Compliance with CBM: From Helsinki to Stockholm', Canadian Institute for International Peace and Security, Paper No. 30 (Feb. 1990); *SIPRI Yearbook 1992 – World Armament and Disarmament* (Oxford: Oxford University Press, 1992); *The Strategic Balance* (London, IISS); Catherine M. Kelleher, 'Co-operative Security in Europe' (unpublished manuscript, 1993); Volker Rittberger, Manfred Efinger and Martin Mendler, 'Toward and East-West Security Regime: The Case of Confidence and Security Building Measures'.

4. There are broader definitions of CSBM. For one which emphasizes the creation of trust and more stable relations between states see 'Regional disarmament and confidence-and-security building measures', *United Nations Disarmament Yearbook 1990,* Ch.XVII.

5. A widely held definition of an international regime states that it is a 'set of implicit or explicit principles, norms, rules and decision making procedures around which actors' expectations converge ...', Stephen D. Krasener, 'Structural Causes and Regime Consequences: Regime as Intervening Variables', in Stephen D. Krasener (ed.), *International Regimes* (Ithaca: Cornell University Press, 1983).

6. For the concept of limited security regimes, see Janice Gross Stein, 'A Common Aversion to War: Regime Creation by Egypt and Israel as a Strategy of Conflict Management', in Gabriel Ben Dor and David Dewitt (eds.), *Conflict Management in the Middle East* (Lexington: Lexington Books, 1987).

7. Stable deterrence balances or successful CSBM, or a combination of both, could stabilize a conflict situation so that war is prevented and the likelihood of escalation to war diminishes considerably. Strategic stability is then achieved.

8. On UNTSO's positive role in maintaining the stability of the armistice agreements, see, *inter alia*: Yehoshafat Harkabi, 'The Armistice Agreement – A Retrospective Look' [Hebrew] *Maarachot* (July 1989), pp.294–5; Arieh Shalev, *The Israeli–Syrian Armistice Regime 1949–1955*; Moshe Sharett, *Personal Diary* [Hebrew] (Tel Aviv: Maariv, 1978). E.L.M. Burns, *Between Arab and Israeli* (London: G.G. Harrap, 1962).

9. On the role of the external powers in the Middle East during that period see, *inter alia,* Nadav Safran, *From War to War* (Indianapolis: Bobbs-Merrill, 1969); Yair Evron, *The Middle East: Nations, Super-Powers and Wars* (New York: Praeger, 1973).

10. See, *inter alia,* Steven Z. Freiberger, *Dawn Over Suez – The Rise of American Power in the Middle East* (New York: Harper, 1990); Yair Evron, *The Middle East: Nations, Super-Powers and Wars.*

11. On the activities of the Egyptian *Fidaiyun* (armed inflitrators) against Israel, see, *inter alia,* Mordechia Bar-On, *The Gates of Gaza: Israel's Defence and Foreign Policy 1955–57* [Hebrew] (Tel Aviv: Am Oved, 1992); Michael B. Oren, 'Escalation to Suez: The Egypt–Israel Border War: 1949–1956', *Journal of Contemporary History,* Vol.26, No.3 (July 1989). On the raid on Gaza by Israel in late February 1955 as an important factor in the escalation between the two countries, see Yair Evron, *The Middle East: Nations, Super-Powers and Wars.* On the Israeli strategy of retaliation and its causes, see also: Shlomo Aronson and Dan Horowitz, 'Tagmul Mevukar' [Hebrew], *Medina u-Mimshal,* Vol.1, No.1 (1971); Yair Evron, 'The Interaction between Foreign Policy and Defence Policy in Israel:

1949-1956' [Hebrew]; *Ha'Zionut*, 1989; Jonathan Shimshoni, *Israel and Conventional Deterrence* (Ithaca: Cornell University Press, 1988); Fred Khouri, 'The Policy of Retaliation in Arab-Israeli Relations', *Middle East Journal*, Vol.40, No.1 (1987).

12. On the political contacts between Israel and Transjordan until 15 May 1948, see especially Abraham Sella, 'From Contacts to Negotiations – The Relationship between the Jewish Agency and the State of Israel with King Abdallah 1946–1950' [Hebrew] (Tel Aviv: Machon Shiloh, Tel Aviv University, 1985). On the coincidental or shared interests of Israel and Jordan see: Yosef Melman *Hostile Co-operation* [Hebrew] (Tel Aviv: Yediot Aharonot, 1987); Aharon Klieman, *Coexistence without Peace* [Hebrew] (Tel Aviv: Maariv, 1986); Ran Yaron, *The Roots of the Jordanian Option* [Hebrew] (Tel Aviv: Sitron, 1991); Dan Shueftan, *The Jordanian Option* [Hebrew] (Tel Aviv: Yad Tabenkin, HaKibbutz HaMeuhad, 1986).

13. On the partial demilitarization of Sinai see Yair Evron, *The Demilitarization of Sinai* (Jerusalem: Jerusalem Papers on Peace Problems No.1, 1975); Yair Evron 'Arms and Security in the Middle East', *Bulletin of the Atomic Scientists* (Feb. 1978); Janice Stein Gross, 'A Common Aversion to War: Regime Creation by Egypt and Israel as a Strategy of Conflict Management'.

14. On the Egyptian remilitarization of Sinai which led to the 1967 crisis, see *inter alia*, Yair Evron, *The Demilitarization of Sinai*. Theodor Draper, *Israel and World Politic: Roots of the Third Arab–Israeli War* (New York: Viking Press, 1968); Janice Stein Gross, 'A Common Aversion to War'; Michael Brecher, *Decisions in Israel's Foreign Policy* (New Haven: Yale University Press, 1975).

15. On Israeli–Syrian relations in Lebanon and on the 'red lines' system see *inter alia*, Michael Bar, *Red Lines in the Israeli Strategic Deterrence* [Hebrew] (Tel Avin: Maarachut, 1990); Avner Yaniv, Moshe Maoz and Avi Kober, *Syria and the Israeli Security* [Hebrew] (Tel Aviv: Sidrat Mirkam, 1991). Yair Evron, *War and Intervention in Lebanon: The Israeli–Syrian Deterrence Dialogue* (Baltimore: Johns Hopkins University Press, 1987); Itamar Rabinovich, *The War for Lebanon 1970–85* (Ithaca and London: Cornell University Press, 1984).

16. On the 1974 Golan agreement, see Arieh Shalev, *Ramat Ha Golan* [Hebrew] (Tel Aviv: The Jaffee Centre for Strategic Studies, Tel Aviv University, 1992).

17. On Sinai I and Sinai II agreements see Yair Evron, 'The Role of Arms Control in the Middle East'; Brian S. Mandell, 'Anatomy of a Confidence Building Regime: Egyptian–Israeli Security Co-operation 1973–79', *International Journal*, Vol.45 (Spring, 1990); William Quandt, *Camp David* (Washington: Brookings Institute, 1986); William Quandt, 'Kissinger and the Arab–Israel Disengagement Negotiations', *Journal of International Affairs*, Vol.9. No.1 (1975); Itshak Lederman, 'the Arab–Israeli Experiment in Verification and its Relevance to Conventional Arms Control in Europe', Occasional Paper 2, Centre for International Security Studies, Maryland University, 1989.

18. On the Israeli–Egyptian peace treaty and its security components see: Shimshon Zelniker, *Co-operation between Israel and Egypt* [Hebrew] (Tel Aviv: Jaffee Centre for Strategic Studies, Tel Aviv University, 1979); Benjamin Neuberger (ed.), *War and Arrangements* [Hebrew] (Tel Aviv: Ha'Universita Haptuhah, 1987); Ezer Weitzman, *The Struggle for Peace* [Hebrew] (Jerusalem: Idanim, 1981); David Barton, 'The Sinai Peacekeeping Experience: A Verification paradigm for Europe', *SIPRI Yearbook – World Armament and Disarmament* (Stockholm: International Peace Research Institute, 1985); *The Peace Treaty with Egypt* (Tel Aviv: Shiloah Centre for Middle East Studies, Tel Aviv University, 1981). For an analysis of the Egyptian considerations leading to the peace process, see Shimon Shamir, *Egypt Under Sadat* [Hebrew] (Tel Aviv: Dvir, 1978); Quandt, *Camp David*.

19. For a useful account of CSBM in Europe see Katherine M. Kelleher, *Co-operative Security in Europe*.

20. See, for example, Ahmed Khalidi, *Middle East Security: Arab Threat Perceptions, Peace and Stability*, Occasional Paper Series No. 3 (Cambridge, MA: American Academy of Arts and Sciences, 1990).

21. See *inter alia*, Arieh Shalev, *Defence Line in Yehuda and Samaria* [in Hebrew] (Tel Aviv: Hakkibutz Hameuhad, 1982); Zeev Schiff, *Security for Peace: Israeli Minimal Requirements in Negotiations with the Palestinians* (Washington: The Washington Institute for Near East

Policy, 1989); Ahmed Khalidi, 'Middle East Security'.

22. On Jordan's deep interest in continued involvement in the West Bank see *inter alia*, Asher Susser, *Jordan's Disengagement and the Middle East Peace Process* (Washington: The Washington Institute for Near East Policy, 1990); Yair Evron, *Israeli–Palestinian–Jordanian Security Relations: The Idea of a 'Security Zone'*, Occasional Papers Series, No. 3 (Cambridge, MA: The American Academy of Arts and Sciences, 1990).

23. On security arrangements on the Golan see *inter alia*, Arieh Shalev, *Ramat Hagolan*.

24. For an extended discussion of possible CSBM in the nuclear field see Yair Evron, *Israel's Nuclear Dilemma* (London: Routledge and Ithaca: Cornell University Press, 1994).

25. On Syrian strategy, see *inter alia*, Michael Eisenstadt, *Arming for Peace? Syria's Elusive Quest for 'Strategic Parity'* (Washington DC: Washington Institute for Near East Policy, Policy Paper No.31, 1992); Basma Kodmani-Darwish, 'Security in the Middle East as Viewed from Syria', Paper presented to the conference on a *New Security Order for the Middle East* (Almeria, 1992). On the implications of the presence of SSM in the Middle East, see Martin Navias, 'Missile Proliferation in the Middle East, *Adelphi Paper*, No.252 (London: International Institute for Strategic Studies, Summer 1990).

26. For a solid Israeli assessment of Syria's strategic objectives, see Dov Tamari, 'The Syrian–Israeli Balance of Forces and Strategic Parity', in Joseph Alpher, Zeev Eitan and Dov Tamari (eds.), *The Middle East Military Balance 1989–1990* (Tel Aviv: Tel Aviv University, 1990).

27. For a discussion of this point, see Yair Evron, *Israel's Nuclear Dilemma*.

The International Politics of a
Middle Eastern Arms Control Regime

EFRAIM INBAR and SHMUEL SANDLER

Introduction

The Middle East has been racked with conflict for most of this century, and remains one of the planet's major trouble spots. The dissolution of the Soviet empire had a limited stabilizing effect on the region, but Middle East conflicts can, nevertheless, be expected to persist for the foreseeable future.[1] The Arab–Israeli conflict is just one of several major disputes that plague the region.

Furthermore, Middle Eastern countries continue to be one of the globe's main consumers of advanced conventional weapons. In recent years the Middle East has also become host to weapons of mass destruction. During the 1991 Gulf War Iraq attacked distant targets in Israel and Saudi Arabia with improved Scud B missiles demonstrating that states in the region possess long-range delivery systems. Post-war UN inspections have revealed also the advanced state of Iraqi chemical warheads production, and the extent of its nuclear bomb effort.[2] The dynamics of weapons proliferation suggest that with the acquisition of a new weapons system by one state, neighbouring countries are unlikely to abstain from joining the race.

Other Middle Eastern countries are relentlessly pursuing a capability to produce and deliver weapons of mass destruction. Iran renewed its nuclear ambitions, while Syria's chemical weapons arsenal is substantial. With the help of North Korea Syria also has established the infrastructure to build long-range missiles. Sale of ultra-modern conventional military equipment, primarily by the US, is another important cause of concern. Proliferation of weapons of mass destruction, their delivery systems, as well as enhanced conventional military capabilities are somewhat surprising in light of current Arab–Israeli peace diplomacy. At the same time, arms control has risen to the top of the agenda of Mideast peace talks in an unprecedented fashion. Since the Madrid Conference (October 1991), this issue has been the focus of intense talks under the rubric of the multilateral group on and Arms Control and Regional Security (ACRS).

The departure point of the editors of this volume is that the structure of the Arab–Israeli conflict is changing toward less enmity, which could be conducive to the establishment of a security regime relationship. The purpose of this article is to examine how the peace process between Israel and its Arab neighbours influences the ongoing arms competition in the Middle East and the opportunity for establishing a regional security regime in the area of arms control. But, first we seek to clarify the concept of 'security regime'.

Security Regimes

Robert Jervis defined a security regime as 'those principles, rules and norms that permit nations to be restrained in their behavior in the belief that others will reciprocate. This concept implies ... a form of cooperation that is more than the following of short-run self-interest'.[3] A security regime can be placed within a spectrum measuring methods of dealing with the security dilemma. At one end, in an anarchical *laissez-faire* system, order is maintained through the distribution of power and deterrence relationships. At the other end of the spectrum, order is maintained by a collective security system in which security challenges are managed by the aggregate power of the alliance members. A 'security regime' falls in between these two poles. It is characterized by acceptance of limitations on the use of force. These constraints can also include agreements on arms control. The new rules of engagement must be observed over time and eventually internalized. A security regime also requires a certain level of institutionalization.[4]

Our definition of a security regime in terms of a managed balance of power differs at least philosophically from a neoliberal approach. We agree that a regime implies an explicit acceptance of norms and rules, as well as establishing institutions to control competition, but we do not agree that the Middle East has drastically changed its game rules or will do so soon. The most optimistic scenario regards Israel as a normal actor in the region. The Middle East is still far away from an 'international society' where each state accepts the other's claim to sovereignty and territorial integrity.[5] The Arab–Israeli arena is on the verge of a transition from a pure anarchic system based on mutual deterrence and recurrent wars to a more managed balance of power that could also be described as a security regime. The transition toward a 'security community', where the use of violence is not considered as a legitimate means of achieving national goals is not within view.[6] It is not realistic to expect Arab leaders to treat Israel differently or better than the manner in which they behave towards each other.

Our aquaintance with past and with present interactions in the Middle East, with the ruling elites and the prevailing political culture, also brings us to reject some of the recommendations originating from several neorealists who recommend nuclear proliferation in some regions as a recipe for stability.[7] It would be 'deadly' wrong to assume that the long peace that prevailed in Europe during the nuclear stalemate can be emulated in the Middle East. A security regime constraining regional nuclear ambitions seems thus a more promising arrangement than a nuclear balance of terror.

The main difficulties in erecting a security regime are verification and defection. Verification needs an agreed apparatus and a certain degree of transparency, which impinges on issues of sovereignity. Any mechanism of verification requires some co-operation over time. Only intrusive verification can allay deeply-rooted suspicions. Fear of defection from the regime, where one party seeks to acquire a strategic advantage to be used against the other, is a constant. Consequently, confidence-building measures (CBMs) are needed, although they cannot alone constitute a security regime.[8] Is the improved political climate in the Middle East conducive to the establishment of a Mideast security regime? This essay, and indeed the entire volume, seeks to explore the possibilities.

The International Environment of a Middle Eastern Security Regime

The last major inter-state military confrontation between the protagonists in the Arab–Israeli dispute took place in 1973, almost 25 years ago. Over the past two decades the intensity of the Arab–Israeli conflict has waned, but war has not spared other parts of the Middle East.[9] Violence engulfed Afghanistan after the 1979 Soviet invasion, and threatened the stability of the Persian Gulf. The lengthy Iran–Iraq War (1980–88) and the much shorter Desert Storm attested to the great potential for armed conflict in the Gulf area. Similarly, the war between the two Yemens in 1994 demonstrated the Saudi peninsula's propensity for war. Indeed, intricate links exist between various conflicts in the regions.[10] Turkey, Iran and Syria share an interest in the future of the Kurdish areas in Iraq. Iran supports the Hizbollah in Southern Lebanon and other radical Islamic operations elsewhere in the Middle East. These are an indication of the intricate linkages between the various conflicts in the region.

From a military perspective, armed conflict in the Middle East has never been only an inter-state conventional encounter: it has also non-conventional and sub-conventional characteristics. In the 1960s, Egypt used chemical weapons in Yemen. In the 1980s Iraq employed chemical warfare against the Kurds and the Iranians; and it threatened to do so again against Israel and the Americans in the early 1990s. At the margins of the Middle East, the Soviet Union was accused of chemical and biological warfare in Afghanistan. Though nuclear weapons have not been used by any party, a nuclear dimension has existed in the past. The 1973 Yom Kippur War ended with an American nuclear alert and with rumours about Israel assembling several nuclear devices. In June 1981, Israel destroyed the Iraqi nuclear reactor and in 1991–92 the Americans attacked the Iraqi nuclear infrastructure.

Low intensity conflict has also plagued the Middle East for years. From its establishment, Israel has struggled with terrorist activities. In the early 1950s the *Fedayeen* actions made the life of the new state miserable and ended only by Israel's 1956 Sinai campaign. Following the Six Day War, the Palestinians initiated a guerrilla war in the West Bank and the Gaza Strip.[11] In 1982 Israel invaded Lebanon and this war turned into a guerrilla war. Since 1987 Israel has faced a Palestinian uprising, the *intifada,* in the West Bank and the Gaza Strip. Since the 1960s, Iraq has conducted a guerrilla war against the Kurds in Northern Iraq, and in recent years also with Iraqi Shiites in the south of the country. Oman experienced a guerrilla campaign in the Dhofar region during the 1970s. Syria ruthlessly killed 20,000 civilians in quelling an Islamic rebellion in 1982. Recently, Egypt has been challenged by terror activities initiated by Islamic fundamentalist circles. Without exception, each party initiating a low intensity conflict was assisted by at least one other Middle Eastern state.

Notwithstanding this regional propensity for violence, in the last two decades the Arab–Israeli conflict has become less hostile in two interrelated dimensions: legitimacy and intensity. Since 1973 we have witnessed an increasing number of bilateral agreements, the most recent involving direct negotiations between Israel and all the confrontation states. Egypt led the way. It signed interim agreements with Israel in 1974 and 1975. The Camp David accords were reached in 1978 and less than a year later the two countries signed a peace treaty. Following the 1991 Gulf War, Israel met face to face with many of its neighbours at the Madrid Conference, where bilateral and multilateral talks were initiated; it signed a Declaration of Principles with the PLO in September 1993; and a peace treaty between Jordan and Israel was reached in October 1994. Israelis were officially present at sessions of the multilateral negotiations which took place in Oman, Katar and Tunisia. This unprecedented intensity of diplomatic activity and Israeli presence in Arab capitals captures the general perception of seasoned Mideast observers that gradually the Arabs have learned to acccept Israel as a *fait accompli.*

Another facet of this process is the decline in the intensity of the conflict. Indeed, no general war has taken place between Israel and its neighbours since 1973. The 1982 Lebanon War was a limited war in several respects.[12] The Israeli–Syrian confrontations were confined to the Beqaa Valley and adjacent territories in Lebanon with no spillover to the Golan Heights.

Moreover, neither sided employed its full order of battle. Furthermore, in contrast to past Arab–Israeli encounters, the Lebanese embroglio did not draw in additional Arab states. Similarly, a few years later, the *intifada* did not trigger any military intervention on the part of Arab states; and the level of violence during the Palestinian uprising remained rather low with only occasional use of small firearms and petrol bombs. For its part, Israel also made an effort to limit the use of force versus the Palestinians.[13]

But this trend towards better relations between Israelis and Arabs is not irreversible. Arab authoritarian regimes have not yet adopted a legitimate mechanism for the succession of power. As far as we know, two major figures in the peace process – President of Syria Hafez el-Assad and King Hussein of Jordan – are ill and not young. It is not clear what will happen in their countries when they are no longer in power. The acceptance of the PLO and its chairman Yasser Arafat in the territories inhabited by the Palestinians has not yet stood the test of either popular elections or governability. Even the good political fortunes of the present Israeli government led by Prime Minister Yitzhak Rabin are not assured, as his support in the Knesset is precarious. Israel is scheduled to hold elections in November 1996.[14]

Another feature that threatens the peace process is the growing appeal of Islamic fundamentalism, particularly in Egypt and Jordan, which have better relations with Israel than other Arab states.[15] In the two countries, as elsewhere, radical Islamic groups oppose the peace process and any reconciliation with the Jewish state. Actually, Islamic fundamentalism enjoys broad support beyond Iran and Sudan – the two Islamic republics – in almost every state in the region including secular Turkey. Ascendance to power of such counter-elites would put great strains on the agreements reached in peace diplomacy and would threaten regional stability.

Growing support for Islamic fundamentalism is also related to deteriorating Arab economies. Arab states are underdeveloped and have difficulties in providing jobs and a decent standard of living for their growing populations. Even countries considered rich, such as Saudi Arabia and Kuwait, have recently faced economic problems.[16] Furthermore, the economic benefits of the peace process are largely exaggerated.[17]

Another regional element that affects the peace process is the existence of national security challenges and subsequent military needs, which are not related to the Arab–Israeli conflict. Syria feels threatened by Turkey, Iraq and Jordan. Likewise, Jordan has good reason to worry about all its neighbours: Syria, Iraq and Saudi Arabia. In a similar fashion, Egypt faces threats from Libya and Sudan. Thus a reduction in the intensity of the Arab–Israeli conflict may not necessarily lead to a reduction in the armaments of regional actors. Egypt, though at peace with Israel since 1979, has not reduced its order of battle. Indeed, it has enhanced its military capability over time by converting to Western equipment. In fact, the improved relationship between Jerusalem and Amman has been accompanied by American promises to sell advanced F-16 jet fighters to Jordan.

The fragility and the reversibility of the peace process, as well as the existence of security threats unrelated to the Arab–Israeli conflict, are of major significance in the attempt to find suitable provisions for a security regime and for arms control. Despite the high correlation between arms races and the occurrence of war, it is by now common wisdom that arms procurement is only a symptom of increased potential for violence; not its cause.[18] It would not be realistic to expect that states in conflict would abstain from acquiring the most advanced weapons they can afford to further their political goals. In a more relaxed political atmosphere, we might expect the acceptance of a regime for regulating arms procurement.

In this respect the role of extra-regional weapons suppliers is very important. The termination of the East–West conflict is a contributing factor in improved Arab–Israeli relations, though it is not clear how it will affect the arms supply to regional actors. Despite the growing capacity for indigenous military production in several countries in the region, all armies are heavily dependent on arms procurement from abroad.[19] The major sources are the United States, Western Europe and Russia. Western Europe and Russia have strong strategic and economic interests in the region, and thus will not allow the region to become an exclusive American zone of influence. Though Russia is preoccupied with domestic problems, it nevertheless remains a major actor with respect to the supply of arms. Moscow is in great need of foreign currency and is willing to sell even its latest model equipment at bargain prices. The fact that several armies in the Middle East are already equipped with Russian equipment and prefer not to undergo a difficult conversion process to Western weapons gives Russia an additional advantage. Similarly, West European producers will fight hard to maintain their share in the weapons market. Two essays in this volume, one on Russia and the other on Europe, point out the slim prospects of these two actors joining a comprehensive arms control effort to stabilize the region. The United States, the hegemonial power, could contribute significantly to the emergence of an arms control regime. Whether the US will be willing and able to act and to establish such a regime in the area of arms control remains to be seen, as Robert Lieber concludes in his article in this volume.

Nevertheless, the regional powers are able to change the nature of their relationship without outside prodding. Indeed, Sadat's visit to Jerusalem in 1977, the Oslo track that led to the Israeli–PLO September 1993 Declaration of Principles, and the 1994 Washington Hussein–Rabin summit were all achieved without American involvement. It can thus be assumed that when the regional actors find it in their interest to agree on an arms control regime they will do so. The American role is not to be minimized, however. In the peace talks, the United States has an important function as a mediator. Similarly, the US contribution to the establishment of a security regime could be critical in safeguarding verification and preventing defection, the two pivotal elements of any security regime.

There are four main reasons why the regional rivals should begin a transition to a security regime. First, the inability of the protagonists to achieve peace on their terms after more than four decades of recurrent use of conventional military force may have convinced them to look for other avenues in order to achieve their national goals. This consideration is related directly to domestic factors and changing political agendas in many Middle Eastern countries, including non-Arab states.

Second, the emergence of a 'new international order' appears to have pushed some Arab states into understanding that their goal of eradicating Israel is unattainable. In the new international constellation the United States, Israel's ally, plays a paramount role, while the Soviet Union, traditional ally of the Arabs, collapsed and Russia depends economically on the West. Israel, while more secure as a result of the victory of its ally, is presently in a position where its traditional deterrence policy has become very problematic.[20]

Third, the introduction of unconventional weapons and delivery systems has considerably raised the price of military conflict. Both sides, the Arab states and Israel, fear that a continuation of an unrestricted arms race will result in their disadvantage. While Israel is afraid of the development of an 'Arab nuclear bomb', the Arab states fear that an overt Israeli nuclear capability will force them to turn their inter-Arab rivalries into a nuclear competition as well. Some of the Mideast regimes that are candidates for acquiring nuclear weapons are more threatening to the rest of the Arab states than Israel has been. Israel has used nuclear threats only in circumstances where its existence has been jeopardized. Therefore, some form of co-operative security arrangements may become desirable to prevent the high risks.

Finally, the international community has in recent years increasingly stressed the importance of global security regimes in the area of arms control. Because of their dependence on the West, regional actors must consider and respond to this. The Chemical Weapons Convention (CWC), the scheduled 1995 renewal of the NPT, the Missile Technology Control Regime (MTCR), the Comprehensive Test Ban Treaty (CTBT), discussions about a freeze in the production of fissionable materials, are all on the international agenda, as Gerald Steinberg points out in this volume. Yet, the regional actors will evaluate such regimes in light of not only the present circumstances, but also past experience.

The History of Arms Control in the Middle East

The record of arms control in the Middle East is not very encouraging, despite the fact that in this volume Yair Evron points out that CBMs have played a useful role in regulating conflict.[21] The United States attempted to limit weapon sales to the Arab–Israeli arena in 1948 by imposing an embargo on arms to Israel and Egypt; yet the combatants found alternative sources for purchasing weapons. The first collective attempt at arms control by the major suppliers to the region, the United States, the United Kingdom and France, started what came to be known as the Tripartite Declaration in May 1950. This suppliers' regime had an institutionalized regulatory mechanism – the Near East Arms Co-ordinating Committee – which was rather effective in preserving a certain balance of military power in the Arab–Israeli arena. It collapsed as the Soviet Union started supplying high quality weapons in large numbers to Egypt and Syria in 1955. The Soviet arms deal with Egypt was particularly destabilizing and served as a catalyst for the Israeli decision to launch the 1956 Sinai campaign.[22] The United States attempted to address the issue of conventional arms control again in 1962 and immediately following the 1967 June War with little success, because the Soviets were simply not interested. While the reluctance of both superpowers to see an escalation between Arabs and Israelis led to occasional moderation in their arms sales to their Mideast allies, competition between the great powers prevented the establishment of a conventional arms control regime. Following the 1973 October war, both superpowers transferred huge amounts of military equipment to the Arab–Israeli protagonists. Today, *expansion* of regional military forces has been replaced in most states by a quest for *modernization* of existing forces, and the Middle East has remained an important target for the military industries from all over the world. Generally, the great powers have lost interest in limiting conventional arms transfers to the lucrative Middle Eastern markets. Indeed, the present international system allows for greater access to modern weaponry and for less constraints upon new sellers.[23] Conventional weapons have so far wrought great destruction in the Middle East. This is why Israel stresses the need for agreed limitations on weapons procurement, force structures and deployment, concerns which attract less attention outside the Middle East.

Today, arms control efforts in the Middle East have moved away from conventional weapons, instead focusing on controlling the proliferation of non-conventional capabilities and missiles. Although the United States and

Russia agreed on the need to control the spread of nuclear arms, they have been unable to impose the NPT – the global non-proliferation regime agreed upon in 1969 – on their Mideast clients. Israel declared in 1965 that it will not be the first to introduce nuclear weapons in the region – its official position to this day – but has refused to join the NPT. The deficiencies of this global regime are by now well known, particularly in those instances where verification is most critical.

Ambiguity in Israel's nuclear policy, opaqueness as it is called nowadays, is the result of a concatenation of factors: strategic, political and domestic.[24] After 1973, the Israeli leadership resisted domestic pressures to adopt an open nuclear posture, and even attempted to reduce some of the ambiguity surrounding its nuclear programme, *inter alia* proposing in 1975, for the first time, a Middle East Nuclear-Weapon-Free Zone (NWFZ).[25] Though other Middle Eastern countries adhered to the idea of a NWFZ, Israel's intent was mainly to score points on the diplomatic chessboard, as Avner Cohen correctly points out in his contribution to this volume. Nuclear weapons are on the agenda of the talks on Arms Control and Regional Security (ACRS). Israel is challenged to join the NPT or to accept a freeze on the production of fissionable material. Jerusalem seems more than ever ready to deal squarely with the issue, though it prefers to delay addressing it until the end of the peace process. Unfortunately, the two nuclear aspirants, Iran and Iraq, are not participants in the multilateral track. As in the past, the United States is committed to non-proliferation. In contrast to the past, the US is an hegemonic power whose desires carry great weight, but the intensity of the American commitment is tempered by other interests.

As noted earlier, chemical weapons were part of the strategic environment in the Middle East for many years. The technological knowhow, as well as the infrastructure for producing chemical weapons, readily exists. The Middle East is one of the few regions in the world where chemical agents have been used in warfare. In contrast to fissionable material that is essential for assembling a nuclear device, the dual-use materials for chemical weapons are easier to procure on the international market or to produce locally.

The 1991 Gulf War rekindled fears of chemical warfare and sparked interest in this issue. The conclusion of the CWC in 1993 was the result of several concerns, analysed by Zanders in this volume, and it catalysed governmental responses to the issue. Within the framework of formulating a new arms control policy, Israel signed the CW Convention in January 1993.[26] But ratification has been delayed until the Arab states join. Most Arab states refuse to do so because they regard chemical weapons as counter-balancing the Israeli nuclear capability, and consequently have linked their adherence to the CWC to an Israeli ratification of the NPT.

Another area pertinent to arms control is missile proliferation. Curiously, as Aaron Karp points out in this volume, the interest in missiles, which can carry nuclear and chemical warheads as well as big conventional warheads, has dwindled. His review of missile capabilities in the Middle East shows, however, that there are increasing threats to stability. This is so because no defence is available, for the time being, against incoming missiles. The MTCR, a suppliers' global regime established in 1987, has only limited impact on the spread of missile technology, while the Global Protection System (GPS) against missiles, which was suggested by the Bush administration, is still on the drawing board.

In the past, there have been tacit understandings between the Arabs and the Israelis to limit use of missiles to the battlefield. In other parts of the Middle East, such as the Gulf and the Saudi Arabian peninsula, missiles have been used with less constraint. After the 1991 Iraqi missile attacks on Israeli population centres, a certain taboo was broken in the Arab–Israeli arena, leaving Israel, the party most sensitive to civilian casualties, at a disadvantage.

Therefore, Israel is quite eager to impose some limits on the procurement and use of missiles in order to minimize the vulnerability of its homefront. It even joined the MTCR in 1992. The Arab states, however, regard missiles as a way to overcome Israeli air superiority and escalation dominance.[27] Missiles coupled with chemical warheads constitute the Arab countervalue option to Israel's missiles and primarily its nuclear potential.

Conclusion

The Middle East is now in a state of flux in both diplomatic and strategic contexts. Much diplomatic effort has been put into the peace process to reach a détente between Israel and the Arabs. This effort also influences the strategic relationship between the parties. Yet both contexts are affected by the developments outside the pure inter-state Arab–Israeli relationship, such as proliferation of nuclear weapons and missiles, as well as a surge in the appeal of Islamic fundamentalism. Under the existing conditions and circumstances, the best the states in the region can aspire to is the establishment of a security regime.

An important component of this regime would be arms control. The cardinal elements of a regime require agreements on joint policy processes guided by agreed principles, verification mechanisms and decision-making procedures. Such a regime would require co-ordination by an institutional infrastructure. The second best option is a tacit security regime evolving in the absence of a formal security arrangement, which might require difficult compromises. Taking into account the long tradition of tacit agreements in the Arab–Israeli context and two decades of nuclear opaqueness in the region, such a possibility should not be dismissed.

The links existing between the various issues on the arms control agenda create difficulties in reaching simple agreements. Another thorny issue not dealt with here is the strategic vulnerability of Israel in the light of the territorial concessions deemed necessary to pave the way for the peace process. Similarly, the existence of additional fundamentalist regimes and other revisionist actors in the region are stumbling blocks in attaining an effective security regime. These actors are located geographically beyond the immediate ring of Israel's Arab neighbours, but are as relevant in the era of missiles to a security regime as are the states at the core.

Nevertheless, the linkages between the various issues of the arms race – conventional, nuclear and chemical weapons and missiles – have created a predicament that calls for the establishment of a security regime. Despite the discouraging record of the past, the peace process, the common fears about the use of weapons of mass destruction and the accompanying arms control talks have changed the political atmosphere. To some extent, the talks have sensitized each side to the concerns of the other. But such 'understanding' will not necesssarily lead to a change in interests and to an agreement. Formidable challenges must still be overcome before an arms control regime is reached in the Middle East, despite the fact that the regional actors may, for the first time, sincerely pursue such an option.

NOTES

1. For an analysis of the post-Cold War international order, see Max Singer and Aaron Wildavsky, *The Real World Order. Zones of Peace/Zones of Turmoil* (Chatham: Chatham House, 1993).
2. Hans Blix, 'Verification of Nuclear Proliferation: The Lessons of Iraq', *Washington Quarterly* (Autumn 1992).
3. Robert Jervis, 'Security Regimes', *International Organization*, Vol. 36 (Spring 1982), pp. 357–78; for a less rigorous approach, see Janice Gross Stein, 'Detection and Defection: Security Regimes and the Management of International Conflict', *International Journal* ,Vol. 40 (Autumn 1985), pp. 599–627. For a review of the regime literature, see Etel Solingen, 'The Domestic Sources of Regional Regimes: The Evolution of Nuclear Ambiguity in the Middle East', *International Studies Quarterly,* Vol. 38 (June 1994), pp.305–37.
4. Efraim Inbar and Shmuel Sandler, 'The Changing Israeli Strategic Equation: Toward A Security Regime', *Review of International Studies*, Vol. 21 (Jan. 1995), pp. 41–59.
5. This concept was coined by Hedley Bull, *The Anarchical Society* (London: Macmillan, 1977). See also Barry Buzan, 'New Patterns of Global Security in the Twenty First Century', *International Affairs*, Vol. 67 (July 1991).
6. For this term, see Karl W. Deutsch *et al., Political Community and the North Atlantic Area,* (Princeton: Princeton University Press, 1957), pp.5–7.
7. Kenneth Waltz, 'The Spread of Nuclear Weapons: More May be Better', *Adelphi Paper*, No. 171 (London: International Institute for Strategic Studies, 1981). For a refutation, see Scott D. Sagan, 'The Perils of Proliferation', *International Security*, Vol. 18 (Spring 1994).

8. See for instance, Johan J. Holst, 'Confidence Building Measures: A Conceptual Framework', *Survival* Vol. 25 (Jan.-Feb. 1983 and Evron in this volume.

9. See *inter alia* Janice Gross Stein, 'Dilemmas of Security in the Middle East: A Prognosis for the Decade Ahead', in Bahgat Korany, Paul Noble and Rex Brynen (eds.), *The Many Faces of National Security in the Arab World* (London: Macmillan, 1993), pp.56–75.

10. On the linkages among conflicts see Shmuel Sandler, 'The Protracted Arab–Israeli Conflict, A Temporal Spatial Analysis', *The Jerusalem Journal of International Relations*, Vol. 10, No. 4 (1988). For protracted conflict, see E. E. Azar, P. Jureidini and R. McLaurin, 'Protracted Social Conflicts: Theory and Practice in the Middle East', *Journal of Palestine Studies*, Vol. 8, (Autumn 1978); Elizabeth Crighton and Martha Abele Mac Iver, 'The Evolution of Protracted Ethnic Conflict, Group Dominance and Political Underdevelopment in Northern Ireland', *Comparative Politics* (Jan. 1991), pp.127–42.

11. For a theoretical treatment of this kind of war see, Stuart Cohen and Efraim Inbar, 'A Taxonomy of Israel's Use of Force', *Comparative Strategy*, Vol. 10 (April 1991), pp.128–9.

12. See Avner Yaniv, *Dilemmas of Security* (New York: Oxford University Press, 1987).

13. Efraim Inbar, 'Israel's Small War: The Military Response to the Intifada', *Armed Forces and Society*, Vol. 18 (Fall 1981), pp.29–50. See also Hillel Frisch, 'The Palestinian Movement in the Territories: the Middle Command', *Middle Eastern Studies*, Vol. 29 (April 1993), pp. 254–74.

14. See the main conclusions of recent books on the 1992 Israeli elections: Daniel J. Elazar and Shmuel Sandler, *Israel at the Polls, 1992* (Lanham, MD: Rowman and Littlefield, 1994); Keith Kyle and Joel Peters (eds.), *Whither Israel? The Domestic Challenges* (London: The Royal Institute of International Affairs in association with I.B. Tauris, 1993).

15. For comprehensive books on Islamic fundamentalism see Emmanuel Sivan, *Radical Islam: Medieval Theology and Modern Politics* (New Haven: Yale University Press, 1985). The most comprehensive recent work is Martin Marty and Scott Appelby (eds.), *Accounting for Fundamentalism,* especially Vol. 4 of the Fundamentalisms Project (Chicago: University of Chicago Press, 1994). On Jewish fundamentalism in Israel, see Eliezer Don-Yehiya, 'The Book and the Sword: The Nationalist Yeshivot and Political Radicalism in Israel', ibid., pp.262–300.

16. See Eliyahu Kanovsky, *The Forgotten Dimension: Arab Economies, Political Stability and the Peace Process* (Ramat Gan: BESA Center for Strategic Studies, Bar-Ilan University, 1993); Fred H. Lawson, 'Neglected Aspects of the Security Dilemma', in *The Many Faces of National Security in the Arab World*, pp.100–26.

17. Eliyahu Kanovsky, *Assessing the Peace Economic Dividend* (Ramat Gan: BESA Center for Strategic Studies, Bar-Ilan University, 1994).

18. See *inter alia* Colin S. Gray, 'Arms Control Does Not Control Arms', *Orbis,* Vol. 37, (Summer 1993), pp.333–48. For the original study linking arms races to war, see Lewis F. Richardson, *Arms and Insecurity*, (Pittsburgh: Boxwood Press, 1960).

19. For the Israeli military industry see Aaron Klieman, *Israel's Global Reach* (Washington: Pergamon-Brassey's, 1985); for the Arab capability in this area, see Yezid Sayigh, *Arab Military Industry* (London: Brassey's, 1991).

20. Efraim Inbar and Shmuel Sandler, 'Israel's Deterrence Strategy Revisited', *Security Studies*, Vol. 3 (Winter 1993/94), pp.330–58.

21. For the arms control experience in the Middle East see Yair Evron, 'The Role of Arms Control in the Middle East', *Adelphi Paper* No.138 (London: IISS, 1977); Alan Platt (ed.), *Arms Control and Confidence Building in the Middle East* (Boulder: Westview, 1990).

22. Moshe Dayan, *Diary of the Sinai Campaign* (New York: Shocken Books, 1967), pp.3–4; For the role of arms races in the 1956 and 1967 wars, see Nadav Safran, *From War to War* (New York: Pegasus, 1969), chs.4–5.

23. Amit Gupta, 'Third World Militaries: New Suppliers, Deadlier Weapons', *Orbis,* Vol. 37 (Winter 1993), pp.57–68.

24. Yair Evron, 'Israel and the Atom: The Uses and Misuses of Ambiguity, 1959–1967', *Orbis,* Vol. 17 (Winter 1974), pp. 1326–43; Alan Dowty, 'Nuclear Proliferation: The Israeli Case', *International Studies Quarterly,* Vol. 22 (March 1978), pp.79–121; Avner Cohen and Benjamin Frankel, 'Opaque Nuclear Proliferation', in Benjamin Frankel (ed.), *Opaque*

Nuclear Proliferation: Methodological and Policy Implications (London: Frank Cass, 1991), pp.14–44.

25. Efraim Inbar, 'Israel and Nuclear Weapons since October 1973', in Louis Rene Beres, *Security or Armageddon* (Lexington: Lexington Books, 1986), pp.61–78.

26. See Inbar and Sandler, 'The Changing Israeli Strategic Equation: Toward a Security Regime'; see also Efraim Inbar, 'Israel and Arms Control', *Arms Control,* Vol. 13 (Sept. 1992), pp.214–21.

27. For this concept, see Herman Kahn, *On Escalation* (Baltimore: Penguin, 1965), p.290; For a discussion of the consequences of the emerging symmetry in countervalue capabilities see Inbar and Sandler, 'Israeli Deterrence Strategy Revisited', p.343.

Documents

A Farewell to Chemical Arms

Address by the Foreign Minister of Israel, Mr Shimon Peres, at the Signing Ceremony of the Chemical Weapons Convention Treaty

Paris, 13 January 1993

His Excellency the President of France, François Mitterrand,
His Excellency the Secretary-General of the United Nations, Mr Ghali,
The Director-General of UNESCO, Mr Mayor,
His Excellency the Foreign Minister of Germany, Mr Kinkel,
The Secretary-General of the Conference of Disarmament, Mr Berasategui,
Distinguished Foreign Ministers,

Dear Delegates,

I would like to thank and praise the framers and organizers of this convention for years of dedication and hard work, and to thank France for hosting this noble event. In spite of all the difficulties, the peace process in our region is continuing and will continue. No party can or should escape it.

We seek to resolve the disputes of the past over frontiers and respond to the call of new horizons of our age. Our vision is a new Middle East, where the skies will be free from missiles, the land free from desert, the waters free from salt, its peoples free from violence and its children free from ignorance.

There is no weapon against unconventional weapons. There are only policies to prevent their use, and preferably their production. We would like to adopt a Helsinki-type approach, where human rights will replace human menaces – a Middle East with a common market and collective security. No nation in the region will enjoy genuine security unless all nations feel secure.

Accordingly, we have formulated our policy on regional security and arms control, once peace has been attained.

We seek to live in a region in which full and lasting peace prevails, based on reconciliation, good neighbourliness, open borders, and trust and respect among nations.

In the spirit of the global pursuit of general and complete disarmament, and the establishment of regional and global arms control regimes, Israel suggests to all the countries of the region to construct a mutually verifiable zone, free of surface-to-surface missiles and of chemical, biological and nuclear weapons.

In order to establish regional security it is necessary:
- to curtail the arms race and prevent the proliferation of destabilizing weapons;
- to build and nurture mutual confidence between states;
- to diminish the levels of suspicion, hostility and conflagration;
- to reduce the incentives and capabilities for launching surprise attacks;
- to enhance crisis management and stability;
- to ensure compliance with arms control accords; and
- to install mutual challenge inspections once peace has been established and endured the test of time.

In the course of the multilateral regional security and arms control process, we will deal with various types of threats and capabilities and intentions, in relation to:
- military and paramilitary activities;
- military and security forces deployment;
- defence expenditures, conventional hardware and weapon systems; and
- ballistic missiles, chemical, biological and nuclear weapons.

Arms control negotiations and arrangements should be mutually agreed upon and include all the states of the region. Implementation and verification mechanisms, the establishment of comprehensive and durable peace, should be region-wide in their application. Priority in this process ought to be assigned to systems whose destabilizing potential and effects have been proven through their use in wars and have inflicted mass casualties.

The Chemical Weapons Convention must refer to our region, and the region at large must adhere to its principles and comply with its provisions. To reduce the conventional arms race and military build-up and prevent unconventional proliferation, the suppliers and exporters should cease their counterproductive policies of indiscriminate arms sales.

We propose to our neighbours to jointly formulate appropriate mechanisms for inspection. We have adhered to the missile technology control regime (MTCR), and expect the CWC to constitute a further step forward. We cherish the principles of universality and equality among nations. Naturally, we expect equal rights of geographic membership in the institutions established by the convention.

We hope that peace and arms control will lead to democratization of the region, which will strengthen the commitment to peace and bring about openness and greater transparency between states. We believe in the Biblical vision that 'Nations will not lift up a sword against other nations, nor shall they learn war any more.' Isaiah was not just a great prophet; he was also a profound educator.

I call upon our Arab neighbours to establish a broad arms control dialogue with us, and I call upon all parties to sign the Chemical Weapons Convention, and build a new Middle East free of the horrors of war.

One thousand years ago in Spain, Jewish–Arab cohabitation and symbiosis contributed to the formation and shaping of world culture for generations. A present-day Jewish–Arab symbiosis may contribute to the cultural formation of the next millennium.

Arms Control and the Peace Process: The Egyptian Perspective

MOUNIR ZAHRAN

Our approach to the multilateral talks to establish regional co-operation is based on the concept of the interrelationship between regional security in the Middle East and international security; an approach which aims at reaching a level of stability necessary to facilitate a constructive regional co-operation.

We have, in our regional talks, to draw inspiration from the European experience and that of other regions but we have also to accept the internationally agreed principles and parameters.

In May 1993, the United Nations Disarmament Commission (UNDC) adopted 'Guidelines and Recommendations for Regional Disarmament within the Context of Global Security' and devoted a whole section to confidence and security-building measures (CSBMs) for regional approaches to disarmament. I shall briefly refer to the main elements that should guide our regional experience on arms control and disarmament in the Middle East which are, *inter alia*: priority objectives, parameters, confidence-building measures including transparency.

Priority Objectives

A 1981 United Nations study on all aspects of regional disarmament defines the objective of regional disarmament as follows: 'Regional disarmament aims at achieving several objectives at once, namely, to promote regional security, and to contribute to the promotion of a relaxation of tension, enhance security and disarmament at the global level.'

Any regional security and disarmament arrangement should accept the 1993 UNDC Guidelines and Recommendations for Regional Approaches to Disarmament. Under Chapter 1, entitled 'Relationship between regional disarmament, arms limitation and global security', it is stated in paragraph 3 that:

Mounir Zahran is the Egyptian Ambassador to the UN in Geneva. This is his address to the BESA Center for Strategic Studies at Bar-Ilan University, November 1993.

Effective measures for disarmament and arms limitation at the global level, particularly in the field of nuclear weapons and other weapons of mass destruction, as well as in the field of conventional weapons have a positive impact on regional disarmament and arms limitation efforts.[1]

In the multilateral peace talks and in particular the 'Multilateral Working Group on Regional Security an Arms Control', the Egyptian side determined the priority objective of the talks as follows:

1. Ridding the Middle East of all weapons of mass destruction, in particular nuclear weapons, and proceeding to eliminating chemical and biological weapons;

2. Preventing an arms race between the countries in the region, particularly in the advanced military technologies with military application including the military uses of outerspace;

3. Achieving a large degree of military transparency in all weapons systems particularly in the priority areas.

It is worthwhile to stress that the projected arms limitation arrangements in the Middle East must be tailored to fit with the needs of the peaceful environment which would prevail in the region. Countries and peoples of the Middle East will transform their relationship from a state of war to a state of peace and good neighbourly relations as a step towards the establishment of a framework of regional co-operation. Thus the arms limitation arrangements which we are seeking in the Middle East in the multilateral talks should envisage the post-war peace-building in the future in accordance with the 'Agenda for Peace' of the United Nations Secretary General.

Hence, there is no place in such an environment of peace and eventual regional co-operation for the policies of security edge or achieving security on the basis of military superiority. Countries in the Middle East should benefit from the experiences of other regions in shaping their regional disarmament and arms limitations agreements. For instance, the CSCE is an example to study with a view to see how far it may be applicable in the Middle East, bearing in mind the fundamental differences that exist between Europe and the Middle East. The characteristics and particularities of each region should be duly taken into consideration.

Parameters

The discussions on regional approaches to disarmament cannot be taken in isolation of the global approaches; they are not mutually exclusive but are indeed mutually reinforcing. There is certainly an interrelationship between regional disarmament and global security, arms limitations and disarmament. Regional and global approaches to disarmament complement each other. Both should be pursued in order to promote regional peace and security. It has been recognized that the regional approach to disarmament is considered to be one of the essential elements in the global efforts to strengthen international peace and security. On the other hand, the effective disarmament measures taken at the global level, particularly in the field of nuclear weapons and other weapons of mass destruction, would have a positive impact on regional disarmament efforts. By the same token, any regional measures should take into account the relationship between security in the region in question and international security as a whole. It is understood that any regional arrangement or measure of disarmament should respect and take into account the purposes and principles enshrined in the Charter of the United Nations. It should be made in conformity with international law including the principle of sovereign equality of all states, non-use or threat of use of force against the sovereignty, territorial integrity or political independence of any state, non-intervention and non-interference in the internal affairs of other states; the inviolability of international frontiers, the inherent right of states to individual and collective self-defence in accordance with Article 51 and the peaceful settlement of disputes in conformity with Article 2 paragraph 3 and Article 33 paragraphs 1 and 2 of the Charter of the United Nations.

It has been recognized that earmarking resources for potentially destructive purposes is detrimental to sustainable social and economic development. Thus, reduction in military expenditure following the conclusion of global, regional and bilateral disarmament agreements would yield additional resources necessary to implement social and economic development projects in the countries concerned. Such disarmament agreements, including regional measures, should aim to establish military balance at the lowest level of armament without diminishing the security of each and every state belonging to the same region. Such measures should also aim to prevent the capability for large-scale offensive and eventual pre-emptive military attacks. Disarmament measures in one region should not lead to increasing arms transfers to other regions or to the displacement of military imbalance or tension from one region to the other in accordance with the experience learned from the CFE. It has been universally agreed that the implementation of regional disarmament arrangements requires the adoption at the regional level of *confidence-building and transparency measures.* It is the understanding of experts in the field that compliance with disarmament agreements including regional measures calls for the adoption and the implementation of verification measures.

It is worthwhile to recall that the basic parameters which guide the talks in the Multilateral Working Group on Regional Security and Arms Control and Regional Security are the following:
1. Achieving a just, lasting and comprehensive peace settlement between all the parties concerned;
2. The process shall be based on Security Council Resolutions 242 and 338 including the principle of 'land for peace'; and
3. The Regional Security and Arms Control Working Group should proceed step by step towards ambitious goals.

Confidence-Building Measures

The United Nations Disarmament Commission (UNDC) adopted a 1981 study on Guidelines for Confidence and Security-Building Measures in its 1993 session. The 1993 UNDC report on this matter stated in paragraph 34 that:

> Bearing in mind the need to maintain and develop an integrated approach to international peace and security, regional arrangements aimed at building security and confidence need not be confined to the military field, but could, as appropriate, also extend to the political, economic, social, environment and cultural fields.

These guidelines have to be accepted by states in their endeavours to conclude regional arrangements for arms limitation and disarmament. Confidence and security-building measures comprise notification of large-scale military manoeuvres, exchange of military data, reduction of military capabilities, open sky arrangements, dialogue and regular consultations, and co-operation in non-military fields such as political, economic, social and cultural areas. Such measures adopted within the context of a particular region could reduce the risk of misinterpretation and miscalculation, thus foster transparency and openness and enhance friendly relations between states belonging to same regions. Such measures contribute to the maintenance of regional and international peace and security. This is the *raison d'être* behind the General Assembly invitation and encouragement comprised in its Resolution 47/52 G in its operative paragraph 10; and invitation to '...all States to conclude, whenever possible, agreements on arms limitation and confidence-building measures at the regional level, including those conductive to avoiding the proliferation of weapons of mass destruction'.

In addition, General Assembly Resolution 47/54 J, in its operative paragraph 5, 'Supports and encourages efforts aimed at promoting confidence-building measures at regional and subregional levels in order to ease regional tensions and to further disarmament and nuclear-non-proliferation measures at regional and subregional levels.'

The negotiation and implementation of disarmament measures in the Middle East has strategic significance because of its conflicts and potentialities and their direct relationship to international peace and security. Therefore, Egypt stressed the importance of following up of paragraph 63 (d) of the Final Document of the Tenth Special Session of the General Assembly Devoted to Disarmament of 1978 concerning the establishment of a nuclear-weapon-free zone in the Middle East, which would enhance international peace and security in the region. All states of the Middle East should according to this initiative declare that they will refrain, on a reciprocal basis, from producing, acquiring or in any other way possessing nuclear weapons and nuclear explosive devices and from permitting the stationing of nuclear weapons on their territory by any third party, and agree to place all their nuclear installations under the International Atomic Energy Agency safeguards and to promote the role of the Security Council in establishing a nuclear-weapon-free zone in the Middle East.

In this context, Egypt has a firm conviction in the importance of eliminating the hazards of the proliferation of all weapons of mass destruction from the Middle East in order to discourage states of the region from acquiring such weapons which lead them to squander resources and opportunities to achieve prosperity for their peoples. This constitutes a grave threat to peace and security, both in the region and internationally. Accordingly, Egypt has put forward the initiative for the establishment of a nuclear-weapon-free zone in the Middle East and President Mubarak's initiative of 1990 for eliminating all weapons of mass destruction from the Middle East. The latter initiative received extensive international support. It was endorsed also by the Security Council in paragraph 14 of Resolution 687 (1991). This initiative constitutes the most appropriate framework for a balanced treatment of all weapons of mass destruction on a reciprocal and even-handed basis. In the views transmitted to the Secretary-General of the United Nations regarding his report entitled 'New dimensions of arms regulations and disarmament in the post-cold war era',[2] Egypt expressed its belief that

> the Security Council must assume its responsibilities under the Charter with a view to developing the appropriate framework to ensure the implementation of the two initiatives, for the consolidation of international peace and security.[3] This is one of the responsibilities of the Security Council in conformity with article 26 of the Charter; a role which has been highlighted by the Report of the Secretary-

General of the United Nations entitled 'An Agenda for Peace'.

NOTES

1. Report of the United Nations Disarmament Commission General Assembly, Official Records, document A/48/42, p.6.
2. Doc. A/C. 1/47/7.
3. Doc. A/47/887/Add.I.

Notes on Contributors

Michael Brzoska is Head of Research at the Bonn International Center for Conversion, Bonn, Germany.

Avner Cohen is Fellow at the Center for International Studies at the Massachusetts Institute of Technology, where he co-directs the Nuclear Arms Control in the Middle East project.

Yair Evron is Professor of Political Science at Tel Aviv University.

Efraim Inbar is Associate Professor of Political Studies at Bar-Ilan University and the Director of its Begin–Sadat (BESA) Center for Strategic Studies.

Aaron Karp is Research Coordinator and Adjunct Professor at the Graduate Programme for International Studies, Old Dominion University, Norfolk, Virginia.

Yitzhak Klein is Lecturer in the Department of Political Studies, Bar-Ilan University, Israel.

Robert J. Lieber is Professor and Chairman of the Department of Government at Georgetown University.

Shmuel Sandler is Associate Professor of Political Studies at Bar-Ilan University and the Director of its Center for International Communication and Policy.

Etel Solingen is Fellow of the Institute on Global Conflict and Cooperation, and Assistant Professor at the University of California, Irvine.

Gerald Steinberg is Senior Lecturer in Political Studies at Bar-Ilan University, and Senior Research Associate of its BESA Center for Strategic Studies.

Jean-Pascal Zanders is Research Fellow at the Centrum voor Polemologie, Vrije Universiteit Brussel, Brussels, Belgium.

Index